313S

MII
RO
THE
LO!

Te

Ple
la

D1531193

BRITAIN UNDER FIRE

Born in 1926, Charles Whiting joined the army as a volunteer in 1943 and served with the 52nd Armoured Reconnaissance Regiment in Belgium, Holland and Germany. After the war he studied at the University of Leeds and later at London, Kiel, Cologne and Saar-brücken. In 1958, he became a university teacher, first in the USA and then in England and in Germany where he was also the German correspondent for the *Times Educational Supplement*. He gave up full-time teaching in 1973 to devote himself to writing.

Charles Whiting's first novel *Frat Wagon* was published by Jonathan Cape while he was at university. Since then he has had nearly a hundred books published ranging from fiction, under the pen name of Leo Kessler, to military history, espionage and linquistics. His most recent publications include *Death of a Division, The Battle for Hitler's Wall, The German Home Front, The Siegfried Line, '44: In Combat on the Western Front from Normandy to the Ardennes* and *'45: The Final Drive from the Rhine to the Baltic*.

BRITAIN UNDER FIRE

The Bombing of Britain's Cities 1940–1945

CHARLES WHITING

CENTURY
LONDON   MELBOURNE
AUCKLAND AND JOHANNESBURG

First published in Great Britain in 1986
by Century Hutchinson Ltd,
Brookmount House,
62–65 Chandos Place,
Covent Garden,
London WC2N 4NW

ISBN 0 7126 1034 0

Printed in Great Britain in 1986 by
Butler & Tanner Ltd, Frome, Somerset

CONTENTS

INTRODUCTION

'Death and sorrow will be the companions of our journey; hardship our garment; constancy and valour our only shield. We must be united, we must be undaunted, we must be inflexible. Our qualities and deeds must burn and glow through the gloom of Europe until they become the veritable beacon of its salvation.'

Winston Churchill, 1940

Of course, then, I didn't know what was being discussed behind the grey-yellow walls of the big hotel over forty years ago. How could a thirteen-year-old boy in short pants, cycling his way to school, know that the fate of the British Empire was being discussed behind locked doors in York's Station Hotel, well away from the prying eyes and big ears of the capital?

That June day so long ago, Secretary of State for War Anthony Eden heard his senior officers air their views on the British Army, which had just been run out of France. They weren't good. Vice-Chief of the Imperial General Staff Dill thought the Army was 'demoralised . . . and may not be steady when the time comes'.[1]

If the Germans came, the brass told each other at that top-secret conference, the regular officers and NCOs would fight on, even if they had to be evacuated to Canada to continue the war there. But not the wartime conscripts. They would desert en masse to their families rather than leave the country. In that summer of 1940, with a German invasion apparently imminent, it was decided in York that the morale of the British Army was definitely shaky. How would the troops bear up when the storm broke over Britain?

In the event, the Army was never put to the test. For the greater part of the war, most of the British Army was safely tucked away in remote rural camps, never hearing a shot fired in anger. Not so the civilians who would man the Home Front.

That same elegant Victorian station from which Eden departed to report his gloomy findings to the new Prime Minister, Winston Churchill, would soon be in flames, as would most of the buildings around it. But it was not the men in khaki who would fight in that battle to come, as the Germans dive-bombed York for five long hours. It was the civilians: the men, women and children. For the next five years, down the length and breadth of the country, they would be the ones who fought the enemy on the only real front before the 1944 invasion of France—the Home Front!

The city centres of every large city in the kingdom, from Hull to Liverpool, from Clydebank to Coventry, would be destroyed. One night nine and a half acres of Central Manchester would be aflame. In Clydebank, seven hundred civilians would be killed and twice that number seriously injured in a matter of hours. In Birmingham the toll of dead would be so great that Assistant Chief Constable Hawkins would confess sadly: 'No one will ever know how many were really killed. They'll just make up a number.'[2] In London there would be one night when the city centre was blocked for an area of ten square miles, no central tube station was working, and there was only one main line railway station linking the capital with the rest of the country. That night Winston Churchill wept.

Today, forty-odd years later, all of us who inhabit the country's big cities—Cardiff, Swansea, Bristol, Portsmouth, Plymouth, Liverpool, London, Hull etc—live in accommodation that was blitzed in the great storm that swept over Britain in the 1940s; or in buildings erected on the sites of those destroyed then.

But not only the cities were struck. Quiet market towns and villages also took their share of 'stick', in the parlance of the time. Places such as Torquay, Weston-super-Mare, Newark, Scarborough, Driffield, Lossiemouth were temporarily brought out of obscurity as the death and destruction wreaked upon their peaceful communities made them 'news'. In the spring of 1941, for example, the tiny mining village of Cwmparc in Wales found itself the target of enemy bombers. Within five minutes, twenty-seven of its citizens were dead—six of them children—and half the village's thousand houses had been damaged or destroyed.

(Right) Winston Churchill inspects blitzed houses in Bristol.

6

The country as a whole had been woefully unprepared for war. Appeasement, fatalism and a blind, unthinking, anti-war attitude on the part of some politicians—who had maintained throughout the 1930s that it would never happen, so why spend money on defence—all had had their effect. Even with that period of grace known as the 'phoney war' the nation's leaders had failed to take adequate precautions against enemy attacks—specifically air attacks.

The Germans already had a well organised civil defence movement covering every remote village, with the citizens ordered to prepare air-raid shelters in the basements and cellars of their houses. Where these were not available in the big cities, the government built vast nine-storey, reinforced concrete structures—with flak guns on their roofs—which could house thousands. They were so strong that Allied engineers could not blow them up after the war. Today they are still there in Hamburg, Bremen, Berlin, Dortmund and the like, forty years later still mocking that five-year brave attempt of 'Bomber' Harris's men to destroy them.

In Britain, thanks to pre-war parsimony and apathy, half the country's population only had the space under the stairs to shelter in. The lucky few had a couple of pieces of primitive corrugated iron placed over a hole in the garden (if they had a garden), called an Anderson shelter; or an extra layer of concrete laid on the roof of their garden shed by the local council. But three-quarters of London's seven million citizens endured the most intensive bombing for nearly a year without any kind of shelter whatsoever!

This lack of air-raid shelters was mirrored in the overall deficiencies of the nation's Civil Defence structure. When the war began, for instance, there were 1,600 different fire brigades, all with their own differing standards of training, pay, equipment, even uniforms. When Portsmouth and Plymouth burnt, brigades from other cities had to stand by and let them burn; their hoses did not fit the local hydrants! For the first two years of the war Civil Defence was in the hands of unpaid volunteers, who had only the most primitive equipment with which to tackle the Luftwaffe's attempts to bomb Britain into submission. In some cases they did not even have helmets, and went into battle with saucepan lids tied to their heads! To deal with the myriad incendiary bombs that the Germans showered on our cities they were equipped with a stirrup pump and a pail of water—and some did not even have that. It is not surprising that many scores of them were blinded when those deadly little stick bombs sprang ablaze.

There was little active defence, too. The few night-fighters the RAF possessed in 1940 were soon withdrawn. They couldn't find the enemy and they got in the way of the anti-aircraft guns. Not that the AA units were much use, either, at least not at first, when their guns were twenty years out of date. No matter how eager and proficient their crews, they shot down nothing. Indeed, most of the country had no fighter or anti-aircraft defence whatsoever. As late as 1942, three years after the war had commenced, a whole row of historic cities—Canterbury, Exeter, Bath, Norwich, York—were subjected to repeated bombing raids *with not one single shot being fired in their defence.*

Even in the last year of the war, the people of Britain found themselves facing yet another ordeal for which they had been unprepared: the V-1 and V-2 rockets, the cruise missiles of the 1940s. By this time Civil Defence had slackened off, local authorities had become lax, and factory workers were striking, thus hampering the flow of shells and new aircraft needed to take up the challenge.

Before the war, shells fuses for the British Army had been made by the Swiss. It took British engineers more than four years to design a fuse that would not explode prematurely and kill the AA gunners firing it; and one year later, when they had finally perfected an excellent proximity fuse for AA Command, the shells themselves were in such short supply that they had to be rationed—six weeks before the end of the war!

Time and time again, the authorities at national and local level were found lacking, smugly complacent, blind to faults, totally unprepared. And the people suffered. By 1940 more civilians had been killed in London alone than in the whole of the British Army up to then. By 1945, 80,000 men, women and children on the Home Front had been killed, another 80,000 seriously injured and twice that number lightly wounded: a total of a quarter of a million. At some time or other during the long campaign on the Home Front, millions had been rendered homeless or were evacuated. In London alone, in the last year of the war a staggering half a million homes were destroyed or damaged one-fifth of the capital's housing. People became refugees in their own country, living rough, sleeping in ditches, forced to rely on hand-outs and rough-and-ready charity. Thousands upon thousands made a nightly trek from the big cities to avoid the bombs, returning to go to work the next morning. In London a quarter of a million spent the nights in the Underground and often paid bribes to 'spivs' for the privilege of sleeping, if that is the word for it, on the hard concrete platforms.

Yet the survivors of the Battle of the Home Front look back at that terrible time with pride and longing, comparing it favourably with the present.

An orphan girl, who lost her father in World War One and would lose her brother in World War Two, recalling her days in the Coventry and Birmingham blitzes, can state confidently today: 'We won the war,

George VI talks to London women who suffered in weekend air-raids of September 1940.

in a way, on the Home Front. The men in the Army said they were glad to escape to camp. We won, we civvies, because we stuck together and stuck it out.'[3]

Another admits: 'We were petrified of course. I was, many a time. But I wouldn't change for anything those years. There was good comradeship all around. I can honestly say they were the best years of my life, those blitz years in Manchester.'[4]

'Traumatic years they were,' another lady writing from the same city agrees, 'with the raids and rationing and restrictions, but they were happy ones. You could leave your door open when the sirens sounded and rush to the shelters to find everything intact when you returned. Then there was a loyalty, a compassion for others, and a spirit which I wish was around today.'[5]

'The times we endured and lived through! First the bombs on Surbiton and then the V-1s and V-2s. The young people of today have no knowledge of it,' writes another lady who went through five years of blitzes. 'Nor do they appear to be even interested in their own freedom bought for them at such cost.'[6]

'It was Churchill who dragged us,' yet another lady recalls. 'That voice of his! Still gives me a thrill all these years later whenever I hear it. He held us together and he bluffed us through to the end.'[7]

But a fickle ungrateful nation soon voted Churchill out of office, apparently forgetting that it was he who had saved them from defeat. Forgetting, too, the dangers that they had undergone on the Home Front and just how ill-prepared they had been; and what a high price in human life and suffering they had paid because of it.

Now, nearly half a century later, the same political parties and pressure groups work on the nation, urging us to disarm, to close our minds to the 'unthinkable' to bury our heads in the sand—just as we did in the 1930s, and with such terrible results.

But those who survived the Battle of the Home Front know that is not the way. But let Edward Sawyer, one of the 29,500 Allied prisoners out of 98,000 who survived Japanese captivity and went through the nuclear horror of the bombing of Hiroshima, have the last word. 'I will never forget that day when Hiroshima was bombed ... Technology has advanced at an alarming pace, but human nature has not changed ... Men, not weapons, make war. The strong will always take what they can and the weak give what they must ... Neutrality is an illusion and unilateral disarmament can only lead us into slavery ...'[8]

1:
BAPTISM OF FIRE, 1940

I didn't really never ought 'ave went,
In London I was really quite content,
I wouldn't have been windy with the planes up
overhead.
Talk of blinkin' aeroplanes, you should have heard
what Father said—
They couldn't hit Forth Bridge, let alone small boys in
bed.
No, I didn't really never ought 'ave went.

Cockney evacuee's lament in 'Lights Up', 1940

Children sheltering in a primitive trench-shelter in Kent 1940.

ONE
'Are we downhearted?'

It was September, 1940. The war had been running for exactly a year. For half that time nothing had happened in the West. The 'phoney war', people had called it and had forgotten about the new conflict the best they could, to get on with their own private lives. Then abruptly, violently, things had started to happen.

The new enemy had overrun Denmark and Norway. The Low Countries had followed. Nothing had seemed able to stop him. He was ever victorious. In June the British Army had been run out of France. A little later Britain's only remaining ally had surrendered. Suddenly the country was alone. Her defeated, demoralised Army now faced the greatest armed force in Europe—perhaps in the whole world.

Almost immediately the Germans carried the war to England. What was later known as the Battle of Britain had commenced. Hundreds of German and British planes battled for mastery of the air over south-east England. But for most civilians the war still remained the grave, upper-class voice of Stuart Hibberd reading the nine o'clock news on the radio, and newspaper placards announcing the latest RAF victories—'*TEN DOWN FOR ONE!*'—as if they were the cricket scores. After all, it was perfect weather for the game: day after day of bright sunshine with flawless blue skies.

But the war was creeping ever closer to the country's capital with its eight million-odd civilians. In mid-August sixty-two people were killed in a short, sharp thirty-minute raid on Croydon. A few days later, on August 24th, some isolated German bombs intended for the aircraft works at Rochester and the oil tanks of the Thames mouth were dropped by mistake on Central London.

Hitler had strictly forbidden that London should be bombed. So, as soon as he learnt of this mistake, the head of the Luftwaffe Hermann Goering issued a stern signal: 'It is to be reported forthwith which crews dropped bombs on the London prohibited zone. The Supreme Commander reserves to himself the personal punishment of the commander concerned by remustering him to the infantry.'[1]

The new British Prime Minister did not know this. If his capital was bombed, Churchill decided, then the German one should be bombed too. On the morning of August 24th, 1940, he ordered a reluctant RAF Bomber Command, which saw no military advantage in it, to attack Berlin.

Thus on the night of August 25th, 81 RAF Hampdens and Wellingtons set out to attempt to bomb the enemy's capital. The pilots were far from happy about the mission. Apart from the 600-mile flight ahead of them, most of it over enemy territory, what most worried them was whether they would be able to find their targets. As Flight Lieutenant John Watson, who later won the DFC in Bomber Command, now recalls, 'In those days we were lucky even to find the town to be bombed—but actually to *hit* the target was little short of a miracle!'[2]

Squadron Leader Oxley, whose target that night was Berlin's Siemens-Halske Electric Works, a prime military objective, found himself unable to locate it. Although the weather was good he was flying too high at 3,500 feet. Had he gone down to 700 feet he might have found it. However, as he reported later: 'I was keen, but not *that* keen! ... I should have brought my bombs back of course, but I didn't. I left them in Berlin.'[3] And Squadron Leader Oxley was not the only one who failed to find his target that night and on the three succeeding nights when the RAF bombed the German capital.

Goering was enraged. He had always promised the German people that they would never be bombed. '*Wenn eine einzige Bombe auf Deutschland fällt,*' he had boasted, '*dann heisse ich Meier!*'* Meier being a common name among German Jews, this was to Goering the ultimate insult; and now, behind his back, he knew the Berliners were mocking him bitterly.

He was not the only one of the Party's *Prominenz* who was angered. On September 4th, five days after the first civilian had been killed by an RAF bomb in Berlin,† Hitler made a surprise appearance at a rally of nurses and social workers at the *Sportpalast*, Berlin. Addressing the rapturous, excited women who had always been among his most devoted followers, he promised an invasion of England soon: 'In England they are filled with curiosity and keep asking why doesn't he come. Be calm! Be calm! He's coming!' Working the

* 'If a single bomb drops on Germany then you can call me Meier.'
† Back in 1939, the first civilian to be killed by an RAF bomb in the whole of Germany was, surprisingly enough, an Englishwoman.

(Right) Goering and Milch.

women up to hysterical enthusiasm as he had done so often before, he brought them to their feet cheering and clapping wildly, as he shrieked, face crimson, eyes bulging from his head like those of a madman, 'When the British Air Force drops two or three or four kilograms of bombs, then we will—in one night—drop 150 ... 250 ... 300 ... or 400 *thousand* kilograms! When they declare that they will increase their attacks on our cities, then we will *raze their cities to the ground!*'[4]

That same night Hitler ordered Goering to plan a massive raid on London.

Saturday, September 7th, 1940, was a beautiful day, remarkably warm and sunny even for that summer of defeat. In London, as if Dunkirk had not taken place and over the coast the 'Few' were fighting desperately against the Luftwaffe, couples hugged and kissed on the grass in St James's Park. Others queued for the matinées. Celia Johnson was to be seen in *Rebecca*; Robert Donat of the beautiful voice and gentle air in *The Devil's Disciple*. Others went to the pictures to see *Gone With The Wind* or, if they were patriotically inclined, Ralph Richardson and Merle Oberon in that 'Epic of the Royal Air Force', *The Lion Has Wings*.

Out in the suburbs, people were picnicking in the parks or watching amateur gentlemen in whites playing gentle, lazy, middle-class cricket. Some went boating on that river whose world-famous contours would betray them this day as it would on so many terrible days and nights to come.

Many of London's 30,000 strong Fire Brigade were off duty, like Bill Whiting, a sub-section officer at Number 63 Post in the City. He had volunteered for the Auxiliary Fire Service (AFS) before the war, thinking that at thirty he was too old for the armed forces. Since then he had spent a boring twelve months or so. Like the rest of the 28,000 wartime auxiliaries, he had yet to fight a fire. Not only was he bored, he also felt that he was being laughed at by the general public. 'A lot of people regarded us as a bad joke,' he recalls, 'something like the Keystone comedy fire brigades of the early Hollywood pictures!'[5] So, with his young wife Doris, he decided to spend this fine Saturday afternoon in Richmond Park.

Another section officer, Louis 'Tug' Wilson, a former motor mechanic, was one of the few who happened to be on duty. He was just as frustrated as Whiting. 'The biggest jobs we had ever turned out for during the year of training and waiting ... had been an occasional chimney fire and a smoke-filled boarding house where a sleepy lodger had set his bedclothes afire with a cigarette ... People used to gather round at our outdoor practices for a good laugh. Most Londoners used to grumble that

Fireboats try in vain to control the fires in London's docks.

14

the whole 20,000 of us were an expensive liability who got £3 a week for riding around in our taxicab trailers and polishing a bit of brasswork.'[6]

But those who had laughed at Tug Wilson and his amateur firemen would soon be pathetically grateful for their help. This motley collection of university graduates, bearded artists, society girls, middle-aged spinsters and all who made up the AFS would soon be in the front line—like London itself. Even as Londoners everywhere were enjoying the sunshine that Saturday afternoon, the storm was brewing . . .

Air Marshal Goering, had made a personal appearance at Cap Gris Nez, near Calais, to salute his bombers going in action against the Tommies' capital for the first time. Vain as ever, with his rouged lips, powdered cheeks and lacquered fingernails 'Fat Hermann' posed for the press wearing a dove-coloured uniform of his own design and, as one photographer noticed, pink patent leather boots—and rolling 'uncut diamonds between his pudgy fingers'.[7] He told the assembled pressmen and photographers that he was assuming personal command of the Luftwaffe in the battle against England. Then, in disgust at this new development forced upon him by the Führer, he took his armoured train—Goering always had a keen eye for his own comfort and safety—back to Paris. Here at Luftwaffe HQ in the Hotel Luxembourg he conferred with his inspector-general and deputy head of the German Air Force, Field Marshal Milch. An inveterate Anglophobe, Milch would persist in his efforts to bring the hated Tommies to their knees long after Goering himself had given up; indeed, he became the father of that most hated weapon of all—the V-bomb.

Now Goering, whose mother had been the mistress of a rich Jewish aristocrat, and Field Marshal Milch, the son of a Jewish father, waited for news of their first *blitzkrieg* on London: the targets being the docks and the East End—packed with thousands of humble Jewish folk.

By this time 625 bombers protected by 648 fighters, flying in tight formation at heights of 14,000–20,000 feet, had already crossed the English coast. They were making their approach from a surprise direction, and the RAF fighter planes failed to locate them. The Heinkels, Dorniers, Junkers flew on . . .

Down below, at Shepperton on the Thames, people looked up at the bright blue sky in surprise. Some, thinking they were British, waved at the planes. After all, no one had ever seen a German bomber over Shepperton before. Then they returned to their game of cricket.

A senior fire officer taking a leisurely tea in the shade on the lawn of his house in Dulwich suddenly noticed

a great rash of black dots in the sky to the east, moving towards London. No sirens had sounded, but there was the distant drum-roll of gunfire. Surely they weren't British? Then he recognised the slim shape of the Dorniers—the 'flying pencils', they had called them in the aircraft recognition lectures. In five minutes flat he was out of his flannels and speeding back to HQ. His wife wouldn't see him again for a week.

It was just after five o'clock when the sirens sounded over London. Throughout the torpid city, basking in the hot September sun, nine thousand air raid wardens took to the streets, shrilling their whistles and everyone to take shelter. No one paid much attention. The sirens were always sounding, they protested, and nothing ever came of it. Why waste this beautiful Saturday?

The raiders started with fire-bombs. Beckton's immense gas works were their first target; then the docks—Millwall Docks, Limehouse and Rotherhithe Docks, Surrey Docks. Then West Ham Power Station. Over Tower Bridge towards the City, Westminster, Kensington . . . On and on they sailed, cutting a swathe of fire through the capital. Never since the Great Fire of 1666 had London experienced a conflagration on such a scale.

'From end to end the dockside was afire,' remembers Tug Wilson, who with his crew had been ordered to

A fire-engine is bombed and blown into a shop front while fighting a fire.

Gate One of Surrey Commercial Docks. It was an unforgettable sight: 250 acres of resinous timber, stacked twenty-five feet high, going up in flames. Fireboats attempted to approach the blaze but in vain; the river was already choked with boats that had been set on fire. 'The water itself seemed alight. That came from the burning barges. Across the water, an island jetty was blazing and from left and right and all around the heat waves struck us in the face like a blow. I felt numb. So did the others, they admitted afterwards.'[8]

Similar fires were breaking out all over London. Within one hour of the start of the German attack the Fire Brigade had logged one thousand calls. All over the great sprawling city, fire-engine bells clanged alarmingly as the engines raced to yet another 'incident'. From north, south and east, thick white clouds of smoke surged hundreds of feet into the sky, where the German bombers circled and wheeled, with seeming impunity, like black fish in a blue sea.

'We had just been out visiting relatives for the day,' remembers Eric Taylor. 'Although we had heard the sirens and also the guns we never for one moment expected to see the terrible sight that met our eyes that evening at about six. We thought the city was on fire. A great big balloon shape of smoke rolled up and up ... It was a most terrifying sight.'[9]

Far off in Richmond Park, Sub-Officer Bill Whiting had seen that ominous glow over London and guessed what had happened. 'The balloon's gone up at last!' he told his wife Doris. 'Come on—let's get back to the station!'[10] At that time wives were allowed to sleep in the fire stations while their husbands were on duty. Together they hurried to the nearest bus stop to catch a bus back to Post 63. Before it was over Bill Whiting's mother and sister would be dead, his house would be in ruins, and virtually all his relatives and friends would have been made homeless too.

At last the fire-bombers departed, the All Clear sirens trailing them across southern London as they headed for the coast.

At St Paul's, the devoted body of fire-watchers stared in brooding silence at the crimson glare flickering menacingly over the East End. Finally one of them said: 'It's like the end of the world ...' Someone else replied: 'It *is* the end of the world ...'

Indeed, for many East Enders, it was.

For two desperate hours, men like Bill Whiting and Tug Wilson fought a losing battle against the all-

17

consuming flames, hampered at every turn by unnecessary obstacles. The years of pre-war apathy, the lack of central organisation, the antagonism of the Labour-controlled boroughs to defence, the poor state of Civil Defence training—all now showed themselves to tragic effect.

Because it was a Saturday the owners of many homes and shops were absent, and firemen were unable to gain access (specialist teams were later created for breaking into locked up premises, but as yet these did not exist). Outside brigades called in to help had to stand by helplessly because their hoses did not fit the local hydrants. Overstretched communications systems broke down, so incident rooms were unable to direct fire-fighting teams to the fires. Because it was not prepared, the East End of London burned.

And that was just the start of it. As far away as the French coast, the fiery glow over London offered the best possible beacon for the next wave of bombers—250 of them, all carrying high explosive bombs.

They arrived over London at precisely ten past eight that Saturday evening, wave after wave of them, having met little or no resistance from the British anti-aircraft defences. Indeed, when a stray piece of flak from General Pile's AA gunners struck their planes, the crews—many of them veterans of Spain, Poland and France—would cry cheerfully: 'Hereinspaziert!' ('Come on in!').[11]

The raid continued until four o'clock the next morning. Bomb after bomb came shrieking down with a banshee howl that struck terror into the heart of many a civilian cowering beneath the stairs or in his primitive Anderson shelter in the garden. Bernard Kop, the writer, then a fourteen-year-old living in the East End's Jewish quarter at Stepney, recalls that day 'like a flaming wound in my memory. Imagine a ground floor flat crowded with hysterical women, crying babies, and great crashes in the sky and the whole earth shaking ...'[12]

But there was no time for fear for those engaged in Civil Defence. Doctors, parsons, air-raid wardens, firemen, unarmed civilians, all found themselves engaged in an uneven battle against professional soldiers armed with those terrible bombs. They *had* to go into the blazing streets to find the wounded, tunneling into rubble-filled houses to rescue those who were trapped. They *had* to risk the falling masonry as they sought to control the panic-stricken crowds of East Enders fleeing their homes, their pathetic bits and pieces wrapped in bundles or trundled on rickety prams. And above all they *had* to fight the fires—all kinds of fires: rum fires, pepper fires, paint fires, as one warehouse after another went up in flames. The firemen's lungs were filled with stinging particles of burning pepper and the fumes of paint and alcohol.

The water pressure started to go. The mains could simply not cope with so many hosepipes. Firemen reeled back in frustration, choking or temporarily blinded, and had to abandon their posts. In the end many hundreds of acres of burning dockland were simply isolated to burn themselves out.

A. P. Herbert, the humorist and MP, then a petty-officer in the Royal Navy's Thames Auxiliary Patrol, never forgot what he called 'my most fantastic journey through London' via the blazing Thames. 'The scene was like a lake in hell. Burning barges were drifting everywhere ... We could hear the hiss and roar of the conflagration, a formidable noise, but we could not see it so dense was the smoke. Nor could we see the eastern shore.'[13]

Many of the firemen simply could not stand the sheer physical strain of holding the heavy hosepipes for hours on end. The hoses slipped and their jets swung everywhere, covering the fire-fighting crews with a sticky mixture of water, petrol and oil. Numb with exhaustion they dropped their hoses and gave up. Others were cut off by a wall of roaring flame and never seen again. A few were found later transformed into shrunken pygmies, their charred clawed hands jutting up like black twigs.

Tug Wilson's crew had at one stage been helped by the crew of a Canadian Army bren-gun carrier; later by a few civilian dockers. But the going had been too tough for them and they had finally disappeared, leaving the AFS crew to fight on alone. Suddenly there was a tremendous explosion which nearly blew Wilson off his feet.

'What the hell was that?' he bellowed above the roar. 'Gas main gone up?'

'No,' his pumpman replied, '*they're bombing us!*'

There was no time to think. They flung themselves to the ground. Another bomb hit the dock and blew great lumps of timber into the sky. A huge wall of water came racing over the dock wall.

'It's started to rain again,' said Eddie Donlevy, one of Wilson's men.

Wilson and the rest of the hard-pressed firemen 'hugged the earth and laughed'.[14]

Who would ever have guessed that a pleasant Saturday off duty might end like this, thought Eric Taylor, watching as firemen tried to fight a fire at a grain warehouse. Suddenly and to his horror 'out came hordes of rats, thousands of the brutes, scurrying across the road to disappear in some drain'.[15] Taylor fled to join the hundreds of East Enders escaping the dying borough.

The fires became worse. At Woolwich Arsenal the firemen fought the flames among boxes of live ammunition and crates of nitro-glycerine as bombs fell all around, directed at London's number one military target. Elsewhere torrents of blazing spirit poured out of warehouse doors. Barrels of rum exploded like bombs. Cascades of white hot flame poured from paint factories. The choking black fumes that erupted from the burning tyres of the rubber factories suffocated anyone

In Balham, South London, a bus topples into the crater a bomb has opened up.

without breathing apparatus. Death and destruction on all sides . . .

Now the first refugees from Silvertown were reaching Woodford, tired, dirty and despondent. Big ebullient Reverend Hunter, from the local George Lane Baptist Church, took charge of them. In the only church in London capable of being blacked out, he fed them the best he could—and then, leading the men and boys into the baptismal chamber where generations of strict Baptists had been baptised by total immersion, he 'dunked the lot of them, Jew, Catholic, non-believer'.

'Baptists they may not be,' he declared happily afterwards, 'but clean they are!'[16]

At last the sirens started to sound the All Clear. As the Civil Defence still fought on, the first attempts to assess the damage were made. A government communiqué, hurriedly prepared by the Ministry of Information, was released:

Fire was caused among some industrial targets. Damage was done to lighting and other public services and some dislocation to communications was caused. Attacks have also been directed against the docks. Information as to casualties is not yet available.

In fact, thousands of properties had been destroyed or damaged. Fires were raging over many hundreds of acres and would continue to do so for days to come. Three main terminal railway stations were out of action. As for the casualties, 430 men, women and children had lost their lives and 1,600 had been seriously injured. The population of a good-sized Kentish village had been totally wiped out!

The new premier Winston Churchill, like the old warhorse he was, went straight to the sound of the guns. Despite the bombs still falling (on his way back to Downing Street, a shop just in front of his car was blown to smithereens) he drove to Silvertown. There he encountered the columns of terrified refugees and the weary, red-eyed firemen still struggling to subdue the flames. Immediately he showed the spirit and fierce determination which would play such a great part in dragging Britain through in the terrible years to come. Stepping out of his car, in spite of the protests of his staff, he put his antiquated square bowler hat on top of his stick and twirled it round above his head. 'Are we downhearted?' he cried bravely.

The cry came back in a roar. '*NO!*'

TWO
'Beat the German buggers'

The grim siege of London had commenced. For seventy-six consecutive nights, save that of November 2nd when the weather was too bad, the capital was raided. Night after night, anything from fifty to two hundred German bombers would attack London. In September, ten thousand high explosive bombs fell on the beleaguered city, hitting Stepney, Poplar, Bermondsey, Southwark, Lambeth, Deptford, Shoreditch, Bethnal Green. The City was also hit and the riverside boroughs as far as Fulham. At least three of these boroughs were struck by a hundred bombs per square mile!

In October the crippling punishment continued. Again ten thousand bombs were dropped. It was the same in November. In the end, more civilians would be killed in London than in the whole of the British Army in action up to that date, namely 30,000, plus twice that number seriously injured.

Although pre-war pundits had in fact predicted that the casualties would be far higher than they actually were, London had been woefully unprepared for such an assault. Apathy, lack of money, and the constant anti-war attitude of the Labour Party throughout the 1930s were now resulting in the deaths of scores, even hundreds, of ordinary working-class people every day.

Whole areas of the city were burned down because there were no fire-watchers present on the premises and the keys of these properties were at home with their owners. There was no national fire service to coordinate attacks on blazes; in any case, most of the pumps and hoses of the outside brigades would not fit London's hydrants so they would have been no use. Even within the 30,000-strong London Brigade there was considerable, unproductive friction between the regulars and the

Auxiliary firemen play on the fire as an electricity repair squad restores London's light and power.

The underground at Aldwych during an air-raid in 1940.

auxiliaries. The former had several changes of uniform; the latter none. Thus when the auxiliaries came back from a fire, they were often soaked and scorched but with no second uniform to change into. The friction went so far that, in some cases, the regulars would not allow the auxiliaries to use their showers!

Even by November there was still only partial protection offered to the hard-pressed Londoners. Only forty per cent of civilians could find shelter accommodation, of which twenty-seven per cent were using either their own cellars or the primitive, rough-and-ready Anderson shelters: two U-shaped pieces of corrugated iron covering a hole in the back garden.

For the rest there were the tube stations. By the end of September 177,000 Londoners were bedding down nightly in the Underground, on platforms made gritty and khaki-coloured by the sand from leaking sandbags. Many started to queue as early as ten in the morning—they were not allowed to enter till four in the afternoon—to stake out a place on the platform, behind the painted line marking the first three feet of concrete reserved for travelling passengers.

London's petty crooks—'spivs' and 'wide boys' as they were called—soon discovered this as a new source of income. Eric Taylor remembers:

I used to send my lad to stand in the queue at the entrance to the tube station at about two in the afternoon. It was a bit risky because of the gangs of spivs who tried to get rid of any competition—by force . . . If you came late you'd virtually had it. The best places would be gone and by eight there'd be nothing left but small patches at the top of the emergency stairs. Not very safe.[1]

One enterprising crook would plant rags at a dozen different spots on the platform saying he had reserved them 'for an old friend'. Then, when he spotted a prospective customer, he would offer them as a 'favour'—*at a price!* The going-rate varied. Oxford Circus and Green Park tube stations ranked as the most expensive because they were clean and had toilet facilities. There the spivs charged two shillings and sixpence a place. Tottenham Court Road, which was dirty and malodorous, its only sanitation comprising 'piss buckets' hidden behind hessian screens, ranked the lowest.

Even in the best circumstances, it was a hard, uncomfortable life in the tube stations. Those who had no blankets slept on newspapers; if they could afford twopence they bought *The Times* because it was the thickest of the wartime papers. Sanitation was poor, sometimes non-existent. At Swiss Cottage, where 'piss buckets' were forbidden, shelterers had to travel to Finchley Park, the next stop, in order to go to the lavatory. People slept cheek-by-jowl like sardines in a can. It was said that more than one marriage was consummated in full public view on the platforms of London's Underground.

The scandalous lack of adequate air-raid shelters was seen by British Communists as an opportunity for political advancement. They still remained uncommitted to the war—after all, Stalin was Hitler's ally at this stage and Russia had taken part in the carve up of Poland that had finally decided Britain to go to war—but seized this chance to promote their cause. They maintained that the rich had fled the capital in panic, leaving the poor to their fate, or were taking advantage of the deep shelters under such places as the Café de Paris and the Savoy—inaccessible to less fortunate folk, of course.

So, on September 15th, they staged a march on the Savoy. Some one hundred East Enders, under Communist leadership, stormed the first-class hotel as soon as the air-raid sirens had sounded a warning. Unfortunately their demonstration was sabotaged by the All Clear that sounded almost immediately afterwards, whereupon they all filed back out—but the East Enders had a whip-round for the elegant head porter and filled his hand with coppers. Baffled and angered, the Communists were forced to retreat.

London's military defences were equally pitiful. The technique of using night fighters was in its infancy and, four days after the siege commenced, they were withdrawn from over London because they got in the way of the anti-aircraft fire. The defence of the capital was now left to AA Command under General Pile. But as this tough, humorous soldier—whose men admired him greatly: 'smashing fellow, we all liked him'[2]—wrote after the war: 'The defences at night were technically unfit for dealing with anything but the bomber of twenty years earlier.'[3]

He did his best, however. Within forty-eight hours of that first major raid he had doubled the number of guns around the capital and ordered his men simply to blaze away with everything they had, whether they had a target or not, once the sirens sounded. This AA barrage was almost completely ineffective, but it cheered up the hard-pressed civilians enormously. That first night as Pile's wife telephoned him, one of the operators in London cut in and said: 'By God, this is the stuff! All the girls are hugging each other!'[4]

Not everyone was so pleased. With the guns driving them away from their targets in the East End, the German planes tended to jettison their bombs on other suburbs. This caused a lot of resentment, even hate mail. One council leader wrote to the General complaining that 'the lavatory pans were being cracked in their council houses by the vibration of the guns and would we mind very much moving the barrage somewhere else?'

Total war in suburbia, 1940.

Up till now it was London's East End that had borne the brunt of the 'blitz', as it was now being called. To General Pile 'it seemed as if the Germans thought that by concentrating on this part of London ... with its large alien population they would cause such consternation and alarm as seriously to endanger the Government's position, if not to force them to make peace'.[5]

At first, indeed, the East Enders' reaction was 'consternation and alarm'—mixed with a growing sense of outrage as they began to understand the extent to which their leaders had let them down, on a national and a local level, by failing to prepare them for such a cruel onslaught. In Stepney, West Ham and other boroughs there was a rising undercurrent of bitterness and anger, which occasionally spilled over into civil strife. Anti-semitism was rampant because it was believed that all the Jews had fled and found safe billets elsewhere. Deteriorating morale resulted in widespread looting of bombed-out homes and shops. Even in the Fire Brigade Bill Whiting noted that three of his men, all wartime conscripts from the East End, had been caught stealing after a raid and sentenced to imprisonment.

Harold Nicolson, working in the Ministry of Information, wrote in his diary that Sir Kenneth Clark of the Home Morale Emergency Committee was expressing serious misgivings about the East End's morale after night after night of bombing: 'He feels that if the Germans make a good peace offer ... we shall find the popular press take the offer up ... I agree that the spirit of London is excellent but it would take little to swing this courage into cowardice.'[6] And on September 17th Nicolson added: 'Everybody is worried about the feeling in the East End. It is said that even the King and Queen were booed the other day when they visited the destroyed area.'[7]

(On September 13th, Buckingham Palace itself had been bombed and the Royal Family had been obliged to seek protection from the blast and debris. This incident was immediately seized upon by the Ministry of Information to demonstrate that there was no gap between the rich and the poor; they were all being bombed equally. A former GPO publicity man then working for the Ministry, J. Brebner invited forty journalists, British and foreign, to see the damage to the Palace, giving the British orders to stress that the 'King is with His people in the front line together'. The Queen was quoted as saying: 'I am glad we were bombed. It makes me feel I can look the East End in the face.')

Churchill, who would make a point of visiting every blitzed city throughout the war, was worried too. He sent the Tory MP Robert Boothby and other high-ranking figures to the East End to test the cockney's morale. Thus Boothby encountered a ragged little boy in one blitzed street who was crying bitterly. Boothby asked him what the matter was.

'They've taken my mum away,' the little boy sobbed.

'Don't worry,' Boothby comforted him. 'They'll bring her back.'

The little boy stared up at him defiantly through his tears. 'No, they won't,' he retorted. '*Not from the fucking crematorium, they won't!'*[8]

The image of the plucky Cockney wisecracking his way through the blitz was little more than propaganda, deliberately fostered by the Ministry of Information. Nevertheless, like the inhabitants of Berlin-Wedding, the working-class district of the German capital that was repeatedly bombed later in the war, the East Enders', morale never completely cracked. Indeed, the experience toughened and hardened them, and drew them together. A real spirit of comradeship developed, a feeling of all being in the same boat together.

Now, as September passed into October, the German bombing of London was moving westwards, leaving the East End behind in ruins, while the middle- and upper-class areas were getting their share of 'stick'. One report claimed a lady was 'hurled into a Mayfair street in her bath'. Madame Tussaud's Waxworks were struck and the famous wax figures were strewn all across the pavement. Bloomsbury was hit and air-raid warden Graham Greene later recorded 'the squalor of the night, the purgatorial throng of men and women in dirty torn pyjamas, with little blood splashed, standing in doorways'.[9]

Virginia Woolf had just moved from Tavistock Square to Mecklenburgh Square when her new house was hit and badly damaged. She was forced to leave London for the country; and later it was said that it was the effect of the bombing which drove her into final madness and suicide. Another writer living in Mecklenburgh Square, John Lehmann, actually saw the bomb that obliged him to leave his home sitting in 'its earth crater, ugly and waiting'—waiting to be defused.

The BBC was hit. The nine o'clock news was interrupted one night by a crash and listeners all over Britain heard a voice whisper to the newsreader that it was 'all right'. Outside it was most definitely *not* all right. One BBC employee thought the scene outside looked like Dante's *Inferno*:

The front of the building was lit up by a reddish-yellow light; the saloon car was on fire to the left of me and the flames were stretching upwards . . . a few huddled bodies were round about and right in front of me were two soldiers: one, some feet from a breach in the wall where a fire seemed to be raging, was propped up against the wall with his arms dangling by him like a rag doll . . . The other was nearer . . . His trousers had been blown off him, I could see that his legs were bare and that he was wearing short grey underpants . . . There appeared to be one or two dark huddled bodies by the wall of the building. I had not the strength to lift any of them. I wondered where the water was coming from which I felt dripping down on my face and soon discovered that it was blood from my head wounds.[10]

On November 7th, after being hit twice, it was decided to evacuate Parliament to 'an unspecified place'; the Palace of Westminster offered too tempting a target. Princess Elizabeth and her little sister, Princess Margaret Rose, were evacuated too. More and more people were fleeing the capital. In Chelsea whole rows of houses belonging to the wealthy were empty, their owners having fled to the West Country.

When Upper Cheyne Walk was bombed, VAD Frances Faviell, who had studied anatomy at the Slade, was detailed to help a Mr Leacock fit the bits and pieces of dead bodies together so that the relatives could see their loved ones apparently intact before they were buried. 'Proper jigsaw puzzle, ain't it, Miss?' Leacock said cheerfully as they commenced their grim task.

The stench was terrible, but the little crew persisted, going out from time to time for a cigarette. 'After the first violent revulsion,' Miss Faviell said later, 'I set my mind to it as a detached, systematic task. It became a grim and ghastly satisfaction when a body was fairly constructed—but if one was too lavish in making one body almost whole, then another one would have sad gaps. There were always odd members which did not seem to fit and there were too many legs. Unless we kept a very firm grip on ourselves nausea was inevitable . . . The feeling uppermost in my mind after every big

The BBC is hit—this is the back of Broadcasting House.

raid was *anger*, anger at the lengths to which human beings could go to inflict injury on one another.'[11]

In that same November, as London's defences stiffened and reports coming back to Germany indicated that the terror raids had failed to break London's morale, Goering and Milch started to look around for other targets which were easier to attack. Already the Luftwaffe had made minor raids on cities throughout the United Kingdom, from Glasgow in the north to Birmingham in the Midlands, from Liverpool in the west to Hull in the east. Now the Luftwaffe planners decided to attack a relatively undefended but important provincial city; the city they chose was Coventry.

On the night of November 14th, 1940, Coventry was bursting at the seams. Within its bounds there were four times the number of people the city had housed before the war. From everywhere people had flocked to get jobs in the booming, well-paid armaments industry. Now the lodging houses and flats around the medieval Cathedral on the hill were packed.

At ten minutes after seven that perfect moonlit night, the sirens began to wail. Almost immediately the first of the German pathfinders' chandelier flares burst above the city, bathing everything in a pure white incandescent glow. The incendiaries started to whistle down.

To those who witnessed it the scene was indescribable. Everything was burning in a sizzling blue-white glare. The whole city seemed on fire. 'I'd just been through the bombing of Birmingham,' recalls Madge Faulkney, who worked on Spitfires at Vickers in Birmingham and who was visiting friends in Coventry that night, 'but it had not been anything like this. Look in any direction you wanted and all you could see was flames, flames, flames . . .'[12]

The unearthly beauty of those flames seemed to mesmerise all who saw them. As the great Cathedral stood outlined in a sea of fire, Miss Faulkney's friends stood on tables to watch the spectacle; it had such an eerie fascination for them.

But as soon as the fire-bombers had departed and the Cathedral itself had been swallowed up by those greedy flames, the rest of the German attackers came zooming in—over 400 of them, unleashing literally hundreds of tons of high explosive.

As the raid went on, hour after hour, the city's essential services broke down. Fire hydrants were buried under the rubble. Water mains were shattered by bombs. Those who were still attempting to fight the blaze had to drag water by hand from the river and the canal. Rugby's Fire Brigade arrived but had to stand by helplessly and watch the city burn. At St Mary's Police Station near the Cathedral, the defeated fire-fighters listened, sick at heart, to the steady drip-drip of lead melting from the great roof.

Even the German attackers were awed by the

Coventry was devastated in the raid in November 1940.

magnitude of that great fire blazing below. At 6,000 feet, Oberfeldwebel Werner Handorf could feel his nostrils prickle as the smell of the burning city penetrated even into the cockpit of his Junkers 88. Hans Fruehauf, a veteran of the London raids, stared down at the sea of flames in horror. 'The usual cheers that greeted a direct hit stuck in our throats,' he remembers. 'The crew just gazed down at the flames in silence. Was this really a military target, we all asked ourselves . . .'[13]

Eleven terrible hours later it was over. The bombers turned and started to fly back east as the sky began to lighten, revealing the city in all its bomb-shattered horror.

Coventry had been devastated. Out of the city's pre-war total of 75,000 dwellings, 60,000 had been destroyed or damaged—along with twenty-seven vital war plants. Every railway line out of the city was blocked. The tramway network was unusable and half the city's buses had been destroyed. The telephones weren't working. Coventry was cut off from the world.

With the electric power lines down, they were unable even to sound the All Clear. Those wardens still capable wandered through the streets in the drizzling rain shouting hoarsely, 'It's all over . . . They've gone . . . It's all over . . .'

Hilde Marchant of the *Daily Express*, who had been through the London blitzes, was one of the first outsiders to report from the stricken scene. Surveying the one square mile of rubble that had been the city centre, she was particularly struck by the thousands of refugees fleeing the city with their pathetic bits and pieces piled on barrows and prams. 'It was a familiar sight, one that I had seen in Spain and Finland,' she wrote later, 'but this was worse . . . These people moved against a background of suburban villas, had English faces, used the English tongue, wore English clothes. They were our own kind.'[14]

Everywhere it was the same: ruins, disruption, death. Madge Faulkney was fighting her way through the crowds in order to get back to her job in Birmingham. She watched numbly as soldiers went before her 'picking up bits of arms and legs and putting them in potato sacks, as if they were working in a harvest field'.[15]

The casualties had indeed been terrible. In those eleven horrific hours, at least 520 men, women and children had died and more than 1,200 had been wounded—the real figures were never established. In the end 420 victims, all unidentified, were buried in a mass grave.

For days, in some cases even for weeks, those who stayed and did not join the panic-stricken exodus from Coventry would lack the bare essentials of modern living—gas, running water, electricity—as the fires continued to blaze unchecked, some of them not being put out until after Christmas.

Mass Observation sent three observers to check on the mood of the survivors. Their report was gloomy. On all sides they heard the same feeling expressed: 'Coventry is finished . . . Coventry is dead.' 'The small size of the place makes people feel that the only thing they can do is to get out of it altogether,' the observers reported.

There were more open signs of hysteria, terror, neurosis observed in one evening than during the whole of the past two months together in all areas. Women were seen to cry, to scream, to tremble all over, to faint in the street, to attack a fireman and so on . . . There were several signs of suppressed panic as darkness approached. In two cases people were seen fighting to get on to cars which they thought would take them out into the country, though in fact the drivers insisted the cars were going just up the road to garage.[16]

During the raid itself many people had been 'staggering about with shock, as though they were hopelessly drunk', remembers H. E. Legg, who was now doing the best he could to help the injured. One incident he still recalls today concerned a man who had been trapped under some wreckage and was obviously seriously hurt. After helping to free him, Mr Legg draped his own coat over the injured man, who 'gritted his teeth and joked that he hoped he'd be playing football on Saturday'; but when they tried to move him he screamed with agony. Finally one of the First Aid men started to work on his injured leg, cutting away the trouser material; and 'as soon as the cloth parted completely the man's leg fell apart as though cut by an axe from thigh to ankle'.

Mr Legg's coat was later returned to him, along with a pound note and a message saying *'Thanks pal, have a drink with me'*. A pathetic hope—for Mr Legg learned that shortly afterwards, during an operation to amputate his shattered limb, the man had died.[17]

At last it began to dawn on the people of Britain, in that winter of 1940, that it was not just the men in khaki who were fighting this war. The civilians, the men, women and children who had stayed at home, were in the front line now.

'This is the *real* war, here in Coventry, and we are the ones—the civvies—who are fighting it,' Madge Faulkney told herself as she finally found a lift back to Birmingham (which would soon be heavily blitzed itself). And she felt a sudden fierce pride and determination. 'We were going to beat them, I knew it in my heart. *If we could stick it out, we'd beat the German buggers in the end.'*[18]

The rubble of Coventry after the raid in November 1940.

THREE
One vast bonfire

Manchester had had a quiet war so far. Apart from the introduction of rationing and gradual disappearance of the younger men from its streets, the war raging in the south had left the northern city virtually untouched. Once, on August 8th, a German plane had flown over the city and dropped a few incendiaries (which caused relatively little damage) plus some leaflets. The leaflets, containing Hitler's 'Appeal to Reason', were still tied up in bundles as if the bomb aimer had been bored with the whole operation; and one bundle landed on a policeman's head, his helmet being the only casualty that Manchester had suffered in nearly fifteen months of war.

Most people's main concern was how to eke out their meagre food rations and find some sort of respite from gloom—very often in drink. 'The quickest way out of Manchester is through a bottle of gin!' they used to say. Cigarettes were not rationed, but they were hard to get. One young office worker, nineteen-year-old A. Neeson —who worked in Lancaster Avenue, in the shadow of the great Cathedral—seemed to spend half her time scouring the local shops on behalf of her chain-smoking boss. Very often the popular brands were reserved for 'regulars' only and she was forced to accept 'lesser brands that no one in his right mind would buy, save a man desperate for a smoke'.[1] But her problem would soon be solved; there would be no more shops.

Even the younger men already in uniform thought Manchester a particularly 'cushy billet' in that second winter of the war. Private Alan Brandt of the Pay Corps, stationed at the Pay Office in George Street, Piccadilly, thought he couldn't have it better: 'Here I was serving in my home town and billeted at home.'[2]

But soon the Pay Office would disappear, along with much more of Central Manchester, and 'what had so far been a rather pleasant sojourn in HM Forces was brought to an abrupt end'.[3] His next three years would be spent in India, a long way from smoky old Manchester.

Of course, in common with all cities, Manchester had mobilised some sort of civil defence at the outbreak of war; but as one boring month gave way to another and there were no alarms, the men had grown slack. By December 1940 the city was taking its duties very lightly indeed. Harry Palmer, then an eighteen-year-old volunteer fire-watcher at All Saints between Piccadilly and the University where he was a student, recalls the Oxford Road pubs being filled with 'unattached ladies, servicemen and husbands out for the night "fire-watching"'.

Oxford Road and Piccadilly were known even before the war as the centres for finding a 'good-time girl' on the way to the Ritz or a straightforward professional whore. They liked also to congregate in Lewis's Arcade on the corner of Mosley Street and Piccadilly. I can picture them to this day: some in smart two-piece costumes, wearing little hats with a lace veil; others in fur coats standing about two yards apart, backs to the windows, and men walking the Arcade looking at the toys and occasionally asking the price—which seemed to be fixed at about two pounds (the price of twenty pints, the way I reckoned in those days). I think a lot of men carried out their 'civil defence duties' there in Manchester before it happened.[4]

The City Fathers, too, were concerned with morality—or rather the lack of it. Alan Jackson, the sixteen-year-old son of an off-licence owner in Ardwick, had volunteered for messenger duties with Civil Defence at the central post in Piccadilly. But 'someone had the idea that young lads like myself should not be spending long hours at night in the company of older men in the middle of a big city. So they had the brilliant idea of putting all the young messengers in one building where they could be supervised properly. Every night then we spent on the top floor of Rylands Building. One bomb, as a result, could have put all messengers out in one go.'[5] Which, as Mr Jackson points out today, would have meant the end of Manchester's civil defence communications system.

But the war was slowly coming the way of the ill-prepared, unsuspecting city. After Coventry, it advanced northwards like some predatory monster greedy for new prey. On November 28th Liverpool was blitzed for the first time. Between December 12th and 15th it was the turn of Sheffield, the country's greatest arsenal. On December 20th, Liverpool and Merseyside took another brutal beating . . .

That same day, Manchester was the subject of what was later seen as a large-scale reconnaissance trip by the German raiders. T. C. Baskerville—who was destined, as he says himself, to become 'the world's longest diarist

Men of the Hampshire Regiment are helping to clear bomb damage in a town in the Northern Command.

as recorded in the Guinness Book of Records'*—noted in his diary for that day:

6.35 The sirens sounded. Soon after a plane came over and guns opened fire. About ten minutes to fifteen minutes a plane is coming with AA guns opening up on him. New candle.[6]

Soon this twentieth-century Pepys would be recording another 'Great Fire'—that of his home town, Manchester.

December 22nd, 1940, was a dark, depressing winter's day, the last Sunday before Christmas. While the Mancunians were busy preparing for whatever festivities they could muster, the men responsible for Manchester's civil defence were meeting to discuss the alarming possibility that trouble was on its way.

Ever since that spring, British intelligence had been intercepting most of the Third Reich's coded traffic. As soon as orders were sent out in code from Berlin, they reached a rusty little tin hut in Bletchley, the small market town sixty miles north of London, headquarters of the Government Code and Cypher School—or 'the Golf Club and Chess Society' as it was mockingly known among the eggheads who worked there. And as a result of their top-secret operations, the code-breakers had recently concluded that Manchester was a likely target for German bombers in the immediate future. It was their report, filtered through various official channels, that

now caused so much alarm among the members of Manchester's Emergency Committee.

In December 1940 Manchester had 193 full-time regular firemen and 1,774 auxiliaries, plus 1,576 part-timers who reported for duty only when there was an air raid. But on December 22nd ten per cent of the regular force were in Liverpool, helping the hard-pressed local brigade. The Committee decided to withdraw their men from Liverpool and drew up an emergency plan for requesting extra firemen and rescue squads from other areas. They made no attempt to alert the local Civil Defence or to inspect the state of the fire-watching teams, which on this pre-Christmas Sunday could well be very slack, with even higher absenteeism than normal.

In the end, nothing really was done. The brigades from outside town would reach Manchester when it was too late. Many Civil Defence workers never turned up for duty; and as for the ordinary citizen, he was left totally in the dark. Like their successors of forty-four years later, who in 1984 banned all military activities from the Manchester Show because it 'should not be a recruiting ground to seduce unemployed youngsters into the armed services',[7] the city's leaders remained complacent and blind to what was about to descend upon them. They would reap a bitter harvest from that blind complacency, very bitter indeed.

Outside the council chambers the unsuspecting citizens were doing their best to enjoy this last Sunday before Christmas. Seventeen-year-old Eileen Hargreaves heard the *Messiah* performed by the Hallé Orchestra, under Sir Malcolm Sargent, for the first time. That stirring music

*At the time of writing Mr Baskerville has been keeping his diary for forty-six years.

telling of peace and love would sustain her through the long night of horror to come.

Grace Crane, a first-aider, also went to hear some Christmas music that afternoon at her local church. To her surprise she found herself being called upon to sing a solo in the carol service because the girl who should have sung it was ill. She did not give her best performance, and she knew it. Later, when it had all happened, the vicar said to her: 'Well, Grace, I've heard of some people's voices bringing on the rain. But yours was so bad that it must have caused the destruction of your native city and my church!'[8] But that was later.

Ada and Harry Mann had more urgent things to attend to. Their seven-month baby daughter was ill and they were taking her to Hope Hospital for an operation. Little did they know as they delivered her to the nurses that afternoon that it would be many long weeks before they saw their child again—and then it would be too late.

Marjorie Riley, fourteen years old, was excited because she was going to celebrate her birthday this day at her Granny's and she knew Granny had prepared a trifle for her—a special treat now that sugar was so short. She and her brother could hardly wait to taste it.

Edith Bethal's husband also had a birthday on December 22nd, and she too was preparing a special celebration meal, waiting for him to return home after his day's duties as a warden. But her husband would not come home this day and when he finally did, he'd find his home destroyed, with only the budgie rescued . . .

Slowly the day passed. By four o'clock it was almost dark. All over Manchester, housewives began to draw their curtains and check their black-out. A trickle of reluctant fire-watchers reported for duty, collected their helmets and gasmasks and set off for their posts. Night-shift workers picked up their 'snap', their sandwiches, and headed for the factories. Here and there, those who had nothing to do settled down in front of the fire and turned on the radio for some early evening's entertainment. 'Auntie BBC', as always on a Sunday, was making a very dreary business of it: sombre music, serious talks, chats by well-meaning padres. Some radio listeners twirled their dials impatiently until they found Radio Hamburg and that familiar voice speaking in oddly accented English. It was Lord Haw-Haw—'the Humbug of Hamburg' as B. Reilly called him, for she was a regular listener to the traitor. Mostly she found him amusing, 'a real good laugh at times'. But this evening what he had to say sent shivers down her spine. This night, he promised, 'the German Air Force would chase the bugs and fleas from Ardwick Circus Cinema'—and that old fleapit of a cinema was just up the road from her house . . .

It was 6.38 pm when the first dreaded wail of the air-raid sirens cut into Manchester's dreary December Sunday. Now the night was fine and cold. There was a stiff breeze blowing, too, something the Germans had hoped for as they had set out from their bases in Holland and Belgium, some 400 planes in all.

Sixteen-year-old John Walker was in the middle of his solo at the carol service in Holy Trinity Church, Platt Street, when the first incendiaries started to whistle down. He was singing the role of the page in that favourite old Victorian carol, 'Good King Wenceslas', and he had just reached the verse

> Sire, the night is darker now
> And the wild wind stronger,
> Fails my heart, I know not how,
> I can go no longer.

As he recalled over forty years later, 'Believe me, at that moment the last words were just too true and that night was certainly my swan song as a treble!'[10] The rest of that night he would spend in the Rectory, with shrapnel hissing through the roof.

Manchester's ordeal had just begun—and it was to last thirty-six long hours.

The first real incident occurred barely seconds after the sirens ceased to howl, when an incendiary landed on the Vine Hotel, near Albert Square. The hotel was rapidly engulfed in a fierce blaze, which served to light up the whole area and provided the German bombers with a clearly visible target at the very heart of the city.

The incendiaries were raining down on all sides, hundreds upon hundreds of them, starting fires everywhere—in Piccadilly, Victoria Street, Miller Street, the Assize Courts outside the notorious Strangeways Prison, Woolworth's, the famed Falstaff Inn, the medieval Shambles. Because so many fire-watchers had simply not turned up for duty, the fires started to gain the upperhand at a tremendous rate, searing across Central Manchester like the flame from some great blowtorch.

Harry Palmer, the young volunteer fire-watcher, was on duty however. He was just 'having a quiet chat when suddenly the whole of the city in my area was ablaze, as hundreds of sizzling white flames erupted from roofs, roadways, gutters'.[11] And, in common with fire-watchers all over the city, all he had at his disposal were a few sandbags and a stirrup-pump—a hand pump supplied from a bucket of water. With these he was supposed to combat a blazing inferno.

He and his friends soon found themselves swamped by the sheer number of these fire bombs. Some of them contained an explosive charge 'which went off just after landing—just long enough for someone to have got near enough to them to get his eyes burnt out in the flash'. He could see them dropping everywhere, 'plopping on to nearby roofs, and you looked across the gap of roadway absolutely powerless as they burned their way through the roof and top floor until the whole building gradually roared into flame and was lost'.[12]

On top of a 100-foot ladder above the burning Royal Exchange, twenty-seven-year-old fireman Les McLouglin, who was fated to be on duty for thirty-six hours solid, looked over his shoulder to see the Shambles in flame. 'It wasn't red hot. It was *white hot!* I thought—I'm better off up here!'[13]

Not far away, the gentle, middle-aged Dean of Manchester, Dr Garfield Williams, found incendiaries dropping on the roof of his Cathedral—and discovered that the water supply had been cut off. There was nothing he could do but stand by and watch. 'We were all marooned in an island in the very centre of the disturbance like a ship in the middle of a cyclone.' Tearing his eyes from the burning roof of the Cathedral, he glanced across Cheetham's Hospital, attached to the church, and saw the same horrific sight that Les McLouglin had seen: the medieval Shambles was 'one vast bonfire and the wind was so filled with sparks as to give the impression of golden rain. There was much more flame than smoke or so it seemed to me, and the roar of the flames was terrific.' And in the midst of this his 'Owd Church', as the Manchester people called the Cathedral, was 'fairy-like, scintillating in the midst of the blaze of fire'.[14]

But there was nothing 'fairy-like' about the great fire raging across the thirty-one acres within a one-mile radius of Albert Square, particularly for those trying to escape.

Ten-year-old Betty Woods had been visiting her grandfather, a caretaker for the Air Ministry in Blackfriars, together with her mother and her little brother, two years younger. Now they were fleeing for their lives, chased by a roaring red wall of flame. They ran helter-skelter over tailor dummies scattered in the road, looking for all the world like corpses; they ran past a burning shop with the charred remains of a wooden model of a dog in its window. (Betty thought it was 'a real live dog' and burst into tears) and past 'groups of dirty dejected people standing on street corners, talking in whispers'.[15] Finally they reached safety. But her brother never recovered from the ordeal. Soon afterwards he developed St Vitus's Dance.

Eleanor and James Schofield also found themselves racing from the advancing flames, hugging close to walls that burnt to the touch and here and there bulged alarmingly with the heat as if they were live things. At last they reached their shelter—only to find it occupied by a young woman in an advanced stage of pregnancy, 'moaning and groaning that she was going to have her baby at any minute'.[16] Out they went again into the streets but none of the vehicles they attempted to flag down would stop for them, their drivers were intent on fleeing the burning city before it was too late. In the end the Schofields managed to stop a Co-Op milk float, whose driver grumbled that it was 'illegal' but finally agreed to take the woman to hospital. Thus the baby

Fire-hoses in action after a raid on Manchester in 1940.

was duly born in the middle of a burning Manchester—courtesy of the Co-Operative Society!

Harold Kelly had been watching 'Carol Levis's Discoveries' in the Paramount Theatre when the raid started. For a while he and the rest of the audience tried to ignore it; but when the 'balcony began to bump and wobble in a very funny fashion' they decided they'd had enough. They fled outside to find a scene of utter confusion. The nearby Princess Theatre had been hit and was blazing furiously. Panic-stricken crowds were surging this way and that. Mr Kelly and his friends took to their heels, heading down Oxford Road towards Portland Street. But the chaos here was even worse: 'It was mass hysteria! Hundreds of people jammed together in sheer terror as Portland Street burned.'[17]

As Mr Kelly summed it up over forty years later: 'We

hadn't been prepared for this.'[18]

It was Coventry all over again: another city falling apart because its blinkered leaders had failed to read the warning signs.

Down in the Central Control Room, located under Police HQ at South Street, a pattern to the raid had emerged as wave after wave of German bombers swept over the burning city. The raiders had obviously been concentrating on the area around the Victoria Exchange, the merchant houses of Portland Street, and the rich Trafford Park Industrial Estate, the biggest in the whole of Europe.

A pattern had also been established for Salford, where the rail centres and marshalling yards had been badly hit, cutting the borough off from Manchester. Stretford, too, was receiving a heavy battering, especially the Old Trafford area. Both places reported 100 fires apiece, thirty-five of them out of control.

It was officially decided to declare the situation 'serious' and, although the damage had already been done, to request help. So, from Leeds and as far away as Birmingham, Newcastle, Nottingham and Cardiff, the fire brigades set out on a long journey over treacherous winter roads, racing to the help of hard-pressed Manchester. Whether the additional 176 crews and pumps would arrive in time, some of them having to cross the icy, snow-bound Pennines on their way, was anybody's guess that night.

By now, however, the raiders were changing their tactics, using a new and untried technique. Relying on the forecast of high winds to spread the blaze, they now began to drop high explosive bombs. The detonation of these HE bombs fanned and increased the flames, turning the blaze into what was later to be called a 'fire blitz', the first of its kind in the history of warfare. For Goering wanted to burn Manchester to the ground— and it seemed he was largely succeeding.

There was a mad scramble for the shelters as the first HE bombs came whistling down, even among those who had earlier refused to set foot in one.

Sixteen-year-old Betty Hopley and her family, however, found to their horror that they could not escape from their house in North Street; behind them in Cheetham Street a series of bombs had dropped and jammed their door. Frantically they screamed for help, thinking they were going to be burnt alive. Fortunately their cries were heard. The door was smashed down by local air-raid wardens and they were hustled into the nearby shelters under the Weinberger and Blond Bros. factories. But Fred, Betty's twenty-seven-year-old brother, was later forced to leave the shelter. Even though he was an invalid, often confined to a wheelchair, he had to take his turn with the others at fire-watching.

The strain proved too much for his weakened heart. Within a few weeks he would be dead.

But death was all around them that terrible night. Fred had no sooner shuffled away than a Mr Scully staggered into the shelter from Cheetham Street, dressed only in a vest and dirty long-johns. He was shaking all over, clearly in a state of severe shock—and with good reason, as Betty Hopley remembers today.[19] He had just lost his wife and all his four children, plus a niece. He was not the only one. Another neighbour, Joseph Malloys, lost his father, mother, brother, two uncles, two of their children and his grandmother—all killed in the same instant by a bomb.

Young or old, they were all caught in the horror of that never-ending night. Six-year-old Dorothy Toldsley had been having nightmares each night that Hitler might bomb her precious doll's house. Even now, as she sat quaking in the shelter below the local Conservative Club, listening to her mother saying that the 'glare and blood-red sky was Manchester burning', Dorothy was worrying about her doll's house. It survived; her home didn't.[20]

On the other side of the city, the Manns had heard some dreadful news: the hospital where their sick baby was, Hope Hospital, had been hit. They persuaded a friend who owned a taxi to take them there. It was a nightmarish journey through flame and exploding bombs. Once the cabbie shrieked, 'Oh my God, my bloody tyres are on fire!' Somehow or other they got through, only to find Hope Hospital 'a smoking pile, with the bedding fluttering out of the windows like flags'.[21] The ward that had housed their baby was destroyed. *But where was she?*

No one knew. No one could give them any information, as the rescue workers toiled away at the smoking debris. It was six weeks before the Manns found their baby again—in Warrington Mental Hospital, of all places, several miles away. And she had been badly burnt: 'The whole of her back from the knees upwards had not a bit of skin left on it. It looked like a piece of liver with yellow blobs on it.'[22] For days on end the sick baby had lain virtually unattended in a drawer. She died soon afterwards.

Even today, the memory still makes the Manns, now both in their mid-seventies, shake with emotion.

There were lighter moments, though, amid all the horror, tragedy and suffering. Marjorie Riley and her brother were quite contented to pass the time in their Anderson shelter, waiting for the All Clear and a chance to sample Granny's tempting trifle, playing noughts-and-crosses and drawing swastikas on the plaster of the latter's broken leg. Granny, however, was bored. She decided to leave the Anderson shelter and secure the trifle before it was too late.

Hardly had she got outside when there was a tremendous explosion. Marjorie and her brother rushed out to find Granny lying on the ground, legs in the air, covered in broken china, with what was left of the precious trifle dripping down her apron!

Fred Neeson, a Civil Defence man, found his way into the Ardwick Cinema, the 'fleapit' which Lord Haw-Haw had predicted the Luftwaffe would finally clear of its celebrated bugs and fleas. He'd been right; the cinema was now on fire—but its lights were still blazing out into the night. Desperately young Neeson sought for the main switch to turn them off, but try as he might he could not find it. So in the end: 'I just had to stand there, feeling a bloody fool, aiming bricks at each individual light bulb to knock it out.'[23]

Sometimes the humour of that terrible night became decidedly macabre. Grace Crane, who was later to be accused of bringing down the city with her singing voice, was on duty at her First Aid post one mile from the city centre when yet another casualty was brought in: an old woman covered in dust and obviously injured about the head. 'Clip her hair,' the harassed doctor ordered, 'so I can have a better look at her head.'

'Not bloody likely!' the old woman snapped defiantly. 'I've just had me hair permed for his funeral—' She gasped suddenly. 'Oh my God,' she exclaimed, *where is Ernie? I left him in the front room when the bomb hit us . . .'*

As Grace recalls many years later: 'I didn't know whether to laugh or cry.'[24]

A. Neeson, who had spent so much time before the bombing looking for cigarettes for her boss, experienced pretty much the same emotion as she watched the survivors from a nearby Army barracks which had been bombed, stagger into her local grocer's where they were being given cups of tea. 'I grabbed for what I thought was my boot,' one of them choked, face still white with shock. 'I found my right one and put it on. Then the left. But it weren't mine. *It had a human foot inside it!'*[25]

Horror, bravery, compassion, patriotism, fear, greed— all the emotions and passions were intermingled that terrible night, without any pattern or order. They were like the night itself, chaotic and confused.

B. Reilly emerging from the air-raid shelter, bleary-eyed and weary, to gasp at what appeared to be a dummy hanging from the roof of the corset factory in Downing Street, Ardwick. 'But it was no dummy. It was a woman whose clothes had been blown off her and her body propelled right to the roof.'[26]

George Roberts, a railwayman, uncoupled a trainload of high explosive shells while bombs dropped all around, thus saving hundreds of lives. He would win one of the first of the new George Medals for bravery.*

Mrs Johnson leaving the shelter under the local girls'

* He is still alive and tough today, although now he is bedridden.

grammar school in Chester Road to find a parachute mine hanging from a tree opposite, her house badly damaged and already ransacked by looters. But in her pantry they had not found her most precious possession that Christmas—'my dozen fresh eggs'.[27]

Thomas Flannagan, a teenager, was wandering through the burning city and watching blazes being fought by what he thought were 'pitifully few firemen'. Presently he came across a lone fireman, little older than himself, pointing his hose at the huge fire raging at the S. J. Watts factory. 'Suddenly a strange feeling came over me. I think you could call it love of one's native land, one's native city. At that moment I loved them both.' He picked his way forward and silently took the hose from the weary fireman. Neither spoke. 'Words would have been superfluous.'[28]

But on his way home he saw two men loading loot from a shop in Swan Street into a van . . .

At last it was over. Eight miles outside Manchester, children watched in wonder as the first snow started to fall. But this was snow with a difference: the 'snow-flakes' were pieces of charred paper from the hundreds of burnt-out offices in the city centre, swirling down from the leaden sky.

Standing in the ruins of his Cathedral with the 'snow' falling on his bare head, Dr Williams reflected: 'I was glad she [his cathedral] was battered about like this. How could she possibly remain unscathed when so much was destroyed? I did not want her saved by a miracle—she must suffer with Manchester.'[29]

And Manchester had indeed suffered, like all the other unprepared cities before her. By Christmas Day, after thirty-six hours of bombing, 363 of its citizens were dead, 455 were seriously injured and thousands were homeless, while the remainder were shocked and shattered by the terrible experience.

All the Emergency Committee could do now was issue a stirring message:

The city of Manchester suffered the effects of the raid with fortitude and determination of the highest character. There was no feeling of helplessness but a general desire to bring every effort to bear to restore normal conditions in the city so far as this was possible.[30]

In fact, most of the survivors faced a Christmas with very little food and no gas to cook it on. There was no pure water and electricity was rationed. There'd be no Christmas shopping because the city centre was sealed off, one square mile of ruins, much of it still burning. Christmas dinner for most was, as Mrs R. Davies recalled many years later, 'an ad hoc affair, cooked mainly in saucepans on the dining-room fire and our "siren suits" were laid ready for the next air-raid warning'.[31]

Christmas in Britain, vintage 1940 . . .

FOUR
'We'll get the bastards for this'

By this time London had been under almost constant attack for four months. Thirty thousand people had been killed; twice that number seriously injured. Half a million people had been rendered homeless. Nearly a million people spent every night sleeping in the shelters. The Hungerford railway arches near Charing Cross Station had been converted into shelters for the down-and-outs and vagrants so that they could be segregated from the rest of the shelter population, due to the fear of epidemics being spread by too many people crowded together.

And yet the city was still very much alive and working. Letters were still delivered, as were milk and bread to doorsteps. Buses, trains and tubes still ran, even if their schedules were sometimes disrupted. Food was still brought from outside the beleaguered city to be sold at Covent Gardens and Billingsgate, though at a cost. The men and women who kept the capital going—the clippies, porters, merchants, postwomen and the like—often worked fifteen hours a day, six or seven days a week, under appalling conditions; indeed, often risking their lives during the nightly raids to ensure that Londoners had their morning 'pinta'.

But London had to contend not only with the bombs, but also with the growing shortages. Imports were down, due to the success of the German U-boat campaign against Britain; thirty per cent less food was now arriving in the country.

The average Londoner's diet was the poorest of the whole war. One person's meat ration for a week might be a single chop. Cheese was down to one ounce per person per week. Eggs were like gold—one per family per week, and there was always the problem of who was going to eat that precious egg: the growing child or the working Mum or Dad? Onions virtually disappeared, as had already the orange and the banana. Later in the war when a child was given one of these rarities, a banana, he ate it skin and all!

Clothing and footwear were becoming difficult to find too. Knicker elastic, like lipstick, was all but unobtainable. Silk stockings could only be bought on the black market, which had become literally a way of life now in London. Shoes were soled and heeled at home with the aid of patent kits of rubber (there was no leather) sold by the local Woolworths. When their menfolk disappeared into the Forces, women unpicked their suits, which they would no longer need now, and turned them into jackets and skirts for themselves; and they made bras out of butter muslin and panties out of mosquito netting!

And still the bombs fell. The majority of Londoners had by now grown accustomed to the noise, the horror, the destruction, the sudden violent death. But not all. Mass Observation in its secret surveys reported that people still panicked at the sound of bombs:

Women scream and huddle together. Suddenly a woman of 25 shouts at a younger girl: 'Stop leaning against that wall, you bloody fool! Like a bleeding lot of children! . . . My God, we're going mad!'
People begin shouting at each other. Sophie, 30, screams at her mother: 'Oh, you get on my nerves . . . Oh, shut up!'
Here the ARP helper tries once again to start some singing. 'Roll out the barrel—' she begins.
'Shut your bleeding row!' shouts a man of 50. 'We've got enough noise without you!'[1]

Looting and violent crime was becoming widespread, too. In the worse hit districts, notices were posted by the police warning that '*Looting from premises which have been damaged by or vacated by reasons of War Operations is punishable by death or penal servitude for life.*' Reading the newspapers of that time, one always finds small paragraphs tucked away inside naming men and women sentenced for looting a few days after any big raid. 'Looting—or better pilfering—always occurred after each blitz,' Bill Whiting, the Fire Brigade officer, confirms today. 'People said, why leave it to some other bugger to pinch? *I'm* having it, mate!'[2]

Criminals, too, were becoming more dangerous and daring. A twenty-year-old nurse in charge of seven tube shelters remembers 'the fear of walking in empty dark streets knowing not a soul was in the tall buildings on either side. The extraordinary loud sound one's own footsteps made when the guns were silent. The memory of kind willing old Charlie (an air raid warden) so recently and horribly knifed and the light-hearted prostitute I walked with one evening of whom the people in the shelters said "Serve her right!" when she was murdered. Another woman who returned from the shelter

These chimney-stacks stand in the rubble of Chancery Lane.

to fetch her purse and was stabbed to death on her own doorstep for a few shillings.'[3]

Starvation, sudden death and savage crime on all sides. But if the average Londoner 'stuck it out', in the phrase of the time, there were some who were growing increasingly critical of the complacent attitude of the various local authorities. They thought that councillors responsible for civil defence and welfare in those boroughs hardest hit lived in a dream world, remote from the hard truths of bombed-out London.

In 1941 after the blitzes had ended, Barbara Nixon, a former actress and now a full-time warden in Finchley, summed it up thus:

It is fair to say that the local authorities fell down on, at least, three questions—water supply, shelters and rehousing. Ours was a Labour borough and before the war had had a good record in rehousing, public health etc ... But as the war developed the local leaders seemed to lose all realisation that they were responsible for and *to* the population; that they were servants as well as rulers.[4]

But the Labour Mayor of Finchley, remote from the needs of his people, finally did receive his comeuppance. One Saturday night he happened to be in Miss Nixon's shelter when a row broke out. A group of local ladies had returned from the pub at the start of a raid to find their usual bunks occupied. There were plenty of empty places, but they wanted their customary places. Wardens tried to settle the row. To no avail. Bottles, brought from the pub for the night, were brandished threateningly. Hair was pulled. People were punched. Clothes ripped.

It was now that Finchley's 'man-of-the-people' decided to settle the matter personally. With dignity, he demanded to know what all this was about.

A huge woman, wearing men's boots, turned and looked down at the fat little man. 'Who the bleedin' 'ell are you?' she sneered.

'My good woman,' he replied, 'I am the Mayor.'

'I don't care if you're an effing 'orse,' the woman snorted. '*I want me bleedin' bunk!*'[5]

So Christmas had passed in the hard-pressed capital. The *Daily Telegraph* had duly recorded that a monster Christmas party had been given for 'night-tunnellers' children' in the crypt of a church where Dickens had worshipped—'a feast of 1,500 cakes and one hundredweight of slab cake, half a hundredweight of jam and three dozen tins of fish paste'. The unknown reporter wrote gushingly, 'What would have delighted Dickens most would have been the sight of a whitebearded roadman minding one of Goering's holes in the road, beside a roughly chalked board of his own design, with the words *Merry Christmas to you all!*'

All suitably festive and encouraging in the best tradition of 'Britain can take it'. But even now as 1940 gave way to 1941, the second year of war, London was still not totally prepared for its last—and most terrible—blitz of that traumatic year.

Its fire-fighting problems had still not been resolved. Every firm in the country employing more than thirty people was obliged by law to furnish a list of fire-watchers, but very few complied; and the new Minister of Home Security, one-eyed Labour leader Herbert Morrison, a former conscientious objector in World War One, seemed oddly reluctant to enforce the law. There was also the problem of London's water supply. In any large-scale blitz one square mile of the capital needed a stupendous *600,000 gallons of water per minute* to keep the flames at bay! Yet a mere 50 kilo bomb could fracture the cast-iron mains three feet below the street and there would be no water. The alternative— the Thames itself—was difficult to reach at low tide, when the waterline was separated from the riverbank by nearly fifty feet of thick black mud.

The younger officers of the London Fire Brigade had been arguing for emergency reservoirs to be built on the spot, ready for an all-out fire blitz, ever since September. Now they had the example of Manchester before them. But the authorities wouldn't budge; emergency reservoirs would be too costly, they said. Instead they provided a series of 5,000-gallon steel dams scattered at remote intervals, 'emergency water tanks' as they were called, which would each supply one pump with exactly ten minutes' worth of water—about as effective as 'pissing against a thunderstorm', according to Lambeth's Assistant Divisional Officer, G. Blackstone.[6]

And on December 29th that thunderstorm was about to descend upon the capital. It was a Sunday night in the Christmas holiday week. Shops and offices were closed and churches were locked, the key-holders at home. Many of the fire-watchers were off duty. Not only that, but there was a strong wind blowing, as there had been at Manchester a few days before—and the Thames was at low tide. London was as ill-prepared for what was to come as it had been on that fatal Saturday in September.

Promptly at 6.15 on the night of this last Sunday of 1940, the fire-raisers of the Luftwaffe's KG 100 appeared above the vulnerable square mile of the old walled City of London: the most perfect target they could have chosen for what they planned this December 29th.

They began to drop their big canisters of incendiaries. Eight hundred of them. The Londoners called them 'Molotov cocktails', a monstrous version of the fire-bomb named after the Soviet foreign minister. At 1,000 feet above the City, the containers broke open and incendiaries started to spill out, scattering over a wide radius, though most of them landed a 1,000 yards short of their target at Southwark. They began to explode, dancing vividly to life in the blacked-out, mostly deserted streets, showering bright white-glowing sparks on all sides.

The fire-watchers went into action at once. Their technique was simple but dangerous: a bag of sand or a dustbin lid would be thrown onto the writhing, furiously spluttering thing to smother it, then any flame would be doused with the primitive stirrup pump. But if the incendiary bomb was an explosive one, it could blind you; and if you were hit by one of the phosphorous pellets that some of them contained, it would burn itself deeper and deeper into your flesh until you immersed yourself in water to cut off the oxygen. If you were lucky a doctor might come by and cut out the merciless pellet before it ate away the flesh to the very bone.

But, strive as they might, the fire-watchers were outmatched, and the City was soon ablaze, from Moorgate to Aldersgate, from Old Street to Cannon Street. As in Manchester, shop-owners and office managers had gone home for the weekend taking their keys with them. The fire-fighters themselves were swamped with hundreds of incidents where they could do nothing but stand and watch buildings burn down because they had no means of breaking in.

Desperately the firemen on the pumps fought the raging fires with one eye on their water gauges, watching the pressure as thousands of gallons rushed upwards to the man on the hose perched high above on a ladder. A sudden jerk on his controls and the man above would hurtle to his death. 'The live thing in your control is only a machine; you're the master, make it behave,' many a hard-pressed fireman reminded himself that terrible night as the whole of the City blazed.[7]

But there was worse to come. In the wake of the incendiaries came the high explosive bombs. Soon, twelve of the City's largest mains were fractured, one of them the 'dirty water' main laid to cope with fire-fighting emergencies between the Thames and the Grand Union Canal by Regent's Park. The water supply began to give out ...

The Guildhall was struck and set on fire. But its fire-crew were alert and began immediately to tackle the blaze. At first it looked as if their efforts would be successful; but as the water supplies dwindled, the greedy flames took over. Slowly the beautiful fifteenth-century structure, the oldest of its kind in England, started to be swallowed up. Falling water levels meant that the firemen's hoses were producing only a trickle of water, 'like little boys peeing on a bonfire' as one man noted bitterly. The crews were pulled out, and the Guildhall left to its fate.

Elsewhere, many firemen were fighting for their very

A house in Holborn is wrecked leaving some furniture still intact.

lives—like Bill Whiting and the crew at Post Number 63, threatened by an encircling ring of fires. They decided to evacuate the building. So, with his wife Doris—who had as usual been sleeping there—and the rest of the crew, Bill leapt aboard the Post's one surviving engine. With a frantic, cursing driver at the wheel, his face glazed with sweat, they raced through burning streets, the house façades swaying and trembling like scenery on a stage. This time, Bill said much later, 'I thought we'd really had it! But somehow the driver got us through and headed for what he apparently thought was the only safe spot in the City—St Paul's Cathedral.'[8]

Already one incendiary had struck the Cathedral's mighty 148-foot dome, but had been put out. The fire-watchers on the roof of the Cathedral knew that if they were unlucky, if just one single incendiary managed to get between the outer and inner domes where the space was packed with old dry timbers, the dome would burst into flames. That first incendiary had landed at a spot where no one could reach it; then, miraculously, the spluttering, burning bomb had tilted sideways and fallen harmlessly onto the Stone Gallery, where it had been immediately put out by a rush of fire-fighters. But would they be so lucky the next time?

Some observers thought that St Paul's could simply not escape destruction. Mary Welsh, the future Mrs Hemingway, was standing on the roof of Landsdowne House in Berkeley Square, watching as the flames grew higher and higher: 'The dazzling pyrotechnic display went up on both sides of the narrow Ludgate Hill, around St Paul's and on into the City.' As the flames leapt from roof to roof, she marvelled at the firemen 'crawling like black beetles up the flame-garlanded walls' and at 'the familiar dome of St Paul's riding the sea of flames like a buoyant ship'.[9]

In fact, another American observer, Ed Murrow, the deep-voiced radio commentator of CBS—who had done so much to present a sympathetic picture of blitzed Britain to the USA—thought that this particular ship had already sunk. He was telling his American audience: 'That church that meant most to Londoners is gone. St Paul's Cathedral, built by Sir Christopher Wren, her great dome towering above the capital of the Empire, is burning to the ground as I talk to you now ...'[10]

But St Paul's was not fated to die this night. All around the Cathedral, the same streets that had disappeared in the Great Fire of 1666 were remorselessly devoured by those fierce, roaring flames—Creed Lane, Ave Maria Lane, Amen Court and all the rest of them. The Cathedral's Chapter House, the Verger's House and the Organist's House, all hard by, were gutted. And yet, as the Dean, the Very Reverend William Matthews, sadly remarked later, 'Six pails of water would have saved any one of them.'[11]

Yet if the old Cathedral was saved, much much more was lost. The heat generated at the heart of this fiery

St Paul's walled in by flame.

40

hissing maelstrom was so tremendous that it would crumble stone walls and cause asphalt roadways to burst into flames. Girders were twisted into grotesque shapes by the heat as if they were made of toffee. Nothing could survive in the path of this glowing, roaring red monster.

At Moorgate Station a terrible fire was raging. The heat twisted and buckled the roof's supporting beams, melting the aluminium fittings and glass so that they oozed to the shattered platforms like pools of silver, and warped the railway lines. Like Cannon Street and London Bridge stations, both on fire, Moorgate was out of action. At London Bridge the heat was so intense that wardens advised the confused, frightened shelterers to cross the bridge to Monument Underground Station. It was risky, but thinking they were going to be burnt alive here, some of them decided to take the chance. They didn't get far. Huge flames were racing across London Bridge and they turned to flee back the way they had come, hosed down with icy water by yelling firemen at the other end.

By morning not a single train would be running within miles of Central London. Along with the rest, Waterloo and Fenchurch Street stations would be closed—debris across the line—and Charing Cross evacuated, for there was a huge parachute mine hanging near it, threatening and chillingly lethal. Communications began to break down ...

Thermals caused by the 1,000°F blaze had by now created terrifying walls of hissing, rushing flame which seared and charred everything before it like a gigantic blowtorch. Towering pillars of fire and smoke high above the blazing city could be seen from as far away as the Luftwaffe bases on the French coast. Such was the brilliance and intensity of the fiery glow that the night was turned to day. Hilde Marchant of the *Daily Express* later reported that she had been able to read a paper by the flames of Ludgate Hill at three o'clock in the morning and see every word.

Ten miles away in Morden, Bill Whiting's brother-in-law Fred was standing on the doorstep of his house looking north towards the stricken city. Bill and Doris 'had had it', he decided; no one could survive that kind of fire. But they did, of course—and one day Fred himself, 'in safe Morden', would find that they were just as vulnerable here as they were in the City; one day he would find his roof down and his house shattered, too.[12]

But if some who saw that terrible blaze were resigned to the worst, others were not. Churchill, with his steel helmet set at a cocky angle, chin thrust out in anger, cigar clenched between his teeth, watched with the SIS man Fred Winterbotham. He had just ordered that St Paul's must be saved at all costs. Now he stared at the flames and growled: '*We'll get the bastards for this!*'[13]

And, on the other side of the city, staring at the fires from the roof of the Air Ministry, Air Chief Marshal Portal and his Deputy Chief of the Air Staff shared a growing sense of anger as centuries of history and culture disappeared before their eyes. Finally the small stocky Deputy broke the heavy silence, broad face set and determined in the reflected glow of the flames. 'Well,' he said slowly, 'they are sowing the wind ...' Portal nodded and turned away, as if he could no longer bear to look, leaving his Deputy continuing to watch, his mind full of dark forebodings.[14]

As the sirens at last sounded the All Clear, and the City continued to burn, a deadly precedent had been set. That lone brooding Deputy Chief of the Air Staff standing on the roof, dappled and patched by the ruddy glow, would make the most of it when *his* turn came. Air Vice-Marshal Arthur Harris—one day to be known as 'Bomber' Harris—would show no mercy. He would make the Germans reap a bitter harvest ...

In spite of the tremendous damage to property which would result in a complete change to the face of Central London after the war, casualties were relatively low. Only 163 people had been killed, and 509 injured. Of these, a very high percentage indeed had been firemen: twelve dead and 250 injured.

This high rate caused much bitterness among the exhausted firemen; not because they did not expect casualties, but because so many of them were unnecessary. On New Year's Eve, Herbert Morrison made a BBC radio broadcast in which he blamed the public for the great fire of December 29th. Over half the fires could have been avoided, he said, if there had been fire-watchers on duty. Soon he would announce compulsory fire-watching for all men between sixteen and sixty, who would be required to report for duty for forty-eight hours a month.

Too late, thought the angry firemen; the damage had already been done. As Frank Lewey, Labour Mayor of Stepney, commented sarcastically, 'Now we are ready—*after* the event!'[15]

In the event, Morrison's new 'Fire Precautions Order' turned out to be almost totally ineffective. It contained so many escape clauses that three-quarters of those who finally registered were exempted from standing watch.

As before, the Government clamped down a strict censorship on news reporting. That Monday, the day after the raids, the *Daily Telegraph* actually said that 'the Nazis failed to cause a second Fire of London' although they admitted that 'some of the City's proudest possessions' had taken a battering. *The Times* headlined its account in accurate if sober fashion: '*FIRE BOMBS RAINED ON LONDON ... MANY BUILDINGS HIT ... FAMOUS WREN CHURCH DESTROYED*'—but they relegated it to page four! And the *Daily Express* was so anxious to add a note of heroic cheer that it even concocted a story about a 'night air

Mr and Mrs Churchill with Brendon Bracken surveying blitz damage in the City of London in 1940.

battle' over London during the raid, although no such battle had occurred!

So Britain passed into the New Year, ill-prepared as ever. None of the terrible lessons learned these last four months had been implemented. AA batteries still went into action to the rousing tones of a bugle signalling the call-to-arms, as if this was the romantic nineteenth century, not the total war of the 1940s. Thousands who should have been fighting on the home front in Civil Defence still 'dodged the column', avoiding any kind of duty unless it was forced upon them or they got paid for it.

The mood in the luxury night clubs and hotels frequented by the rich was bored or sophisticatedly melancholy. In the Garden Room, Mayfair, Jack Jackson played 'A Nightingale sang in Berkeley Square' for diners in evening dress or full service dress who drank iced champagne at 25 shillings a bottle. At the Café de Paris, noted for its so-called bombproof shelter (though it did not save the many killed there in March 1941), Florence Desmond gave a double meaning to the establishment's proud boast when she sang:

> '*I've got a cosy flat,*
> *There's a place for your hat,*
> *I'll wear a pink chiffon négligé gown,*
> *And do I know my stuff—!*
> *But if that's not enough,*
> *I've got the deepest shelter in town!*'

Major-General Harold Alexander, soon to be known throughout the Western World simply as 'Alex', was lunching that New Year's Eve with Harold Nicolson. He summed up his own mood in this wry equation: 'Archie Wilson mops up 40,000 Italians [captured in Libya] and we claim a victory. *In two hours the Germans destroy five hundred years of our history!*'[16]

But in spite of the continued lack of preparations, the complacency of those in power, the bumbling and the muddling through, the feeling of many that war did not concern them, the spirit of the people was hardening under these long months of bombing. It is often said that the British are a tame, orderly people, a nation of shopkeepers with a queue mentality. But they are not! They are an extremely proud and arrogant people.

Up to now they had always believed they could not be beaten. Now it seemed—to the outside world at least—that they *were* beaten. But they weren't. With an almost savage pride they set out, unconsciously and with little direction from above, save for the efforts of the Great Old Man himself, to resist an overwhelmingly powerful and victorious enemy.

And not only in Britain. On that morning of December 30th, 1940, when the weary German pilots returned to their bases in France after destroying the City of London, one of them, Major Bechtle of KG-2, was greeted by three Tommy POWs who were employed in the Kampfgruppe's officers' mess. One of the three British soldiers—a man from Tottenham, London, who had been captured at Dunkirk—asked the same old question he always asked the pilots returning from a raid: 'Where have you been tonight?'

As always Bechtle taunted the Tommies with his standard reply: '*London ist kaputt!*'

This night, however, the London man snapped back: '*Tottenham is indestructible!*'[17]

That unknown Londoner, who now faced five years in the cage as a prisoner-of-war, epitomised the determined spirit of the British people. Even with their few pitiful resources, pitted against an empire that would stretch from the Arctic Circle to the Mediterranean and from the Channel to the Volga, they would fight back; *and they would win.*

II: THE BATTLEFIELD WIDENS, 1941

'It breaks my heart to think of them onions ... We ain't fighting only Hitler, we're fighting some of our people as well.'

Plymouth gardener, interviewed after his garden had been looted during a blitz in 1941

Number 23 Queen Victoria Street in the City of London falls in May 1941.

ONE
But you've got to do something

Back in the summer of 1940, on the early evening of Friday June 28th, a long queue of lorries, vans and horse-drawn carts had lined up along the White Rock Quay at Guernsey in the Channel Islands, peaceably whiling away the time until their loads of 'chips'—12lb baskets of tomatoes—could be swung aboard the waiting British freighters. Although British, many of the farmers and drivers were chatting away in the local French patois, discussing the crop and prices in the mainland markets. That evening the war seemed a long, long way away.

Then, at 6.55 pm precisely, six planes flashed into sight. The farmers' heads shot up. Three zoomed high into the blue sky and raced across the island at 400 mph; within seconds they had vanished. But the other three had something else in mind than simply a demonstration of their power and speed. They began to lose height ...

Suddenly one of the mesmerised farmers recognised that stark black-and-white insignia. '*Jerries!*' he cried, using the English word. In that same instant, the attackers let loose a crackling stream of tracerfire. Panicking farmers threw themselves underneath their vehicles. Others jumped off the pier and splashed into the sea, to be shocked by the coldness of the water, or to lay face-down on the shingle.

Almost before they realised what was happening, the three planes had gone, racing eastwards to France. Behind them they had left a confused mess of dead and dying civilians, their blood mingling with the red pulp of their squashed tomatoes.

Two days later the Germans started to land on the islands in force. Luftwaffe Leutnant X* was the first to land, with orders to co-ordinate the forthcoming operation. Here is how he remembers that moment:

As I approached the Hotel Royal, the site of our HQ, I was filled with satisfaction. Now the British had to stand in line outside it. The people who had regarded themselves as the world's policemen now had to queue patiently, waiting their turn. The sight filled me with joy. I told myself I would never forget it.[1]

Nor would he. Nor would the inhabitants of Britain's south coast. For now the whole of the European seaboard, from Bergen in Norway to Biarritz in France, was in German hands. A few days later the Luftwaffe flew its first attacks against Plymouth, Brighton and Cardiff.

By the spring of 1941, every port in southern Britain large and small alike, had taken a severe beating. Southampton, a prime military target, had been raided time and time again. By January 1941 over 530 civilians had been killed and 3,000 properties destroyed or damaged, particularly in the areas around the city centre and the Vickers Works at Woolston, where the famed Spitfire fighter was produced—not that it had been much help in defending the south coast, the locals thought bitterly.

Bristol, too, had suffered heavily, 1,000 of its citizens having been killed by that same January. And on January 2nd Cardiff was hit by 125 German bombers, which caused the deaths of 299 civilians as well as untold misery, injury and destruction. One six-year-old boy was found buried in the rubble after three days because he was still singing hoarsely. Asked why he sang, he answered bravely: 'My father was a collier. He always said that when a miner was trapped, he sang.'[2]

But this valiant response was not shared by the majority of civilians in bomb-blitzed southern Britain. Their mood was bitter, angry and in some instances definitely shaky.

On January 10th Portsmouth became the target of a particularly intensive raid. By the time it was over, the great naval base had suffered 930 citizens killed, 1,261 seriously injured and 1,621 wounded (naval casualties were never revealed), its seaside suburb of Southsea was virtually destroyed, and the naval installations had been badly hit. Even the city's pride and joy, Nelson's *Victory*, barely escaped destruction. Over 2,000 fires were reported to have been caused by the raid; the city centre was set alight, the harbour railway station was burnt down, the Guildhall was gutted—indeed, the Lord Mayor himself only just escaped with his life.

Mass Observation's investigators, arriving in Portsmouth only hours after the raid, reported widespread distress among the citizens. They also noted that the

The King and Herbert Morrison tour Southampton after a raid.

* My informant does not want to have his name published.

authorities seemed ill-prepared for what was happening to them. The official in charge of post-blitz welfare, for example, 'had a personal horror of communal feeding. He expressed the opinion that it encouraged parasitism and laziness and he did not see "why workers probably earning more than I do should be encouraged by the government".'[3]

As for the people of Portsmouth, the report said:

By 6pm an observer will see that all traffic is moving northwards. The movement begins at about 3.30pm and continues to dusk ... The people are making for the bridge on the main road out of Portsmouth in order to sleep in the northern suburbs, the surrounding hills or towns and villages in the radius of 20 miles. One night after a bad blitz it was estimated that 90,000 left the city ...[4]

It was all too clear what was happening. People were abandoning their place of work early—in some cases altogether. Absenteeism was rife; the industrial life of the shattered city was breaking down. After dark the city was left to the looters and vandals. As the men from Mass Observation concluded sombrely:

Looting and wanton destruction have reached alarming proportions. The police seemed unable to exercise control ... This seems another illustration of the lack of community spirit. The effect on morale is bad and there is a general feeling of desperation* as there seems no solution...[5]

All this while, the south coast's most important port, Plymouth, had been battered time and time again—and, like the rest of the ports on that coast, it had been totally unprepared for such an eventuality. From being a safe haven to which children from the larger cities had been evacuated, once France had fallen Plymouth went straight into the front line. The authorities should have immediately evacuated those who were not needed to keep the city functioning; but they didn't. Indeed Plymouth still remained an area designated as safe for evacuees!

One official report, written in 1941, stated:

It was a blunder on the part of the central government. Plymouth should have been made an evacuation area on the fall of France. Central government had many months to decide on this course of action. But nothing was done. The city paid the price.[6]

Not much was done at a local level, either. Indeed the Emergency Committee running the affairs of the coun-

HMS Newcastle used her ack-ack against German bombers, as no

try's major naval dockyard was a pitiful bunch of old men. It consisted of the Mayor and three aldermen, two of them aged over seventy. One man alone, the Town Clerk, was in charge of the engineers and medical officers, as well as being Air Raid Controller *and* having responsibility for post-blitz welfare! It was hardly a team that could succeed against the might of the triumphant Luftwaffe.

That same critical report—which quickly disappeared into Whitehall's vaults—went on to say:

We had a vivid impression of lack of direction in the blitzed areas, of absence of planning, of confusion of responsibility and problems. Actual and potential dangers of morale are unrealised, far less dealt with.[7]

It is not surprising, therefore, that morale in Plymouth was low. The civilians felt bitter and dispirited. There had been no evidence of precaution taken before the blitzes, nor organised relief services afterwards. There seemed to be no night-fighters available for aerial defence and the only anti-aircraft protection appeared to be that of the guns of the heavy cruiser HMS *Newcastle*, moored in the Sound; and according to the Town Clerk,

* At Portsmouth, however, the only Victoria Cross of the whole long battle was won when Leading Seaman Jack Mantle manning a pom-pom on HMS *Foylebank* kept on firing during a Stuka attack on the port, although seriously wounded, 'He fell by the gun he had so valiantly served,' so the citation read.

r batteries defended Plymouth.

Sir Colin Campbell: 'I never saw her hit anything and the result of her barrage was a shower of shrapnel over the city.'[8] Indeed, most locals thought that the effective defence of their city only started when the Americans started to arrive in the area.

Surprisingly enough Plymouth was represented nationally and locally by two outstanding and powerful figures: Nancy Astor (as MP) and her husband Waldorf (as the mayor). Before the war Nancy's 'Cliveden Set' had been rumoured, to be the centre of appeasement and collaboration with the Germans. Now she and her husband purged themselves of any accusation of being potential fifth columnists by throwing themselves whole-heartedly into a campaign to get things improved in Plymouth. She wrote a stinging letter to *The Times*, demanding a new basis for the organisation of blitz relief after an attack. But in spite of her name and influence, little was done. As Sir Colin Campbell recalled bitterly afterwards: 'No one in Whitehall cared about us or our safety. We were left to get on with it, to bury our dead and clear up the mess. No one warned us what to expect.'[9]

And still the raids went on...

On March 20th, 1941, the King and Queen, plus Robert Menzies, the Australian Prime Minister, visited the battered city in an attempt to raise morale. Someone shouted at the royal party: 'We're keeping our chins up!' And that was about that. The Royals returned with Lord and Lady Astor to their home on the Hoe, took tea from silver plate, and drove through 'cheering crowds', as the papers recorded, to their train. Even as they moved out of the station the sirens started their dreadful wail. The raiders were coming again!

Two hours later the Luftwaffe had launched its most devastating raid yet on Plymouth. High explosive and incendiaries landed all over the city; even St Andrew's, Plymouth's mother church, was not spared. Walls cracked and crumbled in the intense heat, as the wind whipped the inferno into an unearthly roaring vortex. Air currents sucked the flames from the blazing buildings on either side of narrow streets to make lethal, ferocious tunnels. It was the same old story of death, destruction and suffering.

By the time dawn arrived, Plymouth was all but demolished. Twenty thousand premises had been destroyed or badly hit, including the city hospital where fourteen newborn babies had perished with three nurses. In all, 336 civilians had been killed and thousands in-

Mr Widdicombe of Plymouth salvages food from his wrecked home.

jured. And the survivors, as one of them wrote later, 'were hollow-eyed for want of sleep and with vengeance and hatred raging in their hearts against the vile perpetrators of total war'.[10]

Nor were they able to catch up on their sleep the following night. Indeed, this next raid—the 313th that the city had experienced—was even more severe. 'The fires are very much worse than yesterday's attack and damage is likely to be even more extensive,' wrote one reporter in his war diary.[11] And he was right. Whole tracts of the city had vanished. Property to the value of one hundred million pounds had been wiped out.

Frank Booker, assistant editor of the *Western Morning News*, wrote of that night of fire: 'Between Smiths and Costers in George Street, thick plate-glass windows melted, the liquid glass forming pools on the pavement. Solid asphalt pathways became liquid, their surfaces bubbling and wrinkling like boiling water in a cauldron. It was said that gold and silver in a jeweller's shop melted and trickled in a thin but precious stream down the shop front.'[12]

That morning as the bewildered, dirty, scared civilians stumbled through the smoking rubble, the air was filled with the smell of frying bacon—sides of ham that had caught fire in a grocer's shop. Stacks of tins had been fused together into a metal mess, like some grotesque modern sculpture. Cans of corned beef and soup had burst and splattered their sticky contents on the road. The devastation was complete.

Yet even in the midst of such horror, one woman resolutely picked her way through the shattered city, undeterred by the hopelessness and apathy all around her. Finally Miss E. Smith, headmistress of a girls' school, came upon the ruins of St Andrew's Church. She found a piece of wood, chalked the Latin word *Resurgam* on it and nailed it to the lintel of the church. That brave Latin tag—'I shall rise again'—would later catch Plymouth's imagination. You can see it there on the door of the rebuilt church, carved in stone, today. But it was going to be a long time before Plymouth would rise again.

The popular press maintained that they had heard of people in Plymouth who swore that they had caught the sound of Drake's drum being beaten; and Newbolt's jingoistic verse was widely quoted in order to uplift the spirit of the stricken city: *'If the Dons sight Devon, he'll quit the port of heaven and drum them up the Channel as he drummed them long ago!'*

The reality was far different. Mass Observation, hurriedly sent down to observe the scene, reported mass evacuation of Plymouth by the terrified citizens (in the end Plymouth lost half its pre-war population). One observer came across forty people sheltering under ditches and hedges on the edge of Dartmoor (in winter!)—and asked them how they were going to sleep.

'Oh we'll be all right,' they replied. 'The moor soon dries out and then we will roll ourselves up and keep warm.' Suitably impressed, the observer commented: 'I don't know how they kept cheerful because it was frosty and I was dirty, tired and frozen.'[13]

There were hundreds, too, who tramped the surrounding countryside pretending to be homeless and demanding money and food. Nor was morale helped by the many rich people who fled the town for the safety of remote country hotels, although their homes in Plymouth were still intact; this caused much bitterness and resentment among those who had no choice but to stay and fight on.

As March gave way to April and still the terrible raids continued, morale had reached rock bottom. 'The civil and domestic devastation in Plymouth,' opined Mass Observation, 'exceeds anything we have seen elsewhere.'[14] Indeed, although Mass Observation, honest and blunt as it usually was, did not say so, reading between the lines of their report that spring, one has the impression that its investigators thought the raids had finally broken the spirit of the people of Plymouth.

And as if the repeated bombing were not enough, the damage was compounded by unco-ordinated, inadequate, ineffective post-blitz arrangements—a direct result of pre-war complacency at both local and national government levels. When Plymouth's Central Library was set alight, the Swindon Brigade brought in to help had to stand by helplessly and watch a hundred thousand books burn to ashes; their hoses wouldn't fit Plymouth's hydrants! None of the official committees seemed capable of dealing with the ever increasing numbers of anxious, homeless citizens. Even steel helmets were in short supply; Harold Pattison, the city's chief fire guard, remembers a woman in her night clothes fighting one blaze with a colander tied to her head!

Looting became ever more widespread. All abandoned properties were raided and furniture, clothing, bedding, even ornaments were stolen. The police were powerless; they had too much else to do. Few of the looters were ever apprehended and brought to court. People returning home from the 'rest centres' afterwards found that the thieves had even had time enough to steal heavy gas ovens.

Vandalism was equally prevalent; for the children sometimes only went to school one day a week. The *Plymouth Sunday Independent* reported that in one school 'extraordinary damage has been done, furniture smashed, cupboards stored in a locked room rifled, school books, paints etc strewn around and even slates thrown from the roof. There is hardly a whole pane of glass in the premises.'[15]

Civilised living in Plymouth was breaking down. 'One begins to wonder how much longer the mental and physical strain can last,' wrote one journalist at the time. 'Surely we have reached the limit.'[16]

It is hardly surprising, then, in such an atmosphere of tension and insecurity, that people often fell victim to their own wild rumours. One Thursday in April, after days of constant air attacks, a rumour flashed round the city that a Ministry of Information van was touring the streets and warning everyone to leave Plymouth by nine o'clock that night, as there was going to be a major raid. The authorities immediately sent off five vans to deny the rumour, but decided not to use loudspeakers which they thought would only heighten the tension and spread the alarm. But their counter-measure failed; their word-of-mouth denials were simply not believed by the fearful, gloomy population. Once again the reception centres were besieged by panicky civilians (including some officials) demanding to be evacuated at once, before it was too late.

Something had to be done—and soon!

A woman ran naked and screaming across the Hoe. Two men, both with families, hanged themselves in the ruins of their homes. It was reported that more than one mother simply upped and went, unable to bear the strain, abandoning both their men and their children. A direct hit on the petty officers' block at the Royal Naval Barracks killed eighty petty officers. A large underground shelter in Portland Square took a direct hit and seventy-two people died. Lord Astor took to his bed, a sick and weary man. How much more could they take?

Plymouth was by now proclaiming itself the worst blitzed city in the whole of Britain. The city council and the Astors felt central government was not helping enough. They pleaded with Whitehall to do something. So, towards the end of April, after some tension between London and Plymouth, Prime Minister Churchill announced that he would pay a visit to the city, together with Mr Averill Harriman, Roosevelt's personal envoy in Britain.

Nancy Astor received the visitors at Plymouth Station, as her husband was still sick in bed. Together they drove through the city to be cheered as the King and Queen had been cheered a month before. But this was a different city than the one the Royals had visited. Its streets were simply piles of rubble; its very heart had been clawed out by the enemy.

'Your homes are low but your spirits are high,' Churchill told the citizens, though he knew from the reports of Mass Observation that this was not true. Then the tears flooded his eyes, for he was an emotional man, and he was forced to dab them.

Nancy Astor was not impressed. 'It is all very well to cry, Winston,' she said tartly. '*But you've got to do something!*'[17]

(Right) A warning to looters.

TWO: A strong undercurrent of anxiety

An illustration of the cockney spirit. 'Musso's Lake' refers to Mussolini's claim that the Mediterranean was an Italian lake.

Time was running out and there was little the Great Man could offer the blitzed cities save his presence. As April gave way to May 1941 and the Luftwaffe flung its whole weight at Britain's provincial cities, the plight of Plymouth's citizens was shared by people all over the country. Morale everywhere was shaky.

Much show was made by the Ministry of Information that in heavily blitzed Clydeside the workers had called off a strike. 'The most vital sign of unified defiance and determination in Clydebank has been shown by the return of the workers,' said the *Daily Express* in April 1941. 'On Monday this week the Apprentices' Committee decided to recommend all striking apprentices to get back to work, but the bombed-out apprentices had already made up their minds. They had been at the gates of Yarrow that morning trying to get in.' But Mass Observation, investigating this badly hit area where 700 people had been killed in one raid alone, reported that: 'Admirable behaviour is often coupled with a veritable wail of grumbles.'[1]

The citizens of Clydebank had good reason to grumble. They had no real air-raid shelters at all, just brick sheds with reinforced roofs or roughly protected passages in the overcrowded tenements. What's more, the blitz had damaged all but *seven* of Clydebank's 12,000 houses; 35,000 of its 47,000 citizens were currently homeless, and at night its population dwindled to a mere 2,000 when the rest took to the moors. War work at night came to a virtual standstill.

It seemed to be the same everywhere. On May 7th Harold Nicolson wrote in his celebrated diary:

Herbert Morrison is worried about the effect of the provincial raids on morale. He keeps on underlining the fact that people cannot stand this intensive bombing indefinitely and that sooner or later the morale of other towns will go, even as Plymouth's has gone.[2]

In reality, the majority of ordinary men and women in Britain were bearing up, in spite of the raids and the terrible series of defeats inflicted on the armed forces this spring. Just as in Germany later, production was actually rising, despite the bombing, the hardship and the lack of food.

The authorities had little idea of the true mood of the average man. Civil servants, service chiefs, politicians, Labour or Conservative, were hampered by the blinkers of their class or political inclination. They tended to

look upon the mass of the population as infirm of purpose: people who were likely to turn defeatist under pressure; while they were the ones, the only ones, who were resolved to stand firm against National Socialism.

But the Common Man was different. He might well be nervous and shaky, but for the most part he stood his ground. What he disliked almost as much as the bombs was the patronising attitude of such media as the BBC or the left-wing illustrated, the *Picture Post*, propagating the official line that Britain 'could take it'. As one Swansea man commented after hearing the account of a raid on the BBC: 'The people were marvellous, especially the women. They can take it all right. But not like that bloke said on the wireless on Thursday night.

They don't go around smiling all day—the people who have lost friends and relatives, they don't go about grinning.'[3]

Nor did the average man like the chummy, working-class image of 'people being in it together', determined to stick it out 'for a better world'. He knew that Labour, with its pre-war anti-rearmament policies, had contributed to the mess in which the country now found itself. It was Labour that had helped to keep the British Army starved of funds, so that their anti-aircraft guns were twenty years out of date. It was Labour that had often refused to co-operate in pre-war Civil Defence preparations, leaving it to unpaid volunteers from the lower and middle classes.

Now the average man looked askance at the effusions of those same Labour politicians and those 'parlour pinks' ('Live right, act left!') who wrote for such socialist publications as the *Picture Post* and the *Mirror*. Whatever was he supposed to make of pieces like this, by poet Louis MacNeice:

I was in a restaurant when the guns started going heavily—
a deep thudding and vibration that, as often happens, made
me feel as if I were at sea. I went into the street during a
lull; there was a strange flare apparently pinned on the sky,
quite static like a great gilt ornament from a fantastic altar.[4]

What sort of man could describe that flare, which heralded the death and horror to come, as though it were merely a curious bit of costume jewellery? Clearly the average man and woman could expect no great support from such fanciful intellectuals, even if they did claim to be champions of the working class.

But if there were many in Britain who despaired and wondered when it would ever end, time was running out for the Germans, too.

Early in 1941 the men of Hut Three at Bletchley had begun to break coded German intercepts which indicated that Hitler was going to turn his attentions from hard-pressed Britain elsewhere—to Russia. The news placed Sir Stewart Menzies, head of the SIS, in something of a quandary. For most of his intelligence career he had actively *fought* the Russians; should he now compromise his best source of intelligence and let the Russians know that they were about to be attacked?

Winterbotham, who was in charge of the Ultra decoding apparatus' security, asked him what he was going to do. Menzies—or 'C' as he was known in intelligence circles—replied: 'We must let the PM know.'

Winterbotham, who at that time was taking up to thirty intercepts a day to Churchill, asked: 'But what about Stalin?'

'Yes', Menzies agreed, 'can we risk letting him know the source of our information?'

For a while they considered what would be their best course of action. Finally Winterbotham suggested: 'What about getting the PM to write a letter to Stalin stating that it *looks* as if the Germans are going to attack Russia?'[5]

In the end Churchill sent a special instruction to his ambassador in Moscow, Sir Stafford Cripps, to advise Stalin personally of his assumptions based on 'sure information from a trusted agent'; and Cripps duly obliged. But Stalin refused to believe Churchill's warning. Indeed, he went as far as to punish his own agents who were feeding him similar information. In his prejudiced opinion, it was all a 'British provocation'.

So Churchill waited on tenterhooks as more and more Luftwaffe units were drawn away from the Low

An anti-aircraft battery in action near Cardiff in 1941.

Countries and France to the east, expecting the Germans to launch their attack on Soviet Russia at any moment, and praying that this would relieve the pressure on Britain. For not only was he prepared to 'make a pact with the devil himself' (i.e. Stalin), he was also expecting the Americans to enter the war soon.

For months now the Americans had seen repeated newsreels of Britain's suffering, of her bombed-out cities and shattered population. Gradually their isolationist convictions were being undermined. And as time passed, Churchill knew, Roosevelt—himself firmly committed to a war against fascism—would surely persuade his reluctant people to enter the war at Britain's side. It was all a matter of keeping one's nerve until the fortunes of war changed in Britain's favour.

Still the bombing went on. Now Liverpool, which had been under attack since the beginning, was singled out

by the Luftwaffe for one final devastating blow this first week of May 1941. Of all the British targets it was the easiest for the Germans to attack. Flying up the Irish Sea the German pilots had a splendid beacon in the form of un-blacked out Eire, which had remained doggedly neutral, thanks to its premier de Valera. 'God, although I am an Irishman myself, I would have dearly loved to have dropped a bomb on lit-up Dublin many a time!' recalls one wartime bomb-aimer stationed in Wales at the time. 'It was a dead give-away for the Jerries.'[6]

Protests were made to de Valera, but to no avail. Irish lights remained on, and German submarines continued to refuel in quiet bays in southern Ireland, while the IRA went on working with German spies parachuted into Eire, though not very successfully.*

*On April 15th, 1941, when Belfast was heavily raided, however, the volunteer fire brigades of the border area raced through the night to help, neutrals or not.

But not only did neutral Eire help to make it easy to bomb Liverpool, the city with the biggest Irish population outside of Ireland, save New York and Boston; there were also traitors in Britain's very midst, actively helping the Germans. Another RAF man from Liverpool, then helping to train Free French air crew in North Wales, recalls flying at night 'and many a time spotting the beacons lit by Welsh nationalists all along the coast, pointing directly towards Liverpool'.[7] Later his own house was totally destroyed and he thought, 'I'd dearly love to drop a bomb on the buggers.' He never did, of course; and finally the authorities sent a company of Royal Welch Fusiliers into the area to round up the traitors.

By the end of April 1941 there had already been sixty-eight raids on Liverpool and Mass Observation was reporting 'a depressed and sordid atmosphere. This is partly due to its blackness and the number of very poor people seen in its streets and is enhanced by the blitz debris.'[8] The investigators also noted widespread criticism among Liverpudlians of their local leaders, who were 'too easily satisfied with the provisions made' as well as 'inclined to ignore public opinion and to be on the defensive and unwilling to discuss difficulties'.[9]

Although emergency procedures had been improved over the long months since the Liverpool blitz had started, there was still little provision made for feeding people after raids, the shelters were poor and as Mass Observation said, 'what shelters there were were indescribably filthy'.[10] Thousands left the city each night for the supposed safety of the surrounding area. Looting was rife and anti-semitism was strong—the Jews were accused, as they were in London, of using their money to find safe havens away from the city. Yet morale in general was described by Mass Observation as being good, despite 'a strong undercurrent of anxiety'.

But that morale was about to undergo its severest test so far.

It began at 10.43 pm on Sunday May 1st with the mournful wail of sirens across the river and the steady thump-thump of anti-aircraft guns ringed around the port, from which the vital Battle of the Atlantic was controlled.

Ann Diskin, a volunteer fire-fighter wearing a pan lid on her head, tied on with a scarf—as elsewhere there was even a shortage of steel helmets—recalls watching the planes coming in along New Chester Road in what appeared a straight line, following the river. At first, she says, 'it was so quiet we could hear the bomb doors opening'.[11] But not for long. Almost immediately the fifty planes involved in this opening engagement started to drop their bombs in the Sefton Park area.

The biggest single incident of that first night involved the SS *Malakand*, a Brocklebank steamer lying in Huskisson No 2 Dock, with 1,000 tons of shells and bombs amongst the cargo in her hold. Just after the raid started, a partially deflated barrage balloon which had been cut adrift became entangled in the munitions ship's rigging. It burst into flames and fell onto the deck. Captain Kinley, the *Malakand's* master, immediately ordered his men into action. But no sooner had they dealt with the burning barrage balloon than a new hazard emerged: flames from the nearby dock sheds, which had already been hit, were spreading towards the ship. Amid the falling bombs the crew and firemen worked desperately to put out the blaze. As they put out one fire, another bomb would land and start a fresh blaze. Ignoring the danger they fought all night but their lack of equipment started to tell; and soon the Germans, attracted by the fiery glare, started to dive-bomb the ship.

In the end it was decided to sink her and thus reduce the danger of an explosion. But before the men with the oxyacetylene cutters could start burning holes in her side, the advancing flames reached the ammunition in her hold. The giant bomb which was the *Malakand* exploded. The stern end was blasted fifty yards. A four-ton anchor was hurled a hundred yards, crashing into the engine room of a hopper and sinking her. Steel plates from the ship were found *three miles away!* Indeed it was reported later that the blast had been heard at Southport, nearly twenty miles off.

That tremendous explosion seemed to signal the start of Liverpool's seven-day long ordeal, which the Ministry of Home Security soon recognised as 'the enemy's intention to render our port unworkable'.

On May 3rd, there came the great fire blitz. Within two and a half hours, sixty fires were raging inside the city and fifty-six in the suburbs. After four hours the situation, both in Liverpool and Bootle, was reported by the fire authorities to be 'very serious'. Outside brigades were rushed in. As usual their hoses did not fit Liverpool's hydrants. Even Bootle had obstinately refused to standardise equipment before the war, although the town lived cheek-by-jowl with Liverpool. Now both authorities paid the price.

Fireman Rupert Rice, fighting fires at Lewis's and a neighbouring shop, Blackers, today recalls: 'When the water supply finally ran out, horrified firemen found themselves holding empty hoses. Blackers joined Lewis's as debris.'[12]

Inspector-in-Chief of the Fire Services, Commander Firebrace, a tough veteran who lived up to his apt name, was inspecting Liverpool's defences that night and he noted that the strain was telling. 'I actually saw one Liverpool fire officer,' he recorded after the war, 'collapse in the main Control Room. Without any warning he gave a stifled cry and immediately lost consciousness—sheer exhaustion of mind and body.'[13]

Another fireman, Alan Pithstone, recalls 'wading through a knee-deep mass of porridge oats, burst tins of syrup, treacle and tinned fruit' at Lloyds warehouse in order to get to the blaze:

On the way up, an undamaged seven-pound tin of Barlett pears got in my way, so I took it aloft. Then while my mates held onto the jet, I opened the tin and as they both held their heads backwards with mouths open wide, I popped in a pear. Being thirsty and not having food for many hours, they tasted better than anything I have had in my life, before or since, and the full seven-pound tin only lasted as many minutes.[14]

Tom Kelly, Liverpool's deputy fire chief, saw the dawn coming and decided to do something he had never done before in his life. A warehouse had begun to burn, set alight by sparks from the building next door. 'So we opened every door and window in the place and I said

Sorting through the rubble in Bexley Heath.

to one of the men, "Now she'll go!" And we burnt her out* ... It's the only time I ever encouraged a fire.'[15]

It was a time of horror, mass slaughter, and total confusion. Some died instantly from the blast. Others died more slowly, painfully. 'Two young girls just managed to reach our shelter,' a survivor recalls, 'and then they started to die horribly in front of our eyes, choking, gasping for air, as if they were being strangled.'[16]

Irene Drennan, a teenager, watched as Civil Defence workers 'collected the body parts, ears, arms, legs, all to be buried later in the same grave'.[17] These were the bits and pieces of ten relatives all killed in the same house in Towson Street, including young Elisabeth X and her two-day-old baby. Irene's uncle, a badly wounded veteran of World War One, had had a premonition that Towson Street would be hit and, even though his wife had put a deposit down on a little house there, he had refused to move into it. Now he helped to rescue people from the bombed Mill Road Hospital. Working his way through the smoking rubble he came upon the operating theatre. A naked man—a Dutchman, he later discovered—lay on the operating table. All around him were the staff, doctors and masked nurses, and all dead. They had been killed instantly by the blast. But the Dutchman survived because he had been 'put under before the bomb had dropped'.[18]

Mr R. Jenion was working at a munitions factory 'where they took on the blind, the lazy, and even rag-and-bone men'. When the blitz began, the lights went out and hundreds of these 'odds-and-sods' huddled together, quaking in the darkness. Suddenly a faulty detonator went off, no one knew quite how, and one girl was blown to bits. 'All they ever found was her wedding ring,' Mr Jenion remembers; and when her father heard the sad news the next day he hanged himself.[19]

Mrs Gertrude Jameson, then a night telephonist at the Trunk Exchange, had signed the Official Secrets Act because her job enabled her to learn all about shipping and troop movements. As a result it was over forty years before she dared to reveal that an air-raid shelter had been hit in Clint Road and sealed off 'with 400 people inside because they could not be rescued'.[20] This tragic story is confirmed by others. Edith Branwell, aged twelve, emerged from her own shelter after the raid to find the street 'awash with molten margarine and sugar', and still remembers her horror when she heard about the shelter; she was 'heart-broken'. And later, she says, 'we were told they were left there and never buried'.[21] The next day her father went to work as usual at Park Lane Railway Station, and was standing next to a policeman when a bomb dropped. The policeman was blown to pieces in front of her father's horrified gaze. 'He never recovered. Gradually he began to lose his sight and died at the early age of forty-seven.'[22]

May Miles, fourteen years old, was sheltering with another 100 people in the Co-Op shelter in Bootle when it was hit. 'Suddenly there was this terrific explosion,' she recalls today. 'Afterwards it was like all hell let loose. The screaming was unmerciful. The place just caved in. It was chaos. There were no lights. People were fumbling, shouting, screaming...'[23]

Private Francis Clinch, a young soldier with the Cheshire Regiment, was working on Aintree Race-course—preparing it, he had been told by his officer, for the 'incoming Americans'—when the warehouse where the troops slept was hit by a landmine. He was knocked out. When he came round he was surrounded by dead and dying soldiers and trapped by a heavy girder across his legs. Flicking on his cigarette lighter, he looked around: 'I could see an iron door with a lock on it. I thought it might be a way out and I got a brick, smashed the lock and got my fingers behind the door ... I managed to force it just a bit. Then the flames shot in. Both my legs were burnt.' He fainted and awoke to find himself up to his neck in water. He began shouting and fainted again. Finally he regained consciousness 'to the sound of picks and shovels and heard a voice crying, "keep shouting! We're coming down!"'[24]

He was a year in hospital after that and to this day the marks of the flames are still visible on his legs.

And yet, even in the midst of all this horror, the famous Liverpudlian humour was intact. That week Hal Birch was a teenage member of the St John's Ambulance cadets stationed at the Royal Infirmary in the city centre. Together with his pal Billie he was ordered to go and collect a casualty at an 'incident'. All the available stretchers were in use, so when the two cadets got to the smouldering scene they loaded the casualty—a boy of their own age—onto a door and transported him thus back to the hospital where his broken legs could be attended to.

It was Hal's and Billie's routine when entering the main corridor of the Infirmary to kick open the swing doors with the back of their boots and catch them with their elbows. This time the routine didn't work. Just as they entered, a bomb dropped on the hospital itself and the blast came racing down the corridor, knocking the two cadets off their feet. As Hal fell his helmet slammed into the casualty's nose: 'Now he had a broken nose as well as a broken leg. We delivered him and fled, more frightened of what we had done than of the bombs falling outside!'[25]

Later Hal went on operations with the RAF and before he was twenty-one he would have completed a bombing tour of the Ruhr. But he always remembered that broken nose he had inadvertently caused.

Another Liverpudlian who remembers a comic touch amid the tragedy describes how her mother, Mrs B.

*This was done to put out the blaze before nightfall, as otherwise it would have acted as a beacon for the bombers.

Jones, woke her one night in a state of near panic: 'Quick, grab your blankets and your gas mask!' she quavered. *'They're dropping gas!'* So the mother and her teenaged daughter ran to the bathroom and sat there all night long in their hot sticky gas masks, 'trembling with fear'. Next morning the indignant daughter asked the local warden, 'What's all this about gas?'

'I didn't say gas,' he explained. 'I said they'd hit the local *gas works!*'

'We had many good laughs about that afterwards,' the daughter recalls today. 'But there was nothing funny about coming home at five thirty from work and being machine-gunned in broad daylight...'[26]

As always there were some who couldn't take it. Carter Fitzhenry, whose job it was to ferry corned beef from the docks with his twin horses, arrived home from work one day during the blitz to find a note pinned to his door. It was from his wife: *'I can't stand any more.'* She had simply gone off with her two oldest children and made her way to Blackburn where she had family. And 'that was that', says Mr Fitzhenry.[27]

Mr R. Thwaite, then seven, remembers his mother saying miserably, after the water mains had been smashed and they worried about how they would feed their cows on a farm on Liverpool's outskirts: 'Another week of this and we will all have to give in.'[28]

But the great majority were not prepared to give in. They struggled on, contemptuous of those who cracked up or used the bombing to their own advantage. Elsie Smith, who had already lost two brothers at sea, still relishes the plight of two thieves who regularly went looting during the raids. One night they broke into what they thought was a factory and started munching what appeared to be pickled onions. Later as they left they met a passer-by with a torch, which they asked him to shine on the factory sign. 'It read: *St Paul's Eye Hospital.* They had been eating human eyes—and it served them right!'[29]

But Elsie's own baby—born during the blitz—went stone blind, probably due to shock, and died within a few hours.

Tragedy and comedy, mixed inextricably...

On May 8th Liverpool's Emergency Committee learnt that 1,000 bodies had already been delivered to the Webster Road Mortuary, more than half of them unidentified. And, because the power kept failing, the undertakers had been forced to carry out their gruesome but necessary work by the light of hurricane lamps. Anxiously anticipating the future, the Committee acted to ensure stand-by lighting and ordered another hundred coffins (most councils of the bigger cities were using cardboard bags for the dead now).

But the next day's blitz never came. The great offensive on Liverpool ended that night with a minor, scattered raid, and the exhausted, dazed, bereaved and homeless citizens were left to pick up the pieces.

Huge fires still blazed. The living and the dead were still trapped under the ruins. Hospitals and mortuaries were packed with wounded. The docks were in ruins. By the end of that terrible week, fifty-seven vessels from barges to 12,000-ton freighters had been sent to the bottom in the docks. In the city itself most of the damage had been done to offices, churches, factories and the like; but 4,400 private homes had been destroyed, 16,000 seriously damaged and a further 45,000 slightly damaged...

The casualties were tremendous. More than 1,700 had been killed and over 1,000 seriously injured, with twice that number suffering minor injuries. A staggering 76,000 men and women had been rendered homeless, relying on the mobile canteens to serve them a quarter of a million meals. Just short of 300,000 shattered people passed through the city's rest centres.

But even these official figures may be understating the true level of casualties; later estimates suggest that nearer to 4,000 people were killed and a further 3,489 seriously injured. As Harry Hawkins, the Chief Constable of Birmingham, told war worker Madge Faulkney after the big raid on that city: 'We'll never know the full extent of the casualties. The authorities will make up a figure and give it out to the press. It's better for morale that way.'[30]

Whatever the truth, rumours abounded. Not only in Liverpool. As far away as Leek in Staffordshire, a working-class member of Mass Observation would report that week:

General morale very unsteady. This has been a week of gruesome rumours, which were briefly as follows: (1) Trainloads of unidentified corpses have been sent from Merseyside for mass cremation. (2) Martial law has had to be put into operation. (3) Homeless and hungry people have marched around in the bombed areas carrying white flags and howling protests. (4) Food riots are taking place.[31]

In fact, some people seemed to blame their local councils rather than the Germans for what was happening to them. In Bootle, one woman was reported as saying after her home had been destroyed and the rest home to which she was sent was also hit (all but one of these rest homes were knocked out by the bombs), 'I'd string up the whole bloody council if I had my way!'[32]

On the other hand, Hal Birch recalls: 'The spirit was fantastic. I was very proud of my fellow Liverpudlians, who with their well-known wit, came up trumps.'[33]

And Ada Ryder, a teenager about to enter the WAAF, says today: 'I think we all became better people because of it [the blitz]. We worked together and helped each other and Churchill's broadcasts made you feel ten feet tall... We had no weapons at all, but he bluffed us through.'[34]

THREE
'We've won it; we've done it'

The last attack on London started almost as a whim, a lazy idle joke at the end of a long party in the small hours of the morning...

It was a typical Friday evening at the Berghof, Hitler's retreat perched high in the Bavarian Alps looking out across Austria, with all the camp-followers and courtiers assembled as usual for one of those long rambling evenings when they began to wish fervently that the Führer would go to bed: Field Marshal Keitel, head of the German Armed Forces; Eva Braun, Hitler's mistress; Hans Baur, his personal pilot; Martin Bormann, the up-and-coming man known as 'the führer of the teleprinters' because he controlled Hitler's secretariat. The only two who were absent from the *Prominenz* were the commander of the Luftwaffe, Hermann Goering, and Bormann's boss Rudolf Hess, whose fortunes of late had been going into decline: something that Bormann was using to his advantage.

As always there had been the movie—an American film, which would not be shown to the general German public because it was too 'decadent'; it featured 'nigger jazz' and long-legged chorus girls—followed by the usual party fare: the local Enzian liqueur, which even the supposedly teetotal Hitler was known to sip, and those super-sweet Austrian cakes, complete with plenty of whipped cream, in which he indulged himself. On the morrow he would suffer the consequences and commence swallowing the sixty pills a day he needed to keep himself trim and lean; for he had a terrible fear of becoming fat. But tonight he did not care. He enjoyed himself.

The conversation always stopped when Hitler started to speak; but he was not talking much on this particular evening. He confined himself to saying a few words on Wagner, patting his Alsatian bitch 'Blondi', and occasionally poking the great roaring log fire. This night the running was made by Martin Bormann, soon to become Hitler's 'Grey Eminence'; in fact this night was to be the turning point of his career. He pointed out, as Friday gave way to Saturday and the party still continued, that the British needed to be taught another sharp lesson. Hadn't the RAF bombed Germany only the other night with the strongest force ever—400 bombers? They hadn't done much damage admittedly, but Germany's pride was hurt; and Hermann Goering seemed to be little concerned about that.

Baur, Hitler's pilot, whose big mouth would one day land him in a Russian prison camp for fifteen years, now jumped in. He agreed with Bormann. This last raid by a nation which was supposedly on its knees, nearly out for the count after almost a year's intensive bombing, was no good for Germany's international reputation among the neutral nations.

Hitler was not altogether convinced. In exactly one month he would launch his great attack on Russia, Operation Barbarossa, for which he would need every available aircraft. As far as Britain was concerned, he had ordered the Luftwaffe to fly only limited priority attacks, such as the recent one on the Rolls Royce engine factory at Hillington, Glasgow.

But Bormann wouldn't give up. Perhaps he was already beginning to enjoy the power that he could exercise over the Führer. He kept on talking, backed by Baur, who claimed that the Luftwaffe boys were scared to attack London again; the defences had become too tough for them. But *he* wasn't scared, Baur said. Why, *he'd* fly one of the antiquated 'Auntie Jus'* to the Tommy capital and do the job single-handed!

It was a tired old boast but it did the trick. Once again Hitler worked himself up to one of those terrifying artificial rages of his. Hadn't Goering failed him yet again? He'd promised to knock Britain out of the war before he invaded Russia. And look what was happening—that damned drunken sot Churchill with his whisky and cigars was still fighting! But he'd show the Tommies, he'd give them a raid to remember!

Thus it happened that a crowd of camp-followers and courtiers, led by the son of an obscure army trumpeter and a former Bavarian peasant, talked Hitler into ordering the last raid, which would cause almost as many casualties in London as that of the 1906 San Francisco earthquake: 1,436 killed and 1,800 seriously injured. This was the way history was made in that vulgar, cruel, brown-shirted 'One Thousand Year Reich'.

The next morning at eight o'clock, Hitler called General Jeschonnek, Goering's Chief-of-Staff, and snapped out his orders: the Luftwaffe was to stage another raid on London.

It was Saturday, May 10th, 1941.

* The Junkers 52 troop transport plane.

(Right) Goering with boasts and promises.

In spite of the fact that one per cent of the capital's population had so far been killed or seriously injured by the bombs, and some ten per cent rendered homeless, London had by now begun to adapt to the bombs.

Ministry of Information posters everywhere urged people on: *'Go To It!'* they cried. *'Give a Woman Your Place in the Shelter! ... Britain Can Take It!'* But Londoners did not need such official exhortations; they were already carrying on their normal lives the best they could, without paying much attention to the brave patriotic slogans forced in front of their eyes by the MOI.

And this Saturday in May, most of them were looking forward to a break in the dreary routine of war. They would go to the pictures to see Clark Gable in *Boom Town*, or listen to the radio and hope to catch Flanagan and Allen singing their latest jingle on the failure of the blitz:

> *'We've won it, we've done it,*
> *We've beaten them at last*
> *Up in the air ...'*

There was even going to be a cup final at Wembley Stadium.

But not all Londoners shared the common view that this was going to be just another wartime Saturday. For one thing there would be a 'bomber's moon' this night, and word had already been received from Bletchley's Hut Three that for this night the 'X-Beam', which the Germans used to guide their planes to their target, was directed on London.

The Fire Brigade was already alerted and 1,270 fire appliances were standing by in the hundred square miles ruled by the London County Council, with a further 1,242 in Outer London. It seemed an impressive number—some 2,512 appliances. But back in the raid of December 29th, 1940, that same number of appliances *plus* a further 300 from outside had failed to put out the fire in the City. Nevertheless, the hard-pressed firemen were going to do their best. By six that Saturday evening, all leave had been cancelled, every fire chief was dressed in full fire-fighting gear and the stations were crowded with firemen—the old hands of the old London Fire Brigade and the new boys of the Auxiliary Fire Service, but all were veterans now. The minutes began to tick away leadenly. Like soldiers waiting to go over the top, the men smoked and chatted softly, going to urinate in the lavatories frequently, a sure sign of nerves. Soon it would start ...

The 'fire-raisers' of KG-100 wheeled south of Tower Bridge, heading up the river for Waterloo and Westminster. They came in low, cruising at 10,000 feet. It was eleven o'clock and the battle commenced with a roar, as searchlights flicked on everywhere and ack-ack guns opened up. Scarlet flame stabbed the gloom, grey puffballs of smoke started to explode all around the 'fire-raisers'.

They were not deterred from their course, these veterans who had led the raids over every major city in the United Kingdom. They pressed home their attack. 'Get the city alight for the first wave,' they had been ordered before they left and now they proceeded to do just that before the bombers arrived. First the Royal Albert Docks went up flames ... next the railway sidings and sheds at the King George V Docks ... On and on they flew across London, dropping their deadly flares, searching for their priority target—Euston Station.

Incendiaries ploughed through the roof of the British Museum. The rafters between roof and timbered ceiling started to blaze immediately. Within twenty minutes the Roman Britain Room, the Prehistoric Room, the Greek Bronze Room were all well alight and those in charge realised the position was hopeless. The firemen were driven back by choking black smoke and their water supply began to give out.

Now the bombers started to home in on the fires. The first two of the night's many parachute mines, monstrous canisters filled with high explosive, started to drift down towards King's Cross Station. But the breeze caught them and they finally landed in Holford Square, Finsbury, where Lenin had lodged three decades before.

Already half of London was ablaze. Red flames licked the sky above Southwark Bridge, Upper Thames Street, and Cannon Street Station. On all sides they burnt merrily—and the City was running out of appliances!

Desperately the firemen appealed to Chief Superintendent May at Home Office Control for reinforcements. He told the fire chiefs that a further 750 engines from outside London were on their way. But May was less confident than he sounded over the telephone. The new National Fire Service Act had not yet come into force and local fire chiefs were still a law unto themselves, all 1,600 of them, commanding brigades with different pay, different standards of training, even different uniforms. Many of them were still tending to hoard their appliances for local use.

Worse, it was still too early for the fire authorities to decide what the Germans' main target was and where these reinforcements would be most needed; and after a week of fierce attacks on Liverpool, May knew he dared not risk drawing off engines from anywhere further north than Birmingham. Thus the Chief Superintendent waited and waited, while the outside engines raced through the blacked-out country roads—and London continued to burn ...

While yet another wave of bombers came zooming in over the East End, hosing the Church of St Mary of

St Clement Danes is hit in the London Blitz of 1941.

Eton in Hackney with a massive shower of incendiaries, adding to the historic casualties of this terrible night, some startling news was being relayed across Scotland, down through England, slowly working its way to Ditchley Park, Oxfordshire. All along its way it was greeted with shock, outrage and firm disbelief. It simply couldn't be true. *Impossible!*

At Ditchley Park, Churchill—who enjoyed late-night film shows just as much as Hitler—was sitting down with his guests to watch a comedy. It was the latest Marx Brothers film, and later many of his guests would think its title was singularly apt: *The Marx Brothers Go West*.

The only person not watching was a Miss Mary Shearburn. As duty secretary she was boxed up in a small office at the rear of the big baronial hall where the film was being shown, next to the oak front door.

Now just as midnight chimed, the scrambler phone from 10 Downing Street rang. It was an urgent message for the Prime Minister and what a startling one it was. It read: *'Rudolf Hess has arrived in Scotland.'*

'Who's Hess?' thought Miss Shearburn. But the message *was* urgent so she typed it out hurriedly; for even among the elect and friends, top-secret messages were never delivered to the Premier verbally. She threaded her way through the laughing spectators in the darkened hall and asked Mr Churchill to come out.

A few moments later he appeared outside, with a black silk dressing gown over his siren suit, his 'rompers' as he called them, the suit which had already become world famous after he had been shown wearing them in Pathé newsreels. He read the message, chomping on an unlit cigar, a look of incredulous joy spreading over his broad unlined face as he realised what it meant. The Deputy Führer of the Third Reich was in his hands.

It was exactly one year since Churchill had become the King's First Minister, on May 10th, 1940; and it had been a year of defeat after defeat, with virtually every major city in the United Kingdom now in ruins. Even as he stood there, London was suffering its worst raid of that terrible year. And here, for the first time, was evidence that Germany was not all-conquering, frighteningly invincible. Why else would Hitler's Deputy, the man to whom he had dictated his *Mein Kampf* in the early days of the Movement (some even said Hess himself had written much of it) now be defecting to the enemy? Was *this* the first light at the end of the tunnel?

Within minutes he had gathered his advisers around him. 'Gentlemen,' he growled, *'the worm is in the apple . . .'*

Even London's hospitals were being hit as the German raiders swamped all parts of the burning city with their bombs. At Poplar Hospital, East India Docks, a bomb had sliced the building in two, ripping through the ceiling to explode in the ward below. Father George Coupe, who had just held a service there and had stayed on because of the raid, was only one of the many casualties in the confused blacked out mess.

St Luke's Chelsea had also been hit, though casualties here were light: two doctors and one patient. But if the medical superintendent had not thought at the start of the raid that it was too light to remove the 140 patients to the basement, there might well have been a tragedy. For the basement was totally wiped out.

There was a major fire in part of Lambeth Hospital. Porters and nurses ferried their patients to the unscathed maternity wing on stretchers—though one old man stubbornly refused to move until a fireman dashed through the flames to rescue his false teeth and his best suit! The roof of nearby St Thomas's Hospital was also alight; and at the riverside fire station in Lambeth the staff were hard pressed to find enough engines to fight all the fires. Then a verger from Lambeth Palace came running up in agitation, face covered with sweat and dirt. The Palace roof was on fire, too, he announced. Station Officer Charles Davis said he had no engines to spare. But the verger persisted. 'You'll have to do something. The Archbishop of Canterbury is in residence!'

'I can't help the Archbishop,' Davis snorted. 'The hospital is my first concern.'[1]

The verger, swearing angrily that he would report Davis, fled back to his burning Palace.

There had never been a fire like this before. A quarter of a million books were burning at the British Museum . . . a hundred thousand pounds worth of gin in the City Road . . . the Salvation Army Headquarters . . . the roof of the House of Commons . . . bonded brandy and cigars at Waterloo Station . . . the barge *The Silver Wedding* . . . the Royal College of Surgeons . . . the skeletons of kangeroos brought back by Captain Cook . . . fire, fire, fire—everywhere.

One hour after Churchill had received that startling message from Scotland, 'Emergency Working' was ordered in Central London. That meant all the City's appliances were in action. Now the 1,242 fire-fighting appliances from Outer London would have to be moved in immediately. And, as always, the same old failings of the Civil Defence System were simply compounding the catastrophe.

In Farringdon Street, Superintendent Ted Overton watched his firemen breaking down office doors with their axes. He had just spent hours driving up and down Holborn breaking down similar locked doors. Now he cried angrily: 'Why in hell do they have to padlock them? Don't they want us to save their property?'[2]

At a blaze in Fenchurch Street, Thomas Burling shrugged and told a colleague: 'What can you expect? There hasn't been a fire-watcher there in months.'[3] Even some of those on duty failed to respond to the challenge of the incendiaries; instead they retreated to the safety of whatever shelter they could find. In Bishopsgate by Liverpool Street Station, the five fire-watchers actually had to be forced out of their shelter by the police in order to extinguish fire-bombs.

It was the same old story everywhere. Three burning warehouses at Houndsditch were found to be locked and deserted, while the fire-watchers had fled from the fourth. One observer, Police-Sergeant Fred Scaife, reckoned afterwards that in the whole of the City of London the fire-watchers were only ten per cent effective.

Whole streets of eighteenth-century mansions in Chelsea and Belgravia burnt away merrily because their owners had fled the capital and there were no fire-watchers—and it was no different in working-class districts either. Near the Elephant in Pastor Street, houses were ablaze everywhere because their owners had locked up and the firemen could not gain access. On St John's Hill near Clapham Railway Junction, firemen had to hack their way into houses, shops, even factories because they were locked and unattended. At the local Council depot, not one fire-watcher turned up for duty. At one Battersea wharf the fire-watchers got bored with the job and went home, leaving the wharf to burn out.

Once again, the lack of co-ordination or an organised system of communications produced further complications. When the roof of the Palace of Westminster was reported on fire, the first fire brigade officers to reach the scene were shot at by the Home Guard! And when they finally resolved this problem they found that many of the 1,000 rooms were locked up, their keys in the hands of any one of twelve policemen—and it proved a devil of a job to find the right policeman with the right key!

When Buckingham Palace was reported hit, the brigade arrived to find it dark and silent; the Royal Family were at Windsor for the weekend. So the firemen entered the Palace by clambering over the high railings—*and no one challenged them!* Confusion and chaos...

But there was bravery and dedication too. Police Constable Reginald Oakes, a young water-polo champion, walked across a narrow plank suspended between two buildings above a dark abyss forty-five feet deep in Kensington and rescued four people trapped in a fourth-floor apartment. This daring exploit won him the George Medal, one of several awarded that night.

A young accountant, Warden Stan Barlow, ran in and out of the burning synagogue on the corner of Hallam Street and Great Portland Street, time and time again, to rescue people trapped there until the roof fell on him. He survived.

At Battersea Power Station—which surprisingly enough was never hit—two rescue workers, Jack Searle and George Smith, wormed their way through a tunnel less than two feet in diameter to rescue a family some how trapped in there with tons of rubble creaking frighteningly above their heads. It took them two nerve-rack-

Rudolph Hess.

ing hours to chisel away one of the trapped people, a woman who was pinned down by concrete. They did it in the end. But still Smith would accept no relief and had to be hauled out of the debris by an ambulance chief.

For two hours Boer War veteran John Meggs lay on the floor of his room in Islington, quite alone, fighting off a heart attack while bombs whistled down all around the house. Then, as he began to feel better, he did what he always did after an attack; he went for a walk. Just as he started out on his stroll through hell, a bomb sliced into the house and blew it to pieces. He continued his walk.

Bravery, sangfroid and dedication. At St George's Hospital, they gave blood transfusions non-stop for thirty consecutive hours. At the National Temperance Hospital in St Pancras, the lights had all gone, including the operating theatre's emergency lighting, so the surgeons worked on the torn victims of the raid by the light of torches held by nurses. The white-tiled foyer of St Mary's Paddington was awash with blood, which had dripped from the stretchers as the porters brought in one shattered moaning casualty after another. At the

67

Mile End Hospital Sister Margery Vickers found that someone had deposited six dead bodies in her office; but she did not let this traumatic experience interfere with duty. She continued working right through the night and the next day, in fact well into the following night.

Another nurse who remembers that Saturday night says: 'I don't think I was shocked by anything. Perhaps I went through it all with blinkers on. All I can remember was being surprised later—perhaps shocked—to see that all the flowers in Regent's Park had lost their heads. That upset me.'[4]

By two o'clock in the morning, London's infrastructure had about broken down. One by one the railway terminals were hit. St Pancras and Cannon Street had been put out of action just after midnight. King's Cross and Euston had followed an hour later. At a quarter past one Victoria was evacuated when four unexploded bombs were discovered. A direct hit on Paddington caused many casualties. Liverpool Street, too, received a direct hit. All three southern terminals—Charing Cross, London Bridge and Waterloo—were also out of action. Now only Marylebone Station was still working.

The capital was virtually cut off from the rest of the country; and, even within the city limits, communications were all but impossible. The Underground was no longer functioning. In the City of London alone six telephone exchanges had been knocked out. Gas had gone with 700 gas mains fractured, including the biggest gas works in the world—Beckton Gas Works, blown sky-high in a spectacular explosion. Electricity had vanished in large sections of the city. Every bridge across the Thames between the Tower of London and Lambeth was blocked or cratered. One key point after another had been hit.

The alarming news kept flooding into London's control rooms where the harassed controllers, faces glazed with sweat and hollowed out to death's heads in the hissing white light of the emergency lanterns, tried desperately to keep a hold of an impossible situation. Incident after incident, a litany of disaster. When would the horror end? *When?*

But it did. As dawn broke over the smoking burning city, the sirens finally started to wail the All Clear, leaving the shattered streets to the dead and the exhausted Civil Defence men. But if they were exhausted, they burned with anger too.

Quentin Reynolds, the American correspondent who together with Ed Murrow had been in London since the previous summer, sensed a new emotion among the men and women he encountered as he walked the dawn streets. In Whitehall, north to Bloomsbury, on through Trafalgar Square, he sensed it time and time again—the tight-set lips, the glance of implacable hatred, men mut-tering through gritted teeth as they pulled the victims out of the rubble: 'The dirty bastards!'

Reynolds recalled a line from Kipling: 'The English began to hate' ... and now he began to wonder 'what shape that hate would take when the bombers came back'.[5]

But the bombers did *not* come back. Twelve days later, two-thirds of the Luftwaffe moved to Poland for the great attack on Russia. This had been the last blitz for London, the raid that had begun as a whim at Hitler's retreat—but what a deadly whim!

Everything had gone against the capital. It had been full moon. The tide had been low and water had failed. The infrastructure had broken down. Civil Defence had failed. Night-fighters had been unsuccessful, as had the AA guns ... Everything.

And London had paid the price. The butcher bill for the populace was the highest ever recorded, as we have seen. Now the hospitals, fourteen of which had been hit by bombs, were packed with casualties. Eight thousand streets—a third of Greater London—were impassable, blocked with rubble. The Port of London was reduced to one-quarter capacity. Only one main line station was working; 155,000 people were without gas, water or electricity; and there were only six weeks' supply of coal left to keep supplying gas and electricity to those who were still receiving it. Water would run out altogether, it was calculated, if the city were bombed four times.

It seemed hopeless, all so hopeless.

Mary Welsh wrote in her diary:

Today has brought the usual post-bomb misery—the taste of powder in the mouth, burglar alarms ringing incessantly, glass crunching under our shoes in the flat and also outside, clothes in closets and drawers heavy with dust, my eyes red and face old looking and feeling as though it was burning and a terrible job to concentrate my thinking.[6]

Later she and an American friend, Jim Seymour, christened this Sunday, when the smoke covered the sky all day long and shut out the May sun, 'Bloody Sunday'.

In reality, those who had survived should have rejoiced. For they were saved. And if there was any one man who deserved the credit, that man was undoubtedly Churchill.

In April 1941, John G. Winant, the American ambassador to London, had told President Roosevelt:

The Prime Minister's method of conducting a campaign on what one might call a morale front is unique. He arrives at a town unannounced, is taken to the most seriously bombed area, leaves his automobile and starts walking through the streets without guards. The news of his presence spreads rapidly by word of mouth and before he has gone far crowds flock about him and people call out to him, 'Hello Winnie! Good Old Winnie! You will never let us down. *That's a man!'*[7]

An electricity repair squad attends to bent and battered cables.

It was glowing reports like this that finally persuaded Roosevelt he should take America into the war, to help the British people in their fight against fascism.

Naturally enough, Churchill fostered this heroic view of the British. He knew the truth, of course. Privately he might moan that he thought the British soldier had lost his will to fight, but publicly he lauded the virtues of the average man and woman fighting on the Home Front. For he knew just how vital it was to make America—and above all Roosevelt—believe that the ordinary folk in Britain would never give up.

So, in a world broadcast just before that last blitz of May 10th, 1941, Churchill told his American listeners that where 'the ordeal of the men, women and children' had been the 'most severe' he had found their morale 'most high and splendid'. 'Indeed,' he continued, 'I felt encompassed by an exaltation of spirit in the people which seemed to lift mankind and its troubles above the level of material facts into that joyous serenity we think

belongs to a better world that this.'[8]

All good old-fashioned heady stuff which appealed not only to the Americans, but to the British, too, whether they understood the rhetoric or not. Churchill spoke for them. There were still many waverers, but the great majority were hardening. They would, in the phrase of the time, 'see it through'.

On the morning of that 'Bloody Sunday' of May 11th, 1941, Churchill wept over the ruins of the 'Mother of Parliaments'. But in his heart he must have known the tide was changing. Soon his hard-pressed little island would not be alone in its battle against the greatest empire that Europe had seen since the days of the Romans. The Germans had gone. When they came back again, they would be challenged by a different kind of Britain, tough, well-prepared and resolute, which would not be shaken by the terrible new weapons they used. The Britons of the Home Front would meet them—*and beat them.*

FOUR
The 'hit and run raiders'

ATS girls in training for duties in 'mixed batteries' of anti-aircraft guns.

On June 22nd, 1941, the German armies swept across the border into Russia and Operation Barbarossa commenced. Meanwhile the few remaining Luftwaffe squadrons based in France had decided to adopt new tactics. In squadron-strength now—nine, eighteen, twenty-four planes, instead of the hundreds of the winter months— they flew in low over the British coastline and attacked the easy targets: those still undefended by General Pile's AA guns or by the new type of night-fighters equipped with airborne radar.

The days had long gone when one of General Pile's gunners could say of his service in AA Command: 'There we were in East Anglia defending the Midlands, 30,000 anti-aircraft guns firing for over three hundred days and all we could knock down was *two bleeding wild geese!*'[1] For the whole course of the 1940–41 winter blitz, a long-suffering General Pile had been receiving abusive letters about the performance of his gunners, such as the one from a Londoner who wrote: 'As a citizen of London I think the anti-aircraft defence of London is the biggest scandal since Nero!'[2] But by the summer of 1941, Pile had created six new brigades of anti-aircraft gunners and five whole divisions: an enormous increase in his strength. Still finding himself short of nearly 20,000 gunners, in the end he had turned to the women of the ATS. Many were shocked at the thought of women serving side by side with men on remote AA sites. But Pile had persisted and the first 'mixed battery' was set up on May 19th, 1941. It was, said Sir James Grigg, Undersecretary for War, a 'breathtaking and revolutionary' innovation. But Churchill's own daughter Mary joined one of the mixed batteries and the Great Man himself came to Richmond Park later in the year to inspect his daughter on duty.

So Britain's defences had been improved, and the Germans were forced to change their tactics. They now adopted the 'hit-and-run' technique—quick short raids across the Channel or the North Sea. Now they dropped their bombs on such places as Nuneaton, Jarrow, Newark, Scarborough, Brighton, Weston-super-Mare or Tyneside—all easily reached and relatively undefended targets. These attacks were small-scale affairs in comparison with the bombings of the big cities, but they certainly left their mark on the communities that lived through them.

Suddenly men like the Reverend Bob Precious, a former Merchant Navy officer himself and presently running the Mission for Seamen homes in Middlesbrough, found themselves thrust into the front line. Up to now Precious's only contact with the fighting war had been when he and his wife had taken out their 'Mobile Mollies', filled with sandwiches and urns of hot tea, to feed the crew of some badly damaged ship limping into the port. But by the summer of 1941 the hit-and-run raiders were striking Middlesbrough every night. Fortunately, however, casualties were light and the thousand-odd seamen who stayed in the mission homes took the nightly attacks in their stride.

'My first casualty,' says Precious today, 'was my verger who, in his excitement to tell me that a raid was on its way, fell off the kerb and broke his wooden leg!'[3] He also remembers coming across an elderly petty officer, obviously a little the worse for drink, busily sweeping the pavement outside the Mission while bombs dropped all around. 'What on earth are you doing?' Precious asked him in astonishment. 'Steadying me bleeding nerves, that's what I'm doing,' the petty officer answered, and went on sweeping furiously.[4]

The presence of a gentleman of the cloth never seemed to inhibit the rough-tough seamen who were the Reverend Precious's 'customers'. Once he took no less a personage than the Archbishop of York, Dr Temple, aboard a freighter in the port just after a particularly heavy attack. As they came up the plank they were watched by a red-eyed, unshaven, weary-looking deck hand. 'This is the Archbishop of York,' Precious told the sailor.

'How do, chum,' said the deck hand casually. Clearly he was not impressed.

Dr Temple gave the sailor his best smile and asked benevolently, 'And what was it like, my man? How do you feel now?'

'Bloody awful,' the sailor replied. *'We pissed and shat oursens!'*

Precious froze, thinking he would receive an awful 'rocket' from the prelate, but later Dr Temple confessed to him: 'Do you know, Precious, that is the very first time that anyone has ever treated me as a human being.'[5]

A little later that same year the captain of HMS *Wizard* asked the Reverend Precious to hold a special Harvest Festival service on board his ship, to give thanks not for a bountiful harvest, but because another year had gone by and the *Wizard* had been saved from both U-boats and German dive-bombers. Precious agreed, and arrived on board the destroyer to find that her crew had arranged the thanksgiving altar in 'a special naval manner'. Red and green oil lamps stood on the left and right of the altar, to symbolise port and starboard; and, instead of the fruits and flowers of a normal Harvest thanksgiving, the mess itself was draped with garlands of beautiful, fat, glistening kippers!

Unfortunately, during his 'particularly long sermon', the heat from the two oil lamps started to cook the kippers, and a steady dribble of kipper oil began to drip onto the ship's officers. But, says Precious, 'Nobody laughed . . .'[6]

Indeed most of those involved in these minor raids found them to be irritants, something that either annoyed or amused them, nothing more. Teddy Mole, a half-blind 'gunner' serving with a similar bunch of misfits at Lossiemouth, remembers them as a source of fun, a break from the boring routine in this remote place. Once, while Mole was sheltering under his bunk with other members of his hut during a hit-and-run raid, the door was blown off by a bomb. An icy wind blew in and a corporal huddled next to Mole cried, 'Mole, on yer feet and close that bloody door! There's a hell of a draught in here!'[7]

Another time Mole was caught out on the tarmac in a lorry as the raiders came racing across the field, machine guns chattering. The driver hit the brakes hard. The lorry slammed to a stop and one of the misfits, who possessed a glass eye, shot off the back and was knocked unconscious. The station's medical officer rushed out to inspect the injured man. He opened the man's eyelid to check his reflexes and the man's glass eye fell out and rolled onto the tarmac. 'In a very strange voice the MO said, "He's dead . . ." and fainted clean away.'[8]

Not all of these minor raids ended so humorously, of course. In the spring of 1941, the people of Cwmparc, a mining village twenty miles from Cardiff, were preparing for bed when the hills all around were suddenly lit up by incendiaries. The grass began to burn and the village was soon silhouetted against a circle of flames— a perfect target. The German pilots were not slow to take advantage of it. Zooming in at 300 mph, they had dropped their bombs and disappeared within five minutes. In those few minutes twenty-seven people were killed, six of them children, and half Cwmparc's thousand houses had been destroyed or damaged.

Remote though it was, however, Cwmparc was not unprepared. As a contemporary eye-witness reported:

There came into action the fire-bomb fighters, a whole army of them advancing along the main road, emerging from the side streets and whooping some indistinguishable form of war cry as they swooped on the incendiaries with a kind of suppressed fury . . . and extinguished them with a precision and certainty born of months of preparation.[9]

Indeed, that remote Welsh village broke the national record for the speed with which it dealt with its homeless. By noon the following day, everyone had been re-housed. But that particular hit-and-run raid would be remembered in Cwmparc for many, many years to come.

So the country began to settle down to a long, grey, hungry war. Now the great cities were going to be spared the bombs for months, even years to come. The memories of those terrible winter blitzes of 1940/1941 began to recede. The stirring times seemed over; the danger, the fear, the heady excitement. The ordinary man and woman was more concerned now with mundane things like how to get enough to eat, how to clothe themselves, how to find a little happiness in this drab time, when the island itself seemed to sink into a dreary

Churchill's daughter Mary served in a 'mixed battery'—her father has been visiting it.

routine, and it appeared that war would never end.

Now, when it seemed the real danger had passed, a belated campaign was launched to revamp Civil Defence. The 1,000-odd fire brigades were at last organised into a National Fire Service. Compulsory fire-watching was introduced, with everyone from the age of fourteen onwards eligible for duty at his school, office or place of work. The new improved Morrison shelter—a sturdy table-like affair which could be put up in any council

house's front room—was put into mass production. Slowly the memories of the blitz started to fade as the war dragged on and on ... and nothing happened any more on the Home Front.

Not everyone fell into this new complacency, however. Dr R. V. Jones, twenty-eight years old and the SIS's principal scientific officer, was one of those who suspected that the Germans might have something else up their sleeves. In fact his suspicions dated from way back in November 1939, when the so-called Oslo Report made its first strange appearance.

In that month the British naval attaché in Oslo had received an anonymous note offering him some top-level secret information about current German scientific experiments. If the naval attaché was interested, said the note, he should arrange for a slight alteration in the opening format of the BBC's European News. This was duly done; and on November 4th, 1939, a large parcel was mysteriously found in the Embassy's postbox—presumably delivered and compiled by the 'well-wishing German scientist' who had sent the original note.* The parcel, it was found, contained detailed plans for the future of German science, in particular those areas connected with military research. It was sent for evaluation to Dr Jones in London.

Jones was soon convinced that the details were correct; indeed, he wrote a report stating his belief in the authenticity of the strange document, or the Oslo Report as it was now being called. But his colleagues in the Secret Intelligence Service, who had little concept of science, thought differently—as did Churchill's chief scientific adviser, Lord Cherwell. They believed that Jones, a notorious practical joker, had himself been hoaxed . . .

Jones already had a long list of practical jokes behind him when he had entered Scientific Intelligence. In Oxford, for example, he had once hoaxed a certain eminent Doctor of Philosophy. He began by ringing the man several times and hanging up immediately he answered. Some time later he telephoned again and pretended to be a Post Office engineer; there had been a report that there was something wrong with the victim's telephone. The victim readily agreed and Jones, as the Post Office engineer, said he was sending someone round to look at the defective phone in a week's time.

'A week's time!' the victim exclaimed. 'That's awful. Can't you do better than that?'

Jones replied that they were understaffed, but there was something the victim could do. 'It might be just a leak in the earth,' he explained, 'in which case we could fix it from here . . . if you are prepared to co-operate.' Naturally the victim was prepared. 'Well, first tap the phone with something,' Jones ordered. 'A fountain pen, say, and let me hear the sound. That's right . . . Hmmm, can't tell. What kind of shoes are you wearing? . . . Rubber heels. Ah yes, well that's it. You'll have to take off your shoes, if you don't mind.'

So the victim was led through a series of undignified manoeuvres until Jones finally decided he could not 're-pair' the phone.

*In a letter to the author Professor Jones maintains: 'Various post-war claims have been made to me regarding the authorship of the Report . . . I have my own ideas but I would not publish them even at this stage.'

'Oh please,' the victim pleaded. 'If there is anything else I can do, I'd like to try it.'

'Well, all right,' the self-appointed Post Office engineer conceded. 'It's a crude approximation of a test we do with our own equipment. You have to get a bucket of water and lower the telephone into it, slowly.'

Thus the hoax ended with the eminent Ph.D standing shoeless, slowly lowering his phone into a bucket of water![10]

To many, Jones's behaviour seemed juvenile; but Jones himself thought that his concept of the hoax stood him in good stead in tragi-comic world of the SIS in wartime. It was all a matter of building up 'in the victim's mind a false world-picture'.[11]

In November 1939, however, when Jones told his colleagues he believed in the authenticity of the Oslo Report, they thought that the great hoaxster himself had fallen victim of a 'false world-picture'. His analysis of the Report said:

There is a number of weapons to which several references occur, and of which some must be considered seriously. They include: bacterial warfare; new gases; flame weapons; gliding bombs, aerial torpedoes and pilotless aircraft, long-range guns and rockets; new torpedoes, mines and submarines, death rays, engine-stopping rays and magnetic mines.[12]

And over the months and years since he had written that analysis, Dr Jones had found out that many of the experiments mentioned in the Oslo Report had been successful. The Germans now had a new type of radar; the Henschel 293 remote-controlled glider bomber; the directional radio *Knickebein;* radio range-finding, and many others. As Jones himself stated long afterwards: 'As the war progressed and one development after another actually appeared, it was obvious that the Report was largely correct and in the few dull moments of the war, I used to look up the Oslo Report to see what should be coming along next!'[13]

So as the London blitz ceased and those 'few dull moments' turned into longer periods of contemplation in his office in the Broadway Building, Queen Anne's Gate, Dr Jones became increasingly worried. What had happened to the 'radio-controlled or gyro-stablised rocket shell' reported back in 1939 as being prepared to 'fire at the forts of the Maginot Line'? The Maginot Line had been long conquered by the Germans. Had the 'rocket shell' experiment been shelved, therefore? Dr Jones could only wonder; there was little he could do to find out more. The place where the experiments had been carried out, according to the Oslo Report, was still beyond the range of the RAF's reconnaissance aircraft. It was a small village on the shores of the Baltic Sea, a place called Peenemunde . . .

First newspaper clipping (top left):

GERMAN raiders caused an estimated £20,000,000 damage during their four raids on Belfast. They were responsible for 3,343 casualties. They destroyed 3,205 houses, seriously damaged 3,996, and slightly damaged 49,684, a total of 56,885 houses.

The raids were on April 8, April 15, May 5 and May 7. The raid on April 15 was the worst, 83 tons of bombs being dropped, and the casualties were heavier than those caused on any one ~~~ y part of the ~~ ngdom outside

~~ figures re- ~~ the four raids

~~RIL 8—13 killed, ~~jured and de~~d; 47 injured but ~~ detained.
~~PRIL 15—745 ~~d, 420 injured ~~ detained; 1,091 ~~red but not de~~ed.
~~AY 5—178 killed, ~~ injured and de~~ned; 615 injured ~~t not detained.
~~MAY 7—14 killed, ~~ injured and de~~ined.

Second newspaper clipping (middle left):

Raids
The Death Roll 955

OFFICIAL figures support the view that two of the air raids on Belfast in April and May, 1941, were perhaps the most concentrated made by the Luftwaffe on any part of the United Kingdom.

Belfast had four raids. The first, on April 7, and the fourth, on the night of May 5-6, were comparatively light. Those on the nights of April 15-16 and May 4-5 were of long duration and at the time were described officially as "vicious." It was on these two nights that the main damage was done.

The following official statement was issued last night:—

The total civilian casualties in Belfast and its approaches in air raids were 955 killed and 2,436 injured, of whom 657 were detained in hospital.

In Londonderry 12 persons were killed and 29 injured; 17 of the injured were detained in hospital.

In Belfast and its approaches 3,205 houses were demolished, 3,996 seriously damaged, and 49,684 slightly damaged.

In Londonderry 5 houses were demolished, 15 seriously damaged, and 120 slightly damaged.

The statement, it may be noted, does not refer to the damage to churches, church halls, hospitals, the city hall, and large industrial and business establishments.

Here are some comparative figures:—

Coventry.—43 raids; 1,252 persons killed and 1,859 injured; houses destroyed or damaged 54,373.
Hull.—82 raids; casualties about 3,000 (including almost 1,200 persons killed); 86,722 houses destroyed or damaged; people homeless 152,000.
Swansea.—Killed 387; seriously injured 412; slightly injured 439.
Southampton.—57 raids; killed 633; seriously injured 922; slightly injured 986; 43,289 properties destroyed or damaged.
Portsmouth.—67 raids; killed 930; seriously injured 1,216; slightly injured 1,621; properties destroyed 6,625; properties seriously damaged 6,549.
Plymouth.—1,172 killed; seriously injured 1,092; 3,754 houses destroyed; 18,398 houses damaged but repairable; 49,950 houses slightly damaged.
Manchester.—559 killed and 1,778 injured.
Bristol.—Killed 1,230; seriously injured 1,184; slightly injured 1,889.

Top right table:

Town.	Number of Raids.	Civilians Killed.	Houses Damaged.
Fraserburgh	18	40	
Peterhead	16	36	700
Aberdeen	24	68	700
Scarborough	17	30	2,000
Bridlington	30	24	2,250
Grimsby	22	18	3,000
Gt. Yarmouth	72	110	1,700
Lowestoft	54	94	11,500
Clacton	31	10	9,000
Margate	47	19	4,400
Ramsgate	41	71	8,000
Deal	17	12	8,500
Dover	53 (and shelling)	92	2,000
Folkestone	42	52	9,000
Hastings	40	46	7,000
Bexhill	37	74	6,250
Eastbourne	49	36	2,600
Brighton Hove }	25	127	3,700
Worthing	29	20	4,500
Bournemouth	33	77	3,000
Weymouth	42	48	4,000
Falmouth	33	31	3,600
			1,100

Middle table: THE ATTACK ON THE PORTS

	Estimated enemy planes engaged	Total civilians killed in all raids to end of 1941
PORTSMOUTH		
10th March }	110, 120, 50	756
27th April		
SOUTHAMPTON		
23rd November	60	
30th November } (2 nights)	200	558
1st December		
CARDIFF		
2nd January	125	299
SWANSEA		
19th, 20th and 21st February (3 nights)	250 }	352
LIVERPOOL (AND MERSEYSIDE)		
28th November	150	
20th, 21st and 22nd December (3 nights)	500	4,100
13th and 21st March	250	
1st-7th May (7 nights)	800	
PLYMOUTH		
20th and 21st March (2 nights)	250	1,073
21st, 22nd, 23rd, 27th, 28th and 29th April (5 nights)	750	
CLYDESIDE		
13th and 14th March (2 nights)	460	1,828
5th and 6th May (2 nights)	350	
BELFAST		
15th April	100	94
4th and 5th May (2 nights)	110	
HULL		
18th March	75	
7th and 8th May (2 nights)	100	1,0~
17th July	75	

Right table:

THE ATTACK ON THE ARMS TOWNS

Dates of main raids	Estimated enemy planes engaged	Total civilians killed in all raids to end of 1941
COVENTRY		
14th November	400	
8th April	300	1,236
10th April	200	
BIRMINGHAM		
1st November	—	
19th November	350	
22nd November	200	
3rd December	50	2,162
11th December	200	
9th and 10th April	250	
BRISTOL (AND AVONMOUTH)		
24th November	50	
2nd December	100	
6th December	50	
3rd and 4th January	150	1,159
16th March	150	
11th April	150	
SHEFFIELD		
12th December	300	624
15th December } (2 nights)		
MANCHESTER (WITH SALFORD AND STRETFORD)		
22nd and 23rd December (2 nights)	150 }	1,005

III: BAEDEKERS AND BOMBS, 1942

'It is more than the normal civilian can be expected to stand to have three or four raids in a single day, each producing its tale of casualties and destruction, with no visible hits back at the enemy . . . Brighton working-class morale has suffered and the elderly ladies and gentlemen of Eastbourne could hardly be persuaded to continue their customary occupation of sitting and promenading in the sun.'

Sir Auckland Geddes, Regional Commissioner of South-East England, 1942

Troops help clear up after an air-raid.

ONE
A great superhuman meat and potato pie

The war had come to Yorkshire on the afternoon of August 15th, 1940. On that warm summer's day, the little Wolds market town of Driffield was going about its business as usual. The two hotels, the Bell and the Keys, were packed with Yorkshire farmers attending the Thursday corn market and off-duty airmen from the 77th and 102nd Squadrons, who flew out-of-date Whitley bombers from the airfield two miles up the road at Kellythorpe.

But as the ruddy-faced farmers in their thick unseasonal tweeds drank their ale and talked prices, and the aircrew enthused about 'wizard prangs' and the 'Boches' who had 'gone for a Burton', the war was on its way to Driffield.

At 12.30 precisely, fifty Junkers 88 crossed the Yorkshire coast, after hugging the waves over the North Sea to avoid being detected by radar; and, as they sighted their objective, started to gain height once more for the dive-bombing attack to come.

In the Bell Hotel, one farmer paused in his drinking and cocked his head to one side at the sudden noise. 'The RAF must have stepped up its training programme,' he remarked. 'There's a lot of planes up there.'

'Not bloody likely!' a more knowledgeable RAF pilot cried. 'Those are Jerries!'[1] He bolted for the door, followed by the rest of his crew.

The officers of 77th and 102nd Squadrons, who were on duty, had already sat down in the mess for lunch when the first Junkers came falling out of the sky with a sudden startling howl. Teenage Thomas Overfield who saw them coming in for the attack that day still remembers 'that most impressive formation as they lined up for the attack' and 'the whine of those powerful engines as they brought the war to this quiet corner of England'.[2]

Bomb after bomb rained down on the Yorkshire airfield, while low-flying attackers raked the place with their cannon. Aircraft after aircraft was destroyed. One hangar blew up and three others were set on fire. Within minutes the whole airfield on the edge of the little market town was a shambles of blazing hangars and aircraft.

One RAF man, however, was pleased by the raid—a leading aircraftman currently under arrest in the airfield's cells. He was a member of 77th Squadron, which had been badly mauled in the Battle of France. Repairing one of the squadron's aircraft, this ground crew man, who had had absolutely no training, had suddenly been seized one day with a desire to fly. Somehow he had managed to get a Fairey Battle aircraft into the air and had flown it all the way to a southern airfield, where he had successfully landed the stolen plane. But the RAF had been neither impressed nor amused; he had been brought back to Driffield and placed under close arrest. Now a bomb took off one wall of the jail and the intrepid birdman stepped out a free man once more. For a little while, at least.

By the time the raid was over, twelve bombers on the ground had been knocked out, four hangars had been destroyed and Driffield airfield had been put out of action as an operational base until the end of 1940.

The war had come to Yorkshire at last.

Now as 1941 gave way to 1942, Yorkshire, and in particular its coast, remained virtually the only place in the country still subjected to heavy German attacks.

After Driffield had come Bradford's turn. It was not a very severe raid as the blitzes of the time went, but it motivated the wool town's most famous son, J. B. Priestley (who though he didn't know it had been brought into the BBC to give a less upper-class note to its broadcasting) to liken Bradford to 'a giant superhuman meat and potato pie with a magnificent brown crisp, artfully wrinkled succulent-looking crust ... steaming away like mad. Every puff and jet of steam defied Hitler, Goering and the whole gang of them. It was glorious.'[3]

What it all meant had been anyone's guess, but it was folksy and home-spun and must have appeared to the mandarins of the BBC very working-class.

Leeds had been the next Yorkshire town to receive the attentions of the Luftwaffe. The raid had not been very severe. The Town Hall and the City Museum had been badly damaged; and many people had had several unpleasant moments, including one girl student on duty at the University's switchboard. Instead of waking up another student who was supposed to come on duty during an air-raid, she succeeded in dragging out no less

Hitler receives the salute from the Reichstag—in 1942 he was at the height of his power.

a person than the Vice-Chancellor—at four o'clock on a cold winter's morning!

Sheffield's treatment had been much, much harsher. Prior to the war, Professor Haldane had written in his book *ARP*: 'There is half a square mile of Sheffield which is more vital to the production of munitions than any other part of Britain.' The Germans had known that, too, and now they attempted to knock out this hub of the British armament industry.

Decoy lights set up outside the city on the moors had helped to head off the raiders for a while, and the first bombs had dropped on Leash Fen outside Sheffield. But not for long. They soon found the city—some said they had followed the tramlines glinting in the moonlight to the heart of Sheffield.

That night steelworker Mr F. Barrows was watching a 'corny gangster movie' at Woodseat Palace Cinema in Sheffield. He remembers one scene particularly, featuring Edward Arnold as the big gangland boss. '*Shut that door!*' Arnold had just snarled to Robert Montgomery, when the first bomb landed on Sheffield—and the cinema doors blew open! Whereupon, says Mr Barrows, 'the cinema emptied like magic!'[4]

Sheffield city centre was soon ablaze. The Marples Hotel in Fitzalen Square had taken a direct hit from an high explosive bomb. One of Mr Barrow's workmates, a Scot known to everyone at the steel works as 'Mac', was later found in the cellar of the shattered hotel 'together with the other patrons and young whores, floating in boiling wine and beer'.[5]

Up on Airedale Road, young Roy Hattersley had moved into his grandmother's room. They felt a little safer there, for grandmother—an invalid, incapable of taking refuge in an ordinary shelter—was protected by an invention created by the City Engineer's Department:

The joists of the bedroom floor above her head were held in place by four steel columns buried in the foundations of our new, hard-earned, owned and occupied semi-detached. My mother cried a little when they chipped away the plaster to take the end of the girders and I fell into the hole cut in the floorboards to let the tent poles through. In theory, if the house collapsed, the room in which we huddled with my grandmother would remain intact under the rubble. On the night of the first blitz we almost believed it.[6]

But Mrs Hattersley's 'new, hard-earned, owned and occupied semi-detached' remained standing, a suitable symbol of the future Labour politician's proletarian background. Much of the rest of Sheffield did not. By the end of the city's first big blitz, over 8,000 premises had been destroyed and 85,000 damaged; 668 citizens had been killed and 1,590 seriously injured.

But now as the raids ceased everywhere, even in Yorkshire, only one town continued to be bombed; indeed Herbert Morrison nominated it in 1942 the 'most bombed city in Great Britain after London'. That town was Hull.

'*From Hull, Hell and Halifax, the Lord protect us*', sailors had once quipped about the port on the Humber, which they generally regarded as being even duller than Halifax, Nova Scotia. But this Yorkshire port had now become the vital link between Britain's armament factories and hard-pressed Soviet Russia; for from Hull the convoys sailed to Murmansk bringing aircraft, tanks, guns, munitions, food to help the reeling Red Army, currently suffering defeat after defeat. Thus Hull and the surrounding LNER railway network had become target number one for the Luftwaffe in Holland and Norway.

From June 1941 almost to the end of the war, Hull was bombed savagely time and time again. Along the long stretch of the docks, running for several miles beside the Humber, whole streets had disappeared and continued to disappear as the Germans attacked with relentless fury. And with them families were wiped out or scattered as homeless all over England, never to return.

The Websters were a typical tight-knit East Yorkshire family living in Mulgrave Road, near the docks. The newly married sister lived next door and Grandma, who was fiercely independent in spite of her age, lived a couple of hundred yards away in Hedon Road. As always the local council had done little to protect its citizens. In Mulgrave Road all they had was a series of brick sheds in between the houses, in which the men and women sheltered separately because the women objected to the men's smoking.

The bombs that hit Mulgrave Road and St Mark's Street not only flattened many houses, but sent the shelters toppling like a row of dominoes. Denis Webster, aged eight, was killed; his sister Elsie was buried in the rubble and their younger sister frightened out of her life. All she could ever remember afterwards was 'two women, covered in dust and dirt, fighting with each other for a pair of stays in a bombed house'.[7] In one fell blow that raid put an end to the Websters' cosy little life together. Mother and Father were taken in by friends and the sisters were dispersed elsewhere. Never again did the whole family live together under one roof.

It was a fate shared by many other Hull families. Bombed out of their homes, they were hurriedly evacuated to the surrounding villages and seaside towns such as Patrington, Easington and Withernsea. But even there the refugees were not safe from the Luftwaffe.

In Withernsea, Mrs E. Parkes remembers the Luftwaffe raiders machine-gunning her as she took a walk in the fields of the local junior school. Later another bomber jettisoned his bombs over the bowling green, close to the sea. Hurrying to the scene, because she knew it was her grandfather's habit to go there of an afternoon, she found him standing in the ruins of a hut, red-faced with fury and shaking his fist at the German plane streaking for safety across the North Sea. 'You bloody Germans!' he was yelling. 'Look what you have done!'

'But what happened, Grandad?' she asked.

'*This!*' he snorted and turned his back on his anxious granddaughter. 'Kindly look at my best trousers!'

His granddaughter burst out laughing. The old gentleman 'had a two-inch slit the length of his behind'.[8]

But the blitz on Hull was anything but a laughing matter for thousands of sailors and seamen who were passing through the battered port for the 'Murmansk Run', never to return (in all 10,000 of them died trying to take supplies to Soviet Russia). While they waited for their ships, they were subjected to raid after raid.

Ron Jackson, who worked at Dunn & Co, Hatters, at the corner of Monument Bridge and Princess Dock, opposite the Prudential Building, remembers walking down Hessle Road after three streets in the area had been demolished by bombs and seeing 'the dead bodies, some of them seamen, laid side by side while the rescue squads were still digging away frantically for any survivors. But there weren't any. They were all dead.'[9] Later, when he managed to get to work, he found the Prudential Building had been gutted by fire and wild rumours were circulating that so much water had been pumped into the blazing building that Mecca café patrons on the ground floor had not been burnt to death but had been drowned.

Another Hull man, a soldier by the name of Porter coming home on compassionate leave because his home had been bombed, found himself 'running from Paragon Street Station down a blazing empty street' and clambering over 'what I thought were dead bodies everywhere, only to find later that they were dummies blown out of the window of Binns, the big department store'.[10] Ten or so miles away the future Mrs Porter (then a hairdresser, who would meet her soldier husband during one of these terrible raids) was flung down and injured by a bomb as the dive-bombers attacked a local train, packed with working people. Fortunately the train wasn't hit, though as she says today, 'It was a miracle that only five or six people were killed around me.'[11]

Sapper Ebbington of the Royal Engineers was also home on leave, but the reason for his home-coming was a happier one. He had just been awarded the MBE for jumping into Folkestone harbour to rescue a shot-down RAF pilot—who, it later transpired, was a *German* pilot! (But the King still gave him a medal for his bravery.) Now, arriving in Hull, he found that those same Germans were doing their best to destroy it. With no thought for his own safety, Len Ebbington sprang into action. In Mason Street he rescued the vicar's wife from the nearby St Philip's Church, crawling down a drainpipe with the good lady on his back. That done, he ran into the blazing Alexander Theatre and rescued another man. 'But there are still people inside!' he was told.

'Down in the basement!' In he went again and found the place 'flooded with only dead bodies floating around in the hot water'.[12] Then and only then did he give up.

One year later, in North Africa, that brave sapper was killed.

By the beginning of 1942, 1,200 Hull citizens had been killed, 3,000 had been wounded and 146,000 rendered homeless. Of the pre-war total of 92,000 houses, only 5,943 were still undamaged.

The whole sad story of Hull can be summed up in the words of one elderly working-class air-raid warden who came home after a night raid and found 'the street was flat . . .':

My missus was just making me a cup of tea for when I come home. She were in the passage between the kitchen and the wash-house when it blowed 'er. She were burnt right up to the waist. Her legs were just two cinders. And 'er face. The only thing I could recognise 'er by was one of 'er boots. I'd have lost fifteen 'omes if I could have kept my missus. We used to read together cos I can't read messen. She used to read to me like. We'd 'ave our armchairs on either side of the fire and she read me bits out o' the paper. We 'ad a paper every evening. Every evening . . .[13]

The tragedy of war, as experienced by the citizens of Hull.

But outsiders took a more detached view—in some cases positively clinical. The RAF, for instance, watching the destruction caused by the Luftwaffe, estimated that for every one ton of bombs dropped on Hull's built-up areas, some 20–40 dwellings were demolished and 100–200 people rendered homeless.

In a report sent to Winston Churchill in March 1942, Lord Cherwell, the Prime Minister's Scientific Adviser, stated:

Investigation seems to show that having one's house demolished is most damaging to morale. People seem to mind it more than having their friends or even relatives killed. At Hull signs of strain were evident, though only one tenth of the houses were demolished.[14]

Lord Cherwell and those who thought as he did reasoned that the way to bring the war to Germany was to do to the Germans what they were doing to the citizens of Hull: to bomb the build-up areas of all fifty-eight German cities of over 100,000 inhabitants, which housed one-third of the Reich's population, and systematically destroy their homes. Each British bomber, it was calculated, had an average life span of fourteen operational sorties. On each sortie, if it could drop three tons of bombs on a built-up area, it would, by the time it was shot down, have made some 4,000–8,000 Germans homeless. As Lord Cherwell wrote to

Churchill: '*There seems little doubt that this would break the spirit of the people.*'[15]

Sir Charles Portal and Sir Archibald Sinclair, the Air Minister, reported that they found Cherwell's paper 'simple, clear and convincing'. Neither the politician nor the airman seemingly had any scruples about the morality of attacking civilians, driving them from their homes and killing them in order to break the morale of the German people.

But Portal had seen London burning and Sinclair was encouraged by letters like the one he received from Geoffrey Shakespeare, Liberal MP for Norwich (which itself would suffer as a consequence of what was now being planned):

I am all for the bombing of working-class areas of German cities. I am Cromwellian—I believe in 'slaying in the name of the Lord'—because I do not believe you will ever bring home to the civil population of Germany the horrors of war until they have been tested in this way.[16]

The die had been cast. Now it was going to be an eye for an eye.

In February 1942, the man who had stood on the roof of the Air Ministry back in 1940 and sworn that the Germans would reap a bitter harvest from the deadly seed they had sown, Arthur 'Bert' Harris took over Bomber Command.

Harris, brisk, bluff and abrasive, had come up the hard way. Off to Africa at the age of sixteen with five pounds in his pocket he had sought his fortune in farming, gold mining and driving horse teams. In 1914 he joined the Rhodesia Regiment and fought against rebellious Boers and German guerillas, 'living off biscuits which you had to bust with your rifle butt and bully beef which in that climate was almost liquid in the can'. But it wasn't the food that soon made Harris sick of the infantry, it was the marching: 'How we marched! We marched and we marched and we marched, and God knows as far as I was concerned I'd already marched too far!'[17] So, at the end of the campaign, the browned-off infantryman took himself back to England and promptly joined the one service where he would not have to march another step—the newly formed Royal Flying Corps.

He saw action both over England and in France, served in India, bombed rebellious tribesmen in various parts of the Empire, and slowly progressed up the ladder of promotion. In the early days of World War Two he commanded 5 Bomber Group and showed just what a

The picturesque town of Lübeck, Sir Arthur Harris' first target.

forceful personality he was. Eventually, in early 1942, he landed the plum job, as chief of the only part of the British Armed Forces which could effectively take the war to the heart of the enemy's country—Bomber Command.

And by the time Harris arrived at Bomber Command headquarters at High Wycombe in Buckinghamshire, he was firmly convinced that the only way to beat the 'Hun' was to bomb him into submission. 'There are a lot of people who say that bombing cannot win the war', he declared in an interview a few weeks after taking over his new post. 'My reply to that is that it has never been tried. *We shall see*.'[18]

Now Harris, soon to be known as 'Bomber' Harris (and to some as 'Butcher' Harris), set about putting the suggestions of people like Cherwell into practice. This hard, dry, vulgar man—who once told a policeman who had stopped him for reckless driving and complained that he 'might have killed somebody': 'Young man, I kill thousands of people every night!'[19]—decided his first task was to find an easy target, both to locate and to bomb.

He found it in the old German city of Lübeck. The port-city presented no location problems, being on the Baltic coast, and his bombers could fly over the undefended sea to attack. It was lightly defended and was not incorporated in any of the powerful 'flak alleys' such as those of the Ruhr and the southern German industrial cities. And above all, the city centre was made up of many medieval, half-timbered houses which were highly inflammable. As Harris put it in his typical downright manner: 'Lübeck was built more like a fire-lighter than a human inhabitation.'

Harris's former chief radar officer, Group Captain Saward, a latterday apologist for his old chief, today maintains that:

At this time the Baltic ice was beginning to break and the port would soon come into full use for supplying the military requirements of the German armies in Russia and Scandinavia. Also it would be open for import of iron ore and other strategic materials from Sweden . . . These were important enough considerations to have included the town on the recent list of targets to be attacked.[20]

But Harris made no bones about his reason for selecting Lübeck as his target. With characteristic bluntness he stated: 'I wanted my crews to be well-blooded, as they say in fox-hunting, *to have a taste of success for a change*.'[21]

Thus it was that on the night of March 28th/29th, 1942, the RAF's bombers took off from Driffield, where it had all started in Yorkshire, and from a dozen other airfields in Yorkshire and Lincolnshire fields, zooming out across the North Sea—over 300 of them—to come in on a surprised Lübeck from the Baltic.

They did their job well. For a loss of only eight bombers, they started fires which took thirty-two hours to put out, destroying 1,000 dwellings and damaging a further 4,000. And they killed 520 civilians and left 985 wounded.

Next day Goebbels, the German Minister of Propaganda, wrote in his diary:

This Sunday has been thoroughly spoiled by the exceptionally heavy air raid by the RAF on Lübeck. In the morning I received a very alarming report from our propaganda office there, which I at first assumed to be exaggerated. In the course of the evening, however, I was informed of the seriousness of the situation by a long-distance call from Kaufmann [the *Gauleiter* of nearby Hamburg]. He believes that no German city has ever before been attacked so severely from the air. Conditions in parts of Lübeck are chaotic.[22]

And four days later 'the poison dwarf', as the vitriolic undersized Minister was called behind his back, wrote once more:

The damage is really enormous. I have been shown a newsreel of the destruction. It is horrible. One can well imagine how such an awful bombing affects the population. Thank God, it is a North German population, which on the whole is much tougher than the Germans in the south or the south-east. Nevertheless we can't get away from the fact that the English air raids have increased in scope and importance; if they can be continued for weeks on these lines, they might conceivably have a demoralising effect on the population.[23]

Hitler, meanwhile, was enraged. And when the RAF found another easy target a few nights later—Rostock, also on the Baltic and of equally small military value—his rage knew no bounds. Although the Luftwaffe bomber fleet was fully committed in Russia, he ordered that something must be done. But what?

By now most of Britain's major cities were well-protected by Pile's gunners and the increasingly effective British night-fighters. The quality of the German bomber pilots still engaged in operations in the West had deteriorated alarmingly. The 'old hares', as the veterans were called, had long disappeared, dead or broken men. The 'green-beaks' or new recruits had neither the skill, the training nor even, in some cases, the courage of their predecessors. They no longer pressed home their attacks with the necessary determination. How could pilots of this calibre be expected to penetrate the defences of London or Liverpool? Even Hull was becoming too much for them, although it was a 'soft option' which could be attacked from the sea.

Milch, that implacable enemy of Britain—of whom

Sir Arthur Harris.

one of his staff officers once said: 'When Milch pisses, ice comes out'—thought he had the answer. In the same month that Lübeck was so disastrously bombed, the Field Marshal met an aircraft designer who was out of a job.

As Inspector-General of the Luftwaffe, Milch knew just how miserably his air force was now equipped for any attack on Britain. Only a few months before, he had forced Goering's old crony Ernst Udet to commit suicide because Udet had not maintained aircraft production. *'Why did you put me in the hands of that Jew Milch?'* Udet had scrawled in red crayon on the floor, just before he died.

Now this out-of-work engineer Robert Lusser, who had fallen foul of the Heinkel Company as well as Professor Messerschmitt, the doyen of German aircraft design, was offering Milch a new method of attacking the

Tommies. Within a few days of their first meeting, Lusser had designed at Milch's request a pilotless aircraft. It would make no demands on the hard-pressed aluminium industry; it took only 550 man-hours to produce and could run on low-grade petrol. Above all, it did not need a highly trained crew to fly it. The concept of the flying bomb had been born.

But Hitler could not wait for this revolutionary new weapon to be brought into action. He was under pressure on all sides and his prestige was waning. He could not afford to stand by purposelessly and let his cities be knocked out, one by one, by the RAF. He knew, of course, he had neither the bombers nor the crews in the west for any major operation against the British. Therefore a new tactic had to be found to stop the enemy's attacks. And find it he would. Hitler was out for revenge.

TWO
Tip and run

It all started all very inauspiciously.

One afternoon in early April, four Messerschmitt fighter-bombers dropped out of the sky off Torquay, that home of maiden ladies and retired gentlemen, and came racing in at only 150 feet, their machine guns chattering. Almost before the genteel folk who lived there realised what was happening, the Messerschmitts had dropped their bombs and were hurtling eastwards once more back to France. It was reported that more than one lap-dog never got over the shock.

At top level no one took any notice of the raid. Torquay had no military value and its effect on the war effort was nil. A few genteel ladies might be in shock and in due course some irate gentleman would write to *The Times* protesting about the lack of defence at 'this delightful watering place', but that would be about the sum of it.

Four days later the fighter-bombers made another of these seemingly senseless raids: this time on Brixham. A week went by, and in they came again to attack Bognor Regis, the seaside resort to which George V refused to be taken again for the 'cure': '*Bloody Bognor!*' were reputedly his last words on his death-bed. Swanage followed, being raided on two consecutive days. Five days later, four of these impertinent Messerschmitts attacked Portland.

The raids were both puzzling and annoying. At the beginning of 1942, the Joint Intelligence Committee in London had predicted: 'The tactics of the German Air Force against the British Isles are unlikely to differ materially from those experienced during the latter half of 1941.'[1] What were they to make of this new tactic? For his part, General Pile of AA Command was inclined to find the raids 'annoying but at the same time it all seemed a bit pointless'.[2]

By the third week of April, Exmouth, Bexhill, Folkestone, Hastings, Lydd, Dungeness, Poling, Cowes and Newhaven had all been struck by these 'tip-and-run' raiders, as the popular press was now calling them; for they seemed not even really to 'hit' a target, but simply to 'tip' it. All targets of virtually no importance, all raided lightly, and all raided during daylight hours.

Then suddenly the raiders struck at night again, and Pile began to have his suspicions. He guessed that the Germans were going to recommence their night attacks. *But where?* His gunners effectively protected all the country's major cities. Would he be justified in taking away some of his batteries from these cities to defend what had been up to now regarded as 'open towns', placed such as Penzance, Truro, Guildford, Maidstone and the like, all of which were of little military importance? Pile hesitated . . .

Then the Germans struck. Their 'tip-and-run' tactics, as intended, had confused the British defenders; now they took their strategy a stage further. On the night of April 24th they made a short sharp raid on the cathedral city of Exeter with twenty-five planes. The defences there were non-existent, and the Luftwaffe deliberately set as their target the Cathedral and its surrounding area. They swamped the area with incendiaries and heavy calibre bombs of a type they had never used before. The result was heavy damage to the historic city. The choir aisle of the Cathedral was hit, both St James's Chapel and the Sacristy were demolished, and most of the Cathedral's priceless medieval glass went too.

The next morning, Radio Berlin announced that as a reprisal for the bombing of such cities as Lübeck and Rostock, 'We shall go all-out to bomb every building in Britain marked with three stars in the Baedeker Guide.' The 'Baedeker raids' had begun.

The bombing war was escalating. Before it was over, it would reach heights undreamed of even by those who had gone through the fury of the blitzes of 1940/41. The large-scale indiscriminate bombing of civilians in towns and cities everywhere in Britain was on its way.

On the bright moonlit night of April 25th, 1942, a wave of forty German bombers appeared on British radar screens along the whole length of south-western England. They had crossed the French coast . . . The tense anxious radar operators tried to assess what their target could be. They had reached the English coast . . . They were making landfall between the Isle of Wight and Seaton in Devon . . . Were they heading for Bristol, the operators asked themselves. The attackers flew on over Dorset and Hampshire . . .

Over Salisbury, the experienced pathfinders in the lead began to drop their 'Christmas trees', as the Germans called their incendiary flares. A lane of hang-

Women and children in Exeter after the Blitz in May 1942.

ing fire appeared in the night sky, guiding the heavily laden bombers that were following the pathfinders. On the ground the sirens started to sound their chill wail.

In Bath, the firemen began to tumble out of their bunks and the Civil Defence prepared to go on duty, grumbling as usual that they were in for another long night in Bristol. For that's where they thought the Germans were heading; in the past they had rendered help to the hard-pressed Bristol force many a time.

As the flares hung brightly over Bath, illuminating its gracious eighteenth-century houses in their glowing garish light, Ron Shearn, one of the many ARP men who had been alerted, was not particularly alarmed. He, too, thought the Germans were heading for Bristol. Suddenly he saw, in the light of a glittering flare above the town centre, the dark sweep of a plane. Next minute it was zooming down and ugly black eggs were falling in profusion from its belly. This time the Luftwaffe's target was *Bath!*

Wave after wave of bombers filled the sky over the defenceless town. Not only did they drop bombs, some of them came down low enough to use their machine guns on anyone foolish enough to be on the streets, which were now as bright as daylight. A warden running home to alert his wife found her dead, crumpled on the cobbles. She had been riddled by bullets as she fled for the shelter. Ambulances, mostly driven by women volunteers, were shot up as they raced with casualties to St Martin's Hospital, where Dr Fritz Koehn, a Czech refugee, ran the medical team. By the time Bath's two-day blitz was over, Koehn's team alone would have dealt with some 200 wounded.

At last the bombers seemed to be going—though in fact they were simply returning to France, to refuel and come in for a second attack.

Already the old spa town was suffering grievously. This night the Germans were using a new kind of bomb; it was equipped with a short-delay fuse, so that when it exploded it caused a great deal of blast and splinter effect. The very features that made Bath attractive—the Georgian structure in Bath stone, which was only six inches thick and lightly held together by thin mortar; and its pleasant situation between green hills, which increased the blast effect—helped to create greater destruction than would normally have been the case.

The tall buildings, many occupied by several families, were easily pushed over by the blast or simply collapsed like a pack of cards. All over the town people were buried alive. An urgent appeal went out to Bristol's Civil Defence for their special listening teams, trained to find such people.

Ron Shearn was detailed to stand guard over a pile of bodies, just brought out from the shattered terraces

Civil Defence workers rescue what they can of the belongings from this home.

An anti-aircraft spotter.

of Lower Bristol Road, while crowds of dazed bewildered civilians streamed through the streets. Suddenly, in the flickering light of the fires, one of the bodies seemed to move ... Shearn took another look. It was the body of a little girl, about three years old. He summoned one of the hard-pressed ambulances and asked for the child to be taken to hospital. The driver wasn't too sure. 'Better look after the living, chum,' he said.[3] But Shearn insisted—and he was right, the child was alive. Today that unknown little girl will probably be a housewife in her mid-forties with children of her own, a whole lifetime saved by a man she has never known.

But others were not so fortunate. A little later, Shearn and his colleague Harry Boone, who only had one arm, heard that a house in Beechen Cliff Place had taken a direct hit, and people were suspected of being buried beneath the smoking rubble. Together with four soldiers from the Home Guard, they tunnelled for hours until they finally found them. All five were dead. Three of them belonged to the same family: Mr and Mrs Blackburn and their daughter Cherry. As the little girl was released from the rubble, they found that her father's arm—he had just come home on leave from the RAF the previous day—was curled protectively around her. It had been a vain hope.

Another family had been trapped in the ruins of the nearby Half Moon pub. For two whole days the Bristol squad probed for them with their sound detectors—long poles to which microphones linked with earphones were attached. At last they heard a faint tapping. The Bristol men started digging at once and in the end brought out a 'smiling mine-host', William Small. But as they dug deeper they found his brother Henry and his wife Kate, both dead.

High above the blazing town, a German war correspondent watched the raid and made his notes for a feature which would appear on the morrow in the Führer's own paper, *der Volkische Beobachter*, under the blazing red headline '*Annihilating Reprisal Attack on the English Town of Bath: Lübeck and Rostock Avenged!*'

On the British coast the first searchlights grope restlessly in the night sky and show us the way. The Tommies do not yet know for whom the attack is intended. They think they are well protected in Bath. We roar down from the sky.

'*Now!*' The first flare bombs from our leaders light up the land like day. Beneath, the River Avon winds through the countryside like a silver thread. Here below us is the great loop in the middle of which the town lies. And now the first small incendiaries go down.

Suddenly in front of us there's a great towering flame, which dazzles us even in the cockpit with its flaming red! A huge cloud bursts up from below, sinisterly lit by the greedy self-devouring flames. A gas holder has exploded in the gas works!

In a second the fire spreads and casts a flaming light over the city. We go down still lower. Beneath us we see rows of burning houses. Smoke rises from them and thickens into a black cloud which lies over the town in a threatening pall. We can recognise the streets as well. Fire and destruction are raging in them! Our commander searches calmly for a new target. We fly over it.

'Bomb doors open. *Let go!*'

Heavy bombs fall. Then waiting—a strained pause. Once again there is a flash below and where all had been dark before there is a sudden light, an unpleasant light for the English. *Annihilation!*

The bombs have exploded and met their target. Fresh formations are coming up behind and new explosions continually occur. One wave after another visits this town with death and destruction.[4]

It was a typical piece of National Socialist prose, full of bombast and Wagnerian undertones, clipped harsh sentences, replete with many exclamation marks; and clearly calculated to please Hitler. It signalled that his message had been delivered: bomb the 'soft options' in the Reich and we will do that to your cities too!

General Pile had got the message all right, without even reading the piece. While Bath was still counting its dead—some 400 of them—Pile was anxiously trying to guess which cities would be hit next. Where should he switch his guns?

After poring over his maps, he finally made a snap judgement. The 'soft options' with some cultural value, that he guessed might be future targets were: Penzance, Truro, Hayle, Winchester, Taunton, Basingstoke, Salisbury, Aldershot, Andover, Ilford, Maidstone, Tunbridge Wells, Ashford and Canterbury. Not all of them were of great aesthetic value, but he reasoned that some of the lesser ones might be attacked by aircraft splitting off from a bigger Baedeker raid.

Next night 65 planes attacked Bath again! There was a great outcry from the hard-hit town, which felt itself completely undefended and was bitterly angry—especially because there was a military objective in the area that had warranted AA defence, namely the Admiralty Foxhill site.* On that second night, a Sunday, nearly 10,000 'trekkers', as they were called, fled their homes and slept in hedgerows, their heads covered with clothes so that the German pilots could not spot the white faces.

As Pile admitted himself: 'Unfortunately, though quite excusably, we were waiting in the wrong place.'[5] He tried again, building up his AA defences the length

* After the war it was discovered that the German raiders had possessed aerial photographs of the Admiralty complex.

and breadth of southern England, rushing guns to every possible target, creating a new sense of urgency among the Home Guard rocket and gun batteries which had been recently set up to assist the regular gunners:

Nine-barrelled rocket projectors were also deployed as we wanted the enemy to fly as high as we could make him, and we ordered these weapons to be used freely, even at the expense of accuracy! It was technically a retrograde step. This was how we had started in London, but the need was urgent and there was little or no time to spend in emplacing and calibrating radar sets accurately.[6]

But again the Germans out-thought the defenders, even though the British had the advantage of Ultra and the whole existing German spy network in Britain was controlled by MI5. For now they studiously avoided the prepared defences of the South and concentrated their attack on an old target, but with a viciousness it had never experienced before . . .

Norwich, that ancient East Anglian city, known to most outsiders for its famous cathedral and equally famous sharp English mustard, had been a target for the Luftwaffe even before London had been blitzed.

Since the very first year of the war, the Norwich sirens had sounded daily and often nightly, too. Local photographer George Swain, who was always out in every raid trying to get pictures for the local paper, even at the risk of his own life, says: 'I remember Londoners staying here who said that they were glad to go home for weekends and get some sleep!'[7]

On July 9th, 1940, one of these hit-and-run raids had left 26 citizens of Norwich dead and many more injured. Their names were shown on a list in the local public library. Almost weekly thereafter, other names had been added to that sad list (in the end there would be 330 names on it, plus those of 1,100 wounded).

Often the locals shopping in St Stephens or in Market Place would look up, startled by the sudden roar, to see the sinister black shape of a Dornier or Heinkel streaking across the city. Because Norwich was completely undefended, many of them believed that an attack on the city was a 'novice run' for inexperienced German pilots. But when the sirens sounded the warning at eleven o'clock on the night of Monday, April 27th, 1942, the frightened citizens of the old city soon learned that these were not novices; these were the professionals—and they were coming into attack in force.

Mrs M. Holmes, whose husband was already on duty as a warden, scurried down to her shelter, following her little dog Scamp which was already in there, quivering with fear. As always, she says, 'he had known of the raid before me and had set off howling miserably'.[8] The dog and his mistress were just in time. Seconds later, by the eerie light of chandelier flares, the Germans started to drop their bombs. By dawn Mrs Holmes would have lost more than half a dozen friends and neighbours.

Norfolk Hospital was hit. The night shift arriving at Colman's Mustard Factory was decimated by flying shrapnel. A party of ATS recruits just arrived at Yarmouth Station reeled to all sides, a mass of flying arms and khaki-clad legs, victims of a direct hit.

Photographer George Swain, racing through the streets on his bicycle, saw 'smoke and flames rising. Flares were hanging in the sky and red tracer bullets were making spurts and lines of fire everywhere. Bombs were whistling down.' One bomb, in fact, landed so close that it flung him from his bike. 'Something that felt like a sandbag slumped on top of me and said "Sorry, old man ..."'[9] But nothing would stop the intrepid photographer. Winded and not a little scared, he hopped back on his trusty iron steed and set off for the scene of the action.

George Swain was not the only one who had to conquer his fear this night. Home Guardsman A. Percy, recently discharged from the Army and now the local force's weapons training officer, always carried his trusty 1918 vintage Long Lea rifle with him. Now as the bombs fell all around the Michelin tyre depot in Prince of Wales Road where he worked, he rushed out to see 'a German plane so low that I could see the rear-gunner'.[10] It was too tempting. He ran to his car and, as the plane circled slowly, picked up his rifle and took aim.

Now the plane was over the old Hippodrome. Mr Percy didn't hesitate. With practised ease, he took first and second pressure—and fired. In the very same instant that he felt the first satisfying kick against his shoulder, the plane dropped its bombs. The blast wave slapped him across the face like a blow from a flabby hand and made him close his eyes. When he opened them again, the tyre depot had vanished and the area around the Hippodrome was blazing fiercely. But over forty years later, Mr Percy still wonders, *Did I hit the devil, or didn't I?*'[11]

It is doubtful. None of the twenty-five aircraft which took part in that raid is recorded as having been shot down. How could they be? There were no guns and the night-fighters were scrambled too late. So the Germans bombed relentlessly, shattering houses and offices in Oxford Place, Surrey Street and around the station, the centre of the destruction.

As dawn broke on that beautiful warm spring morning, the Civil Defence set to work trying to rescue the trapped, fighting not only the smouldering ruins, but the hundreds of refugees streaming out of the city for the surrounding countryside. For they were terrified that the Germans would come again this night—as indeed they did.

Mrs M. Holmes was one of them. Among her little group of 'trekkers'—mostly women—who would sleep this Tuesday night on the golf course, was a young girl in an advanced state of pregnancy. She was making heavy going, and in the end the women stopped an Army lorry and asked the driver to take the unfortunate girl to the nearest village. The driver refused and drove off. Angrily the women shouted after him, waving their fists with rage. He changed his mind and stopped. Hurriedly catching up with him, the women pulled back the canvas flap for the girl to get in—and suddenly understood his reluctance to take passengers. For there, in the back of the lorry, lay 'a huge live bomb which the driver had been ordered to take into the country for exploding at double-quick time!'[12]

Not everyone left the city, of course. Nineteen-year-old office worker Barbara Dowdesdale was determined to go to work in spite of her parents' protests. She boarded her usual morning 89 bus to journey to her offices in the city centre. But it was diverted so many times by signs saying 'Road closed' or 'Unexploded Bomb' that she began to think that 'it was all like a board-game of go back and start again'. But in the end she got there, and so did all her colleagues: 'Within the hour everyone had appeared, some dirty and all heavy-eyed, but all glad to see each other alive again.'[13]

Also fighting his way through the shattered city that morning was Mr Percy, the Home Guardsman, making his way to the bombed-out Michelin tyre factory. In Dereham Road, as he threaded his way through debris, downed telephone lines and punctured fire hoses spurting water everywhere, he came across 'a lone old man, sitting on a battered chair on the pavement. Behind him was his house, flattened. He gazed sadly into nowhere.'[14]

The intrepid photographer George Swain was still taking photographs in spite of having run about the city, back and forth, all night. Now he was outside the Hippodrome, which had been shattered by the bombs that Mr Percy had seen falling. The stage manager had been killed outright, two house managers had been flung down the main steps, and the star of the evening had been so badly hurt that he died before the Civil Defence workers could reach the theatre. He had been the trainer of a troupe of performing sea-lions, which last night had delighted the audience by blowing horns, balancing on balls and merrily clapping their flippers in time to the spectators' applause. But now, as Mr Swain stood there viewing the scene, 'from inside the theatre came a terrible sound—a wailing worse than the whistle of a bomb. It was from one of the sea-lions which the bomb had released. I shall never forget the noise it made, flapping in its ungainly way through the dark empty theatre, crying for its master ...'[15]

Thus ended the first week of the Baedeker raids. In all cases the defenders had been caught off guard. As a result, three venerable cities had been wrecked—Exeter, Bath and Norwich. Nearly 1,200 people had been killed,

Princess Elizabeth learns motor mechanics with the ATS, watched by her parents and her sister Princess Margaret.

twice that number seriously wounded, and thousands rendered homeless, refugees in their own country. Now the question uppermost in the minds of ordinary men and women in tourist towns from Stirling to Salisbury was: where would 'Jerry' strike next?

Meanwhile, in bomb-shattered Bath, young Private Davies searched ceaselessly among the debris of his home at 32 Kingsmead Street. His wife Millie and his three young children—June (five), Pam (two) and John,

his six-week-old son—were down there somewhere and he was determined to find them.

For seven days and seven nights, without sleep and living off cups of tea and sandwiches he was handed by the women of the Civil Defence canteens, he searched and searched frantically until he found them. They were all dead—Millie, June, Pam and John.

Apparently Private Davies walked away without a word. He was never seen again in Kingsmead Street.

THREE
All that was left was brought in in a bucket

York

Waggonwerk (L.N.E.R.) und Verschiebebahnhof

Genst. 5. Abt. Oktober 1941
Karte 1:100 000
GB/E 10

GB 82 59 b c
Nur für den Dienstgebrauch
Bild Nr. 602 RI 199
Aufnahme vom 4. 10. 39

Länge (westl. Greenw.): 1° 06' 10" Breite: 53° 57' 30"
Mißweisung: − 11° 14' (Mitte 1941) Zielhöhe über NN 10 m
Maßstab etwa 1 : 18 000

River Ouse

1. Fabrikations- und Montagehallen, massiv, parallele Satteldächer — etwa 79 300 qm
    etwa 350 qm
2. Kraftanlagen, massiv, hohe Schornsteine — etwa 2 700 qm
3. Materiallagerplätze
4. Nebengebäude, massiv, versch. Dacharten

Ausbesserungswerk
5. Werkstatthalle für Personenwagen, massiv, parallele Satteldächer — etwa 9 000 qm
6. Reparaturwerkstätten mit Maschinenhaus an der SO-Ecke, massiv, parallele Satteldächer, Schornstein — etwa 14 200 qm

Personenbahnhof
7. Empfangsgebäude, massiv, versch. Dacharten — etwa 3 700 qm
8. Bahnhofshalle mit 5 Bahnsteigen, Eisenkonstruktion, Glasdach — etwa 22 900 qm

Güterbahnhof
9. Güterschuppen, massiv, parallele Satteldächer — etwa 19 500 qm
    etwa 7 200 qm
10. Verladerampen — etwa 13 900 qm
11. Wohngebäude, massiv, versch. Dacharten — etwa 7 500 qm
12. Betriebs-u. Nebengebäude, mass., versch. Dacharten etwa 60 qm
13. 2 Lok.-Schuppen, 55 und 45 m — etwa 500 qm
14. Wasserturm, massiv, Satteldächer
15. Stellwerke, massiv, Satteldächer
16. ansch. Behälter, z. T. mit Erdwall umgeben, etwa 5 m
17. Drehscheibe

Bebaute Fläche etwa — 180 830 qm
Gesamtausdehnung etwa — 1 155 000 qm

GB 10 257 Flughafen York

94

By April 28th, 1942, York was growing weary. It was another grey day in a long series of grey days. Back in September 1939, when war broke out, it had all seemed very exciting: the first stomach-churning wail of the sirens; the rush for gas-masks (their containers supplied courtesy of Messrs Rowntrees, the local chocolate manufacturers); trenches dug in the moats of the famed Bar Walls; the Minster's medieval glass being removed to a 'secret location' where it would stay for nearly twenty years.

That had been two and a half years before. Since then the days, the weeks, the months, the years, had dragged by in slow grey weariness. The war had become one long battle of privation and shortages. Patient housewives in curlers queued outside empty butchers' shops, whose windows bore the white-painted legend: '*Offal Today—Ration Books A to J*'. Their men in 'reserved occupations' or 'too old to fight' swapped their cloth caps at night for steel helmets in the Home Guard or Civil Defence. Even their children, if they were fourteen or over, did their stint too, as fire-watchers.

All the same, the war seemed strangely remote. It was the headlines in the *Yorkshire Evening Press*, now reduced to five pages, or the dramatic, fruity voice of Bob Danvers-Walker in the newsreels, 'knocking the Hun for six' or 'whacking the Wop'. Indeed, the Home Office had just ordered an inquiry into the cost of York's Civil Defence and Mr A. Cooke, the youngest chief of Civil Defence in the UK, had been called up and was currently square-bashing at the RAC training depot at Warminster. On this Tuesday in 1942, the war seemed to have passed the northern city by.

Yet as that grey day drew to a close and the blackouts were being put up, those who read their *Evening Press* carefully might have spotted a hint of what was to come. The headlines that night were of a kind that the reader had long become accustomed to: '*Fuel rationing proposed in the House ... US Gift to York, City Receives from American Red Cross, Huge Cases of Second-hand Clothing ...*' All very routine and boring. But that night's leader bore the headline '*Reprisals*', and its warning was clear:

The air raids on Bath, followed by the raid on Norwich, remind us of the need to 'keep our powder dry' on the ARP 'Front'. Any night, any place may expect to face the strenuous test of its preparedness and the stamina of its citizens, who, if they are wise, will not lay too much stress on their hitherto surprisingly consistent run of luck.[1]

Indeed, York's 'run of luck' was over.

The reconnaissance photo of York given to German bomber crews. It shows that the station was their target.

They came zooming in from the east. They crossed the coast at Flamborough Head above Bridlington, which before the war had been one of the most popular seaside resorts for the city's working class. On across the broad rolling acres of East Yorkshire, the isolated farms stark and black, clearly outlined by the bright light of a 'bomber's moon'.

In the leading Junkers 88, *Oberfeldwebel* Hans Fruehauf, who had recently returned from a spell on the Eastern Front, thought the pilots were flying high. But then, he told himself, in Russia the Luftwaffe always flew low. There was nothing to stop them there. Here, there were the feared Spitfires and the new Mosquitoes; and those RAF pilots knew what they were doing.

The observer-gunner spotted the silver snake of the River Ouse and craned his neck to find the landmark they had been told about at the briefing. Suddenly he had it; the great silver mass of a huge church, clearly visible above the flat plain of York. 'It was beautiful,' he remembers today, 'standing there above the city, bathed in the cold moonlight and so close that I felt I could have reached out and touched it.'[2]

But as the first 'Christmas trees' began to float down on their parachutes to illuminate the silent city, Hans Fruehauf forgot the beauty of the night scene. There were other—and very unbeautiful—things to be done now.

First-aider Violet Rodgers and her friend Dr Alice Lewis were awakened by 'an unpleasant thud' somewhere nearby in the Clifton area of the city. They sprang out of their beds, telling themselves that after 780 alerts 'this was the real thing at last'.[3] Hurriedly they set off for their post in Alderman Morrell's house opposite Lumley Barracks in which a Signals unit was stationed, running through streets 'lit up by the strange unnatural glare of magnesium from incendiaries burning on the roofs everywhere'.[4]

There they found all their comrades already lying on the floor—dozens of them, all packed in rows 'like sardines'—while the calm Scottish voice of Dr Moss told them over and over again, 'Lie down lasses, while you have the chance ... Lie down everybody ...'[5]

Time was running out. The bombs would soon be falling. The two young women hit the floor and clamped their helmets to their heads.

Meanwhile, city coroner Colonel Innes-Ware had left his wife to deal with a panic-stricken Signals officer billeted on them—the hysterical man was waving his revolver around and shouting: 'They're dropping parachutists, I tell you!'—and the children, seized his bicycle and started pedalling furiously to his post. There had been no 'Purple', the codeword, to alert him for duty; but he was old soldier enough to know the real thing. For two and half years York's Civil Defence had practised for this night. Now, 'like soldiers going over the top for the first time', he and York's 1,000-old wardens were going into action.[6]

Even before he reached his post he could see that St Peter's School was on fire and that incendiaries were dropping all along Bootham, the main road leading into the walled city. Soon, he knew, the high explosive bombs would follow. They did. He arrived at his post just as his deputy, a Mr Colman, set off bravely on his first patrol.

He didn't get far. There was a high-pitched hysterical shriek as the first stick of German bombs dropped through the air. The Colonel flung himself to the ground. Mr Colman was not so quick. He was killed outright. Other wardens close by were killed, too. Some simply disintegrated; in fact, one was identified later solely by the unusual signet ring on his little finger.

Back at Colonel Innes-Ware's command post, reports were flooding in of fires and damage to premises the length of Bootham, that long Georgian street which had once housed York's rich Quakers. A lone fire team was sent to do what they could. Driver F. Fox volunteered to man the pump while his mate Arthur Broadhead ran to check if the hose was correctly attached to the hydrant. As Mr Fox recalls today:

I was watching the pipe filling with water when there was an almighty bang and I was flung to the ground. A bomb had fallen between me and the pump. A small piece of shrapnel had caused a very superficial wound on my leg ... Arthur Broadhead was blown to pieces.[7]

Sergeant Fruehauf recognised the railway station immediately as the pilot came in for a second run. It was their primary target. At the briefing, while they had pored over a photograph of the station and the surrounding complex that had been taken the previous October, the crews had been told: 'Knock out York's signalling system and you'll paralyse the LNER's traffic to Hull and other north-eastern ports. You can bet nothing will reach the Ivans* via Murmansk for weeks to come!'[8] Now he and the rest of the crew tensed as the curved roof of the old Victorian station loomed up, all around it the square bathed in the lurid red light of the flares. This was it!

The crowded 10.15 express from London had just steamed into York Station when the sirens sounded. The station's loudspeakers immediately announced that a raid was imminent, advising the passengers to leave the Edinburgh-bound train. But the soldiers who had fought so determinedly for places at King's Cross and who were now crammed into lavatories, sprawled out in the luggage nets and packed elbow to elbow in the cor-

ridors of the train, were not going to abandon their hard-won places so readily. Ignoring even the threats of the Assistant Station-master Mr Lyon, they stuck it out.

Then a 250-pound bomb came shrieking down to explode at the far end of the station, followed an instant later by a shower of incendiaries. That did the trick. The soldiers abandoned the train in terrified haste, as the station roof, the train and even the track burst into flames.

A shunter was organised. Somehow or other he managed to get some of the train's blazing coaches coupled up to his little steam engine and trundled them away through the flames. But that still left six behind, all blazing furiously. Another shunter raced up, driven by Signalman Simpson whose signal box had been hit. While the woman porters ran up and down the platform, kicking blazing incendiaries onto the lines, he managed to drive away a burning parcel van and twenty other carriages.

Meanwhile, as fires roared all around them, two firewatchers scooped up the money at all the ticket office tills, thrusting it into a handy wellington boot. Then as the flames grew even higher, they fled to the Royal Station Hotel, where two years earlier Eden and the top brass had predicted gloomily that the Army would run away. The LNER would lose no money on this raid!

Now the attackers concentrated their full fury on the station and the main line running east to the coast. A bomb struck the roundhouse where twenty locomotives were parked. Every one of them was ripped and scarred by flying shrapnel; even *Sir Ralph Wedgwood*—the pride of the LNER, the streamlined Pacific locomotive named after the chairman of the Railway Executive Committee, whose nephew would one day bitterly oppose military defence—was tossed on its side like a child's toy.

Not only the railway's 'iron horses' suffered, however. A second bomb had struck the station's stables and they were already ablaze. Stableman Mr Martin and two policemen rushed to save the animals, dodging the flying hooves as they reared and whinnied in terror. Fumbling with haste, they managed to loosen the halters and urged the horses outside with a hard slap on their massive flanks. One by one the terrified beasts were led away to safety by the three sweating men, their faces blackened by smoke. Then Mr Martin glanced ruefully at his prized 'dig-for-victory' garden, to which he had devoted so much loving care and which had now been ruined by the horses' hooves. 'At that moment,' he says today, 'I was more saddened by the sight of my garden than I was of my house blazing away merrily a couple of hundred yards away.'[9]

Now the Guildhall in the centre of the city, a hundred

* German nickname for the Russians.

The Sir Ralph Wedgwood—one of twenty locomotives the Germans destroyed at York Station.

yards from the Minster, was fully ablaze. After London's Guildhall had been gutted in the blitz of December 29th, 1940, the 500-year-old structure had become the oldest in Britain. But it, too, was fated to perish. By an irony of fate, the new roof erected in 1939, after years of saving and appeals, acted as a tinder box. Burning fiercely, it came crashing down, and with it, the priceless medieval stained glass.

The firemen desperately fighting the blaze (under machine-gun fire from the raiders) started to back off as the flames gradually spread to nearby buildings. At the very last moment, the verger of the nearby St Martin's remembered that a young Army officer was scheduled to be married at the church at nine o'clock the next morning. With flames leaping up all around him, he dashed into the vestry to rescue the church registers. Thanks to him, the happy couple would be married—in the nearby St Helen's Church with the city still smoking all around them—only sixty minutes late.

The casualties were beginning to mount. Former head of Civil Defence, now Trooper Cooke—who would one day fight in Normandy, but who was presently on leave in York—cycled into the burning city to see if he could help. His first stop was at the mortuary, which in 1939 he had been instrumental in setting up for just such an emergency. Then the Government had recommended that York should acquire a supply of papier-mâché coffins for the victims of any air raid. The city council had turned down the suggestion; they weren't having 'York people buried in anything as cheap as that'.[10]

Now Trooper Cooke stood in the 'Bodies Room' and watched as they brought in the dead. Forty-odd years later, Mr Cooke recalls the ghastly scene: 'One mother, dead, with her child locked in her arms, also dead, mixed up with brick rubble lying on a stretcher. In a couple of cases, all that was left was brought in in a bucket.'[11] He was soon roped in to help with identification of the shattered bodies, telling himself as he worked at his grim task how typically English everyone was—'quiet, subdued, unemotional'.

The raid had been going on for nearly two hours now and *Oberfeldwebel* Hans Fruehauf's plane was ready to leave. Fuel was getting dangerously low. The pilot swung northwards following the railway line out of the blazing city centre. Suddenly Fruehauf noticed a tall brick building, poorly camouflaged, to their port side. He recognised it immediately from his target map; it was Rowntree's Chocolate Factory—not important enough to waste the last of their bombs on.

Unknown to Fruehauf and his crew, however, Rowntree's Chocolate Factory happened to be the only military target in the whole area. Although German Intelligence and indeed most of York's citizens did not know it, the traditional anti-war Quaker family, the Rowntrees, had formed a new company in 1940 under the innocuous name of County Industries Ltd. For the past two years now, in the heart of the chocolate factory, shifts of local girls had been filling shell casings with high explosive!

So Fruehauf's plane dropped its last remaining bombs on the nearby railway bridge. Then, Fruehauf remembers, the first 'Tommy night-fighter appeared on the scene and our pilot raced for the cover of the clouds and the coast. We'd had our belly-full. We were off!'[12]

One of the first night-fighters on the scene was the Hurricane piloted by Pilot-Officer Yves Mahé of the Free French Air Force, who had stolen a plane in 1940 and flown to England to join de Gaulle.

Mahé swooped down on an unsuspecting Heinkel III, busy machine-gunning the streets of York below. His first burst missed. The Heinkel broke to the right. But the German couldn't escape the Frenchman. Mahé came zooming in again, machine guns chattering, and riddled the Heinkel with blazing red tracer. The German rear-gunner attempted to fight back. To no avail. Now the Heinkel was on fire, thick black smoke pouring from its starboard engine.

'I gave the Hun a taste of his own medicine,' Mahé told the reporters the next day, in the characteristic style of the times, 'and his fire ceased. I fired again, and followed the Heinkel as it spiralled down, but near the ground I lost sight of it in the smoke that hung over the city.'[13]

Mahé had had his first 'kill'. It would earn him the *Croix de Guerre*—presented by no less a person than General de Gaulle himself—and a civic welcome to boot, complete with tea and cucumber sandwiches, at the 'Mayor's Parlour' in York's Mansion House.

At 1,000 feet they started to bail out of the crippled Heinkel. One by one their chutes snapped open—and one by one each of the German crewmen was unlucky enough to be struck by the plane's tail as it spiralled down to its destruction. Momentarily they all blacked out. When they came to again, they realised to their horror that they were drifting straight for the silver snake of the Ouse. Burdened by their chutes and heavy flying gear they could easily drown . . .

Desperately they fought their shroud lines. Now they began to drift right into the centre of the blazing city. The prospect of landing there among probably enraged citizens did not attract them either. They had all heard stories of bomb-crazed Tommies killing German aircrew who bailed out.* So they struggled to control their chutes, gradually being dispersed by the wind, until finally the first of them landed outside York.

Among the first to land was a young gunner, twenty-two years old. After the snarl of engines and the whine of bombs he found the silence eerie, even a little frightening. For a while, he confessed later, he thought of attempting to escape. But how? In the end he surrendered tamely to a village air raid warden who turned him over to the York police.

On questioning it turned out he came from Rostock, the attack on which had produced, together with the attack on Lübeck, this series of reprisal raids on British cities. But this young gunner had heard nothing of the raid from his mother who still lived in Rostock. 'What do you think of Rudolph Hess?' one of the policemen asked their captive.

'Ach, long dead and buried,' the boy snorted. 'Dead and buried . . .'[14]

Still the bombs came raining down. A Catholic convent school was hit and two nuns killed instantly. It was not the only one. Five others were hit including St Peter's, now on fire, which had once been attended by that most notorious fire-raiser of them all—Guy Fawkes.

One York woman remembers standing by the ruins of her daughter's school a little later and seeing on the opposite verge one of her plimsolls and some of her books. 'Had she been at school . . . she would have been blown to pieces and no trace of her left.'[15]

At the local Blind School in the medieval King's Manor in the centre of the city, several buildings were ablaze. The blind boys and girls had filed out obediently, hand on the shoulder of the person in front, down into the crypt where even now they could smell the acrid smoke and hear the crackle of the flames. Were they going to be burnt alive?

Fifty yards away at the Old Folks Home, Mrs Martin—ninety-one years old—was determined that her

---

* Several of my informants had stories of bailed-out German aircrew being shot by the Home Guard (and British pilots as well). But on the whole they seem to have been treated well.

old friends were not going to suffer that fate. With tracer striking the ground all around her, she led them to safety into the home's gardens, while above this scene of death and destruction the Minster towered unharmed, its walls coloured a blood-red hue by the flames at its base, looking to some that terrible morning, like a symbol of the ancient city's ability to survive even this . . .

Finally, as dawn began to flush the sky to the east, the All Clear was sounded at last and the Civil Defence authorities could start to take stock of what had happened to the totally undefended city that night. The raid had lasted over five hours, and in all that time, not one single anti-aircraft shell had been fired at the raiders. The twelve AA guns that General Pile had allotted to York had not arrived in time.

Within the city's boundaries seventy-four men, women and children (fourteen of them) had been killed, ninety-two seriously injured and 113 slightly wounded. RAF and Army figures were never published, but five soldiers had been killed and an unrecorded number wounded while helping the Civil Defence (which itself had lost four men). In all, just short of 300 people had been killed and wounded. There had been damage to 9,500 of the city's pre-war total of 28,000 houses, and most of York's historic buildings—save the Minster—had been hit in various degrees of severity.

Violet Rodgers, the first-aider, ventured into the city that morning to find Civil Defence workers still fighting fires and digging through the rubble to rescue people who had been trapped. Bootham, the major Georgian street in the city, she later described as 'a sight to make a historian weep. Glass, glass everywhere, crunching under our feet. Every house had staring empty windows, tiles off the roof, the walls all pitted with machine-gun bullets.'*[16]

But as the young woman reached the end of the street, its whole length blocked with pumps and fire engines, she caught sight of the medieval pile of Bootham Bar gleaming white and undamaged in the sunlight which was now beginning to shine through the smoke. 'It was like a symbol of endurance, the continuity between the ancient city's long past and the certainty of the future. York would endure!'[17]

The Reverend Harry Radcliffe, the curate of nearby St Olave's Church and currently an air-raid warden, was animated by less noble thoughts that morning. He had just made a startling discovery. One hour ago, searching for survivors in the smoking debris of a shattered house just off Bootham, he had been calling out in his usual gentle manner, 'Is anybody there? ... Is ...' when a coarse angry voice had grumbled: 'Of course I'm bloody well there—and you're standing on me legs ... Now bloody well hurry up and get me out!'

*For those interested in such things, the scars of those bullet and shrapnel holes can still be seen.

The reverend gentleman did his best; frantically digging through the rubble he at last managed to pull 'an old codger from the debris, who didn't have a word of thanks to say to me for my efforts'. And now as he rested and enjoyed a well-earned cup of tea from a mobile canteen, he discovered that 'that old codger had, while I'd been pulling him out with all my might, *nicked my wallet!*'[18]

The raid on York had roused Churchill into making an angry speech, denouncing, in that familiar snarl of his, the German raids on all these old cities. On May 10th, 1942, two years to the day since he had taken office, he said:

He [Hitler] warns us solemnly that if we go on smashing up the German cities, his war factories and his bases, he will retaliate against our cathedrals and historic monuments—if they are not too far inland. We have heard his threats before. Eighteen months ago in September 1940 when he thought he had an overwhelming air force at his command, he declared he would rub out—that was the actual expression, *rub out*—our towns and cities. And he certainly had a good try. Now the boot is on the other foot.[19]

The Prime Minister went on to threaten:

We have a long list of German cities in which all the vital industries of the German war machine are established. All these it will be our stern duty to deal with, as we have already dealt with Lübeck, with Rostock and half a dozen important places. The civil populations of Germany have, however, an easy way to escape from these severities. All they have to do is leave their cities where munitions work is being carried out—abandon their work and go out into the fields and watch their home fires burning from a distance.[20]

The warning was crystal clear. One month and one day exactly after York was attacked, Bomber Harris—soon to be known to his bitter decimated bombing crews as 'Butch' (short for 'Butcher') Harris—despatched 1,000 bombers, 400 of them from Yorkshire, to hit the ancient Rhenish city of Cologne. In that raid 469 citizens were killed and over 4,000 injured; 45,000 people were rendered homeless, with 13,000 houses destroyed and 6,000 badly damaged.

This, then, was the real start of total war, which Dr Goebbels would demand from the German people a few months later in his infamous '*Wollt Ihr den totalen Krieg?*'* To which they replied with a fervent hysterical cry of '*Ja!*'

After the first thousand-bomber raid in history, Churchill signalled Harris triumphantly: 'It is the herald of what Germany will receive, city by city, from now on ...'

*'Do you want total war?'

FOUR
'Bloody pits or t'bloody army'

The Baedeker raids continued into May 1942. Norwich was hit again and Exeter too. Cowes was struck for the first time. Canterbury had its first real blitz; then the next night the Germans came again—and to Ipswich and Bury St Edmunds too. The following night they came for Canterbury once more. Damage was severe, though the cathedral was saved.

A military objective at Poole was attacked ... Then for a little while there was a lull, but only for a little while. Before the end of June, Nuneaton, Great Yarmouth, Weston-super-Mare had all been attacked.

Pile sent his AA batteries flying back and forth across the length and breadth of England and Scotland, trying to meet the challenge as the public outcry at the lack of defences grew ever louder. It was a hopeless task.

Again as spring 1942 gave way to summer, the Luftwaffe changed its tactics. Now the Germans were hitting the south coast from Deal to Dawlish and beyond; and there were only *38 guns* to defend the whole length of the coast when Pile estimated 189 were needed!

The harassed General went to visit one of the south coast towns himself to see what its AA arrangements were like. He found the sun shining on the Regency houses, and along the promenade 'where concrete blocks and barbed wire and occasional positions gave a hint of the battlefield, invalids strolled or hobbled or were drawn in invalid chairs'.[1] Suddenly this peaceful scene was shattered:

Swerving over the pier, behind which they had come undetected, almost skimming the surface of the water, came two or three aircraft racing towards the shore with all their guns blazing. Shells tore at the promenade and shattered the Regency houses, the planes banked steeply and were gone before the AA gunners could even bring their weapons to bear. From the streets at the back of the town by the gasworks there came the sound of the bombs falling. The enemy were gone, racing out to sea again as the sirens sounded behind them a belated warning.[2]

Yet again General Pile was reminded of the short-comings of his command, which was a direct result of the whole country's attitude to the war and the way its leaders had prepared them for it. 'Always the story was the same,' he wrote afterwards:

The supply of equipment was never sufficient for success until great damage had been done. The fact that the British always win the last battle and pride themselves on the fact—as if in some way it was more creditable than winning decisively at the first encounter and saving a lot of lives, time, trouble and expense—was largely the outcome of this supply position. We couldn't win the first battle because we were never ready, so we made a virtue of necessity and drew what comfort we could from the cliché.[3]

In truth, General Pile, on whom the defence of the country mainly rested this middle year of the war, lacked money, manpower, equipment and fighting morale. Once, when Pile set up a scheme to improve efficiency and offered a prize for good suggestions, he was swamped with ideas but found he had no money to pay the prize. It was the same when his soldiers prepared models for their aircraft recognition classes. In a weak moment Pile had offered to pay ten pounds for the best models. But the Army refused him money for this scheme, so in the end he had to pay out of his own pocket.

His sources of manpower were rapidly dwindling. Many of his Class A gunners were being shipped overseas and by July 1942 the supply of ATS* for the mixed batteries had dried up altogether. The Ministry of Labour ordered civilians in reserved occupations to be conscripted into the Home Guard and made into AA units in their spare time.

Pile liked and respected those Home Guards who had volunteered back in 1940, but he was not impressed by the conscripts. He asked for more volunteers—particularly in Wales, in such towns as Swansea and Cardiff, where there had been so much criticism of the lack of defence back in 1940/41—but his appeal, as he said himself, 'fell on the deafest of deaf ears'; so he had to make do with the conscripts.

And a sorry bunch they turned out to be. Absenteeism was rife, yet there was no way that Pile could take disciplinary action against men who were civilians. Local Home Guard commanders regarded the requirement to transfer men to AA Command as a heaven-sent opportunity to dump all their problems on Pile:

* Auxiliary Territorial Service (forerunner of the WRAC).

Air-raid damage in Cologne.

Those men who are to be found in every unit: the halt, the maimed, physically and intellectually, the troublesome men, the men always in detention or absent without leave, the barrack room lawyers, they could be easily spared. With barely a qualm they were certified as operationally suitable and the scruffy crew would be shipped off with the utmost dispatch and with a great lifting of hearts on the part of the senders.[4]

The Home Guard historian of the 71st Monmouthshire Heavy Ack-Ack Battery admits bluntly that the reaction of most of the local miners on hearing they were to be conscripted into AA Command was: 'Bloody pits or bloody Army, man, *not bloody both!*'[5] And in one case Pile came across a Home Guard battalion commander who, when asked to supply men for the anti-aircraft artillery, was found to have included on his nominal roll 'the names of many men long since dead'; he had evidently wanted the prestige of commanding a battalion, even though most of it did not exist!

In truth, the nation was war weary. There had been too many defeats and too many shortages. Apart from the Baedeker raids and the coastal hit-and-run raiders, there was not much to spur them into defiance. Victories were non-existent.

No one was exactly starving, but rationing had reduced the national diet to a drab starchy minimum: potato cakes, 'Woolton Pie', corned beef hash, dried egg pancakes and the like. People were pasty-faced, constantly yawning, easily tired.

The civilians envied the troops their lack of worries over food and clothing and grumbled that while overseas the British Army was on the run again in the Desert, they seemed to be doing nothing, having a good time in the safety of the UK.

Indeed, it is an astonishing fact that the vast majority of men in uniform had seen no action whatsoever, although this was the *third* year of war. To the civilians they appeared to be in the services just for a kind of extended holiday, packing the city centres of a weekend, getting drunk and chasing the girls—not only the men, in fact, but the ATS, WAAFs and WRNS, too.

The latter were often seen to be over-indulging in drink, and alarming stories circulated among the civilians about their filthy language and even filthier habits. There was talk of how many of them deserted and 'walked the streets' to earn their living; how there was an increasing number of pregnancies in their ranks; and now VD was increasing. For the first time since World War One, posters went up on bill-boards drawing public notice to this 'social disease', explaining the symptoms and what to do if you contracted it.

Even those in Britain actually doing the fighting, the men of 'Bomber' Harris's command, were not all as brave and as resolute as the general public thought these carefree, hard-drinking 'RAF types' to be when they saw them in the pubs and clubs of their cities. Morale never became a major factor in Bomber Command as it did in the US Eighth Air Force a year later, when scores of pilots simply flew their planes to neutral Sweden and Switzerland during raids over Germany to avoid any further combat. But a larger number of air crew did have their records stamped with the letters '*LMF*' (Lacking Morale Fibre) and were court-martialled, transferred to the infantry or sent to the 'Aircrew Refresher Centres' at Sheffield, Brighton or Bournemouth—in reality open-arrest detention barracks. There they either learned to 'soldier on' or were posted to the Army or the coal mines.

The Reverend Radcliffe, who had had his wallet 'nicked' in the York raid, was now a padre with a Canadian bomber squadron 'somewhere in Yorkshire', where one of his first duties had been to talk to a shaken young pilot who refused to fly on a raid. If Radcliffe could not persuade him to fly, he would be court-martialled for 'Lack of Morale Fibre' and disobeying a direct order. 'I talked him into it all right,' the Reverend Radcliffe remembers sadly more than forty years later, sitting in the quiet of his study and surrounded by the photographs of 'my boys' who were killed in action over Germany that year, 'but the poor boy never returned. He was shot down and killed on his first raid.'[6]

Many of those at the top, after three years of defeat, thought the British soldier had lost the will to fight and surrendered far too easily. The first time General Pile met Sir Stafford Cripps, in October 1942 during a tour of a mixed battery stationed at Southsea, the politician asked Pile point-blank, over his usual vegetarian lunch, 'What is wrong with the Services?'

He was not the only one. Churchill himself felt that the great slaughter of World War One must have had its effect. In this war, the average British soldier did not seem to be as ready to die for his 'King and Country' as he had been in the Old War. But Churchill knew how vital it was for the hard-pressed Home Front—which in a way had been the only real front for most of the war—to retain its confidence in its servicemen. When this question of what was wrong with the services was put to him, he side-stepped it by turning any criticism into a matter for a vote of confidence, which he always got with an overwhelming majority.

That June, for instance, a Tory member of the House, Sir John Wardlaw-Milne, had put down a motion of censure against the government over its conduct of the war. That month the plight of the Empire was very

In Berlin, the dead are laid out for identification by their relatives

serious. The British Eighth Army was on the run in the Desert, the Suez Canal was threatened, and in Cairo the scared brasshats were burning their secret papers and preparing for flight.

Hurriedly Churchill prepared to meet the threat posed by the motion. He despatched Brigadier George Harvie-Watt, his Parliamentary Private Secretary, to negotiate with Emmanuel Shinwell, the Labour Party's eloquent spokesman, a Scottish Jew with a tongue like a cobra's.

'The chief has a lot of worries now,' the Brigadier explained, trying to enlist the support of the Labour Party. 'He doesn't deserve to be annoyed by attacks in the House. You mustn't forget the Prime Minister has great military gifts. His ancestor *was* the Duke of Marlborough.'

'If military genius can be handed down like that,' Shinwell said tartly, 'then I should be a good critic. My ancestor was Moses!'[7]

But Shinwell duly rallied the Labour Party behind Churchill; and in the end, the same MPs who had applauded Chamberlain's appeasement—and hissed and booed Churchill for having advocated rearmament and standing up to Hitler—voted against the motion of censure, 476 to 25 in Churchill's favour. He received 'a great ovation in the House', it was recorded at the time.

Churchill was saved. There would never again be such a concerted effort to get rid of the Great Old Man—at least, not until after the war, when the nation that he had saved from the gas chambers and slavery (for that is what would have happened if Britain had been defeated) showed their gratitude by voting him out of office ...

So as Churchill cajoled, bullied, inspired his war-weary nation into fighting on, the dreary little raids continued along Britain's coasts, and Bomber Harris stepped up his campaign to bomb Germany into submission— 'squeeze 'em till the pips squeak', as he once barked in that harsh no-nonsense manner of his.

But already the pips *were* squeaking. These small-scale raids on Britain were not enough to appease Hitler's anger at the way Allied bombers were beginning systematically to wipe out Germany's major cities. Where were the *Vergeltungswaffen,** he was demanding of his scientists, which would make the Tommies pay for what they were doing to the Reich? Where were the tools of revenge—*the V-weapons?*

For Pierre Ginter, the whole business had begun when he had been expelled from the Goetheschule in Luxemburg for refusing to join the Hitler Youth. Since 1940, the citizens of this tiny principality, which had

* Revenge or retaliation weapons.

been independent of Prussian domination since 1867, had been regarded by their new Nazi occupiers as *Reichsdeutsche* and thus required to serve the Reich, just like any other German. But Ginter, whose name was as German as was the dialect he spoke, did not agree. He subscribed to the national motto: '*We want to be left alone*'. Unfortunately the occupiers would not leave the quarter of a million Luxemburgers alone. Thus in early 1942, when the German authorities called Pierre Ginter up as an eighteen year old to do his six months' *Arbeitsdienst* (Labour Service), he had no choice but to obey; he duly crossed the border into Germany with hatred for the Germans in his heart.

One day in October 1942, Ginter was on parade with his comrades at the remote experimental station of Peenemunde on the Baltic Sea. The parade was to honour 'Fat Hermann'—Reichsmarschall Hermann Goering—who was coming to witness the launching of one the new hush-hush 'aerial torpedoes', which scientists here in Pennemunde were apparently working on. But the torpedo exploded prematurely and the visit was cancelled. Ginter spent the rest of that day sweeping up the debris caused by the explosion, idly wondering whether these torpedoes would ever come to much. It seemed unlikely that they really were 'the wonder weapons which will bring England to her knees', as Ginter's captain boasted. And when the captain told his young conscripts that these missiles would be 'capable of flying 300 to 400 kilometres', Ginter merely laughed.[8]

A week later the grin was wiped off the young Luxemburger's face when he saw one of the white-painted A-4 rockets make a perfect take-off and vanish into the skies. According to their commanding officer, it landed exactly as planned—in the Bay of Danzig, several hundred kilometres away.

The incident gave Ginter cause for thought. Mentally he compared the distance allegedly flown by the 'aerial torpedo' with the distance from the Continent across the English Channel. The matter puzzled him sufficiently for him to mention it in a letter to his pal Camille Sutor, who had remained behind in Luxemburg. Himself only nineteen, Sutor wrote back and suggested Ginter should 'take a good look at everything'.

Ginter decided he would do more: he would find the plans of this experimental station. He guessed that the likeliest place to find them was in the *Arbeitsdienst* company office and so, in order to get into the office, he volunteered for night telephone duty. His sergeant was surprised; Ginter had never volunteered for anything before. But the young Luxemburger explained that he had a lot of letters to write, and since the lights went out at nine thirty in his barracks room, this was the only way he could write them in peace.

The NCO was satisfied with the explanation and so the next night Ginter found himself on duty in the office, his writing paper spread out in front of him on the desk. But he did not find much time to search for the plans. Every few minutes or so, a young officer would come in and ask for a number—usually that of their girlfriend.

Around midnight, however, things started to quieten down and Ginter decided it was time to look for the plans. Idly he picked up a copy of the National Socialist periodical *Das Reich* which lay in front of him. Beneath it were the office keys! He wasted no more time. Now he started to open the cupboards. He found soap, spare foods, documents of all kinds, but no plans. He had just opened the first of a series of low cupboards when the door opened and an officer came in.

He stared at Ginter suspiciously. 'What are you doing?' he snapped.

Ginter sprang to attention and tried a bold front. He knew what the Germans thought of people like himself—'Booty Germans', they called them contemptuously. 'I'm stealing from the Reich Labour Service,' Ginter said bravely.

'*What?*' the officer exploded.

'Yes—I'm looking for more writing paper, sir.' Ginter indicated his paper-strewn desk. 'Mine's run out and I've got a lot of letters to answer.'

His boldness paid off. 'I see,' the officer said. 'All right, get me this number ...'

So while the German officer sat on the desk talking to his girlfriend, the young Luxemburger wrote with a hand that trembled, '*Meine liebe Mutter ...*'

At last the officer left and Ginter was able to complete his search. In the end he found the plans and spent the rest of the night and the following night copying them, as well as the site's anti-aircraft defences.

For the first time, a foreigner had obtained access to one of the Third Reich's most preciously guarded secrets. The question was—what was he going to do with it?*

Now as Christmas 1942 approached and Pierre Ginter prepared to go home to Luxemburg with that precious notebook hidden in his case, the young men of the *Arbeitsdienst* celebrated their last Christmas Eve in the service. Ginter would be going home to Luxemburg, but most of the young men with him would soon be conscripted into the Army. So, in typical cloying, sentimental, *gemütlich* fashion, they celebrated in front of the Christmas tree, its candles flickering, with poems and carols and little presents carefully wrapped up in coloured paper, and one bottle of beer per man. '*Stille Nacht, Heilige Nacht*', they sang, these doomed young men, for most of them were destined to die on the Russian Front in 1943.

Meanwhile, singing along bravely with the rest, young

*In a letter to the author just before his death, Albert Speer—Hitler's minister of armaments and war production—maintained it was impossible to prevent espionage because of the millions of foreign workers in Germany, though he had 'warned Hitler of that danger'.

A water-cannon in use in Germany after an air-raid.

Pierre Ginter had come to a decision. First, as soon as he arrived back in Luxemburg he would 'take a dive' (in other words, would not allow himself to be conscripted into the Wehrmacht to die 'for Folk, Fatherland and Führer'); and secondly he would show the Peenemunde plans to Camille Sutor. Camille would know what to do with them; Camille had always been the smart one. The first hard information of what was going on at Peenemunde was about to commence its long arduous journey to London.

But even as Pierre Ginter made his momentous decision which would alert the British authorities to this terrible new weapon, one day to be known as the V-2, a few miles away from where he and his comrades sang the old carol that afternoon, the V-1 had already just passed the experimental stage.

That afternoon Milch's and Lusser's brain child was launched from a ramp outside Peenemunde and hurtled out over the Baltic Sea. It was recorded that it behaved perfectly and soared off into the winter sky exactly as planned.

It was Christmas Eve 1942. Soon these new weapons of death and wholesale destruction would be ready for launching against Britain's cities.

IV: SCALDED CATS AND DOODLEBUGS 1942/43

'We cannot exclude the possibility of new forms of attack on this country ... Should they come, they will call for ... a further display of the firmness and fortitude for which the British nation has won renown.'

Winston Churchill, 1943

The V-2 assembly line.

ONE
'As bad as the beaches'

An early version of the Tempest—these aeroplanes were particularly successful in shooting down V-1 cruise missiles.

They were called the 'scalded cat raids' by the popular press because the bombers—Messerschmitts and the new Focke-Wulff 190s—came zooming in at roof-top level in twos and threes, dropped their bombs and streaked for home even as the sirens began to sound the warning. Deadly metal cats that fought and fled.

On the night of January 17th, the Luftwaffe came back to London for the first time since July 1942. Out of the seventy-five fighter-bombers employed in this surprise raid, only thirty managed to penetrate the capital's defences. That night Pile's gunners fired a tremendous barrage of over 11,000 rounds.

The barrage certainly frightened the 'scalded cats', as the shot-down aircrews reported later during their interrogation. But it frightened Pile a little too. A considerable number of rounds either exploded prematurely, killing the gunners, or failed to explode at all, falling to the ground and killing and injuring civilians 'who continued to walk about the streets during the raid and had no one to blame but themselves'.[1]

Again Britain was unprepared. Before the war all the clockwork fuses used by the Royal Artillery had come from Switzerland. When that source of supply was cut off, Britain had been forced to make her own fuses. Yet even after four years of war, the country still lacked the engineering skills and resources to produce a reliable fuse!

Indeed, the faulty AA shells did more damage and killed more people in London that January than the German raiders. As one observer of the London scene wrote that month:

Many people have been killed by our shrapnel in the past few days. The wardens begged people to go inside and on Wednesday, during the daylight raid, people were pushed into Marks and Spencers in Oxford Street and made to stay there, as the Hyde Park guns were in full cry. In the park itself the wardens were hastily opening up the trench shelters. A friend from our office was there airing a dog and when the warning sounded everyone scattered. She was in conversation with an old lady who refused to budge. The noise of the guns was really terrific and my friend, Mrs Winnal, was really frightened but she didn't care to leave the old lady alone. They were near Queen Victoria's statue. Poor old Queen, I wonder what she would have said if she had been alive.[2]

Probably 'We are not amused'. At all events, the Londoners were not. They had thought that the bombing was over, or at least that the authorities should be able to protect them better than this after all the years of combat and experience on the Home Front.

Yet here were the Germans again—and now, on January 20th, they had the temerity to attempt to bomb London by *daylight!*

Sixty fast fighter-bombers were involved, though only a dozen of them reached the capital. The raid again caught the defenders off guard. There was no time even to raise the balloon barrage. So the 'scalded cats' were able to race across the patched-up roofs of the East End, drop their bombs and flee, with hardly a shot being fired at them.

Their bombs hit a school at Lewisham just as the teachers were assembling 150 children for the daily school dinner. The children and their teachers simply didn't have a chance; the whole structure fell down upon them. Forty children were killed outright and forty more were injured, plus six of their teachers. Frantic parents tore at the smoking rubble with their bare hands in an attempt to rescue their kids. One week later, 10,000 people turned out for the mass funeral.

Now the Luftwaffe gave London what Mary Welsh called 'a deafening refresher course of the blitz'— thirteen major raids up to March 3rd, when the bombers' arrival coincided with the evening rush-hour traffic.

At Bethnal Green tube station the howling sirens sent a mass of people swarming down the stairs. Suddenly, at the top of the stairs, a woman carrying a baby was jostled by a frightened old man and fell. She collapsed against the people in front of her. They, in their turn, also tripped. More and more people, caught by surprise, were sent toppling. Their screams and cries of alarm were heard down below on the platform, where the first-comers thought a bomb must have landed on the station. They panicked. Some of them struggled to get back up the stairs, clawing through the mob of confused frightened people.

Later, survivors said that the terrible scene below the surface took several minutes to build up. But in the end a mass of struggling, shrieking, screaming men, women and children fell like a human avalanche into a quivering heap of bodies below. One hundred and seventy-eight people were killed, many of them school children, and sixty were seriously injured. All of them had died of suffocation—while above on the ground the Luftwaffe had killed a mere four people with their bombs.

Next day the *Daily Telegraph* would write soothingly:

There were no bombs. There was no panic ... The disaster was simply and tragically a case of people pushing their way down ... The pitifulness of the tragedy is heightened by the fact that the shelter itself was in no sense overcrowded. Indeed, only a few feet beyond the stairs of death was a circular hall, fifty feet in diameter, that was practically unoccupied.[3]

Of course there were bombs and fear and panic. Returning to London from the United States that spring, Mary Welsh was 'dismayed at the grayness of face among my friends and their air of weariness in speech, thought and movement'. As for herself, she could barely control her fright when the AA guns started blasting away at Hyde Park. 'Conversation continued around me casually and cheerfully. I had to sit on my hands to

Tower Bridge in the Blitz.

hide their shaking.'[4]

Rosemary Black, a rich young widow living in St John's Wood and working for Mass Observation, also noted how the 'scalded cat' raids were affecting the nerves of the average Londoner. Even the noise of General Pile's tremendous barrage upset her:

Each burst of shellfire seemed to thunder and shake the house as only big bombs did in the good old days ... With one thing and another, I was more shaken than I ever remember being. Both physically and mentally I felt completely incapable of rising to meet any emergency which might occur. Frankly I was completely limp with terror, and after the all-clear had gone, I felt too weak and shaken to so much as turn over the bed. I don't feel I can *possibly* face up to a renewal of the blitz, if this horror is what the future holds in store for us.[5]

The future held much worse than the 'scalded cat' raids, but a nervous Mrs Black was not to know that, of course. Not yet.

In that January when the Germans launched their new attacks on London, Ginter returned to Luxemburg carrying his notebook with the information of what he had seen in Peenemunde. Camille Sutor (who had only fourteen months to live before he was shot resisting arrest by the Gestapo) saw immediately that his friend had discovered something important. 'We've got to get this to London!' he said enthusiastically, and urged Ginter to rack his memory for every single detail of what he had seen in Peenemunde.

In the end, the information was passed on to the head of Luxemburg's little resistance movement, Dr Schwachtgen, code-named 'Jean l'Aveugle' ('Blind John'). Dr Schwachtgen tumbled to the significance of what Pierre Ginter had seen much more quickly than many of the highly trained Civil Service brains in London who would finally receive his information. He realised that the 'aerial torpedo' which Ginter had observed being fired at Peenemunde was a space missile. Immediately he had five copies of Ginter's report made, one for himself and four to be smuggled by different couriers to London.

A little later Dr Schwachtgen was arrested and deported to Germany (he survived). But his work was done. The information he had passed to London was the first hard confirmation that the Oslo Report was correct.

On the same day that two V-2s were successfully fired at Peenemunde, June 29th, 1943, Churchill called together the Cabinet Defence Committee to discuss what should be done about the Peenemunde problem.

The underground Cabinet War Room was crowded with the top brass, civilian and military: Eden, Attlee, Morrison and the rest—plus the members of the Sandys Committee, which had been set up to investigate this new threat from what appeared to be space missiles.

Duncan Sandys, an ex-artillery officer and Churchill's son-in-law, opened the meeting with a dramatic discussion of the 'white-painted rockets' that aerial reconnaissance had discovered at Peenemunde. He stated that he was convinced that they posed a major threat to Britain's home front.

Morrison, who was in charge of that front, disagreed. He felt that the Secret Service reports about Peenemunde were too numerous for such a top-secret German undertaking. Information such as that from Ginter—and from other Luxemburgers working at Peenemunde—was surely a plant, intended to frighten them.

Lord Cherwell was equally dubious. He suggested that the whole business was simply an 'elaborate cover plan', aimed at hiding some more sinister German machination.

Churchill, who had listened in silence so far, now turned to the SIS hoaxster and said: 'Now, Dr Jones, may we hear the truth.'

Jones demolished Cherwell's arguments one by one, introducing a new source of information: a German officer, now a prisoner-of-war, who had been listened to in his bugged cell telling a fellow prisoner how Hitler had demanded that the rockets should be employed at once.

Churchill was convinced. It was decided that further aerial reconnaissance should be flown over Peenemunde.

But Dr Jones had now made an implacable enemy of his former teacher, Lord Cherwell—formerly Professor Lindemann—who, being of German extraction himself, had that German *Urtrieb*, the capacity for hate. From now onwards, in his position as Churchill's principle scientific adviser, Lord Cherwell would hamper all efforts to prepare some defence against these terrible new weapons.

Six weeks later, on August 14th, the first attack was launched on Peenemunde. Feigning a raid on Berlin, and aided by two renegade Germans in the Luftwaffe's fighter control in Arnhem who misdirected German Fighter Command, Bomber Harris's men took Peenemunde completely by surprise. By dawn Peenemunde was blazing from end to end. When Colonel-General Hans Jeschonnek, the Luftwaffe's Chief-of-Staff, heard the news he shot himself, leaving behind a note stating:

'I cannot work with Goering any more. Long live the Führer!'[6]

Thereafter the Germans dispersed some of the more important experimental sections of the devastated plant to the Harz mountains, to Poland and to southern Germany and started all over again. The rocket attack which Jones had warned of did not materialise.

As the months passed and nothing happened, Lord Cherwell regained his confidence. Young Jones had been wrong. There were no long-range rockets. If there was anything it was some kind of glider bomb, of the type currently being used against British troops in Italy, which would have a limited speed and fly at the same altitude as a normal plane. Pile's AA gunners or fighter command, Lord Cherwell decided, could quite easily cope with any development of that kind.

Dr Jones, on the other hand, was growing ever more certain that he was right. Indeed, by September he was beginning to suspect that the Home Front was facing *two* threats: not just the long-range rocket being developed at Peenemunde but some kind of short-range missile too. On September 25th he felt confident enough to sum up his conclusions thus:

It is probable that the German Air Force has been developing a pilotless aircraft for long-range bombardment in competition with the rocket, and it is very possible that the aircraft will arrive first.[7]

He had hit the nail on the head! While the Wehrmacht developed the V-2, the Luftwaffe under Milch had been developing what would become the V-1; and it would indeed arrive first.

Although Lord Cherwell was still doubtful, Churchill believed that Jones's conclusions could well be accurate—especially in the light of the threatening speeches made that autumn by both Goebbels and Hitler, promising terrible new weapons to be used against the British.

One month later, photo reconnaissance planes were sent out to survey the whole of north-western France within a radius of 150 miles of London. By November 22nd, ninety-five concrete structures had been discovered: flat-roofed, windowless buildings some 260 feet long, though only 10 feet wide. Because of their shape they were nicknamed 'ski sites'. But what were they intended for? They were too narrow to accommodate a winged aircraft, and it would be difficult to manoeuvre a rocket round the curved section. And what was one to make of the six pairs of 'studs', apparently made of concrete and set 20 feet apart?

The star of the RAF's photographic interpretation unit at Medmenham was Section Officer Babington-Smith, a daughter of the director of the Bank of England. It was her task, that November, to pore over the photographs of these mysterious 'ski sites' and see if she could spot any very small aircraft, smaller than a fighter, that might fit into these curious structures.

Miss Babington-Smith remembered a series of aerial photographs taken the previous June. These she retrieved from the unit's photo library and set to work on them:

And sure enough, I did find a midget aircraft on those splendid photographs ... I named it 'Peenemunde 20', as its span was 20 feet, but there was precious little I could say about it. The midget aircraft had the aggravating cotton-wool look that all light-coloured or shiny objects acquire on aerial photographs.[8]

On December 1st, still looking for more 'Peenemunde 20's', her trained eye was caught by some odd-looking structures, which several months before had been interpreted by others as 'something to do with dredging equipment'. But that 'dredging equipment' she now suggested to her chief, was really 'a catapult for pilotless aircraft'. *She had found it! She had discovered the V-1 and the means to be used to launch it!*

Dr Jones was not best pleased by the sudden clamour of congratulations that now surrounded Miss Babington-Smith; after all, he had been the one to propound the theory in the first place—in effect, he had pointed the way for her. And now Miss Babington-Smith was to be awarded a decoration; even the German-made lens with which she had made her great discovery was to be preserved for posterity! So he decided, great hoaxer that he was, that he would take her down a peg or two ...

Assuming his best upper-class lady journalist's voice, he telephoned Miss Babington-Smith, pretending to be the representative of 'a well-known woman's journal'. Would the 'heroine of the moment' be so kind as to allow a photographer to take her picture for their next number?

'Like a queen', Jones described her reaction years later. Yes, she certainly would be ready to be photographed.

But of course the photographer never turned up; and as Professor Jones relates, his *schadenfreude* still obvious today, so long after the event: '*No doubt she is still waiting!*'[9]

Those who knew about this terrible new threat walked around London, as 1943 gave way to 1944, with a nasty prickling sensation down the small of their backs. Every time a plane flew over, they would look up tensely, nerves tingling electrically. *Was this it?*

One of those in the know was the future Lord Snow. As he later recalled:

It wasn't so bad for the generals and the Cabinet Ministers because although they knew the menace that was threatening London, they were able to talk about it among

Launching a V-2—the guidance mechanism is meticulously adjusted.

themselves. We who lived the lives of ordinary Londoners and moved around with ordinary people could not. It was a curious feeling being with friends in a pub at night. They would begin to talk about the invasion, they would voice their apprehensions about the slaughter which might soon be facing our troops—and of their own guilt in being safe in London when it happened. And one couldn't succumb to the temptation and say: 'Don't feel guilty. You will be in a hell of a dangerous place yourself any moment now. *London might be as bad as the beaches ...*'[10]

TWO
Diver ... diver ... diver ...

Again London was unprepared.

It was now a year since the authorities had begun to learn what the Germans had in store for them. But the Cabinet Civil Defence Committee had fought and lost the battle against the demands of the forces and war industry for labour. The barrel was being scraped clean and there were no men available for Civil Defence in the emergency soon to come. In fact, Morrison had been forced to accept a reduction of Civil Defence to 293,000 by the end of 1943, with a further 50,000 men cut during the first half of 1944. Montgomery simply could not find enough infantrymen for the Invasion campaign soon to come. Now Morrison's youngest and most experienced men found themselves called up into the forces.

There were other shortages too. Steel ran out for the production of the highly popular and effective 'Morrison shelters', and the last order for 50,000 had to be cancelled. But if the mandarins of Whitehall would not help Morrison—and, indeed, turned down his plan for a mass evacuation of the population of London in case it started a panic—they *did* look after their own.

On the last day of 1943, the Ministry of Works stated that priority in shelter building should be given to those intended for civil servants. In particular, those deep shelters being built in certain sections of the Underground should be reserved for government servants, 'even if this course would be likely to lead to protests from certain sections of the civilian population'.[1] In case these irate civilians tried to force an entrance, the chief engineer had designed 'a simple method of blocking up entrances which could be put into use at short notice'.[2]

It was little different in AA Command. General Pile had been informed of the new threat in October 1943, and although he did not share Cherwell's optimism that there was nothing to it, there was little he could do but work out a contingency plan. He dared not yet move his guns from the cities in case they were attacked by conventional aircraft—as indeed they were, during the spring of 1944, in what was called the 'little blitz'. He had worked out that it would take him about eighteen days to deploy his guns to any new site, but had been pacified a little by the information that he would receive a month's notice of any danger. So he waited and hoped his guess that London would be the main target of these new revenge weapons would be right.

D-Day came and went. Still no flying bombs, or whatever they were. Cherwell grew ever more confident that they wouldn't come at all. Jones stuck to his guns. He had even made a prediction of when they would arrive, based on Hitler's reaction to the landings in Normandy. He had calculated that Colonel Wachtel's artillery regiment, which would fire the V-1s, would take seven days after the Invasion to be in a position to do so, once Hitler had given the order to commence firing. One of Jones's colleagues took him at his word. Jimmy Langley made several five pound bets with those in the know that the first bombs would arrive on D-Day plus seven—June 13th, to be exact!

Just after one o'clock that morning, a clear, cold moon-lit night, the officers of General Schill's 81st Infantry Division were assembled in a field in Normandy. To the west the sky flickered a fitful red with the explosions of the permanent barrage, where the Americans and the British were trying to break out of their bridgehead. Already elements of General Schill's infantry division were in contact with the enemy there.

Small, bespectacled Captain Wehr, who had already won the Knight's Cross in Russia, stood shivering with the rest, wondering why they had been assembled at this god-forsaken hour. He was soon enlightened. '*Meine Herren,*' the General snapped crisply, 'this morning we launch our revenge attacks on England. Our wonder weapons are already in action. Look!'

Dramatically the General pointed to the sky. As Herr Wehr recalled many years later: 'Suddenly there was a strange put-put sound like that of a two-stroke motor-bike. A dark object slid into view. Like a steel cigar, trailing flame behind it.'[3] It was the first sight that he had of the new 'wonder weapon', the V-1, one ton of high explosive carried at 400 mph, steered by a magnetic compass. But this particular one's compass was obviously not very good:

Abruptly it changed course. Instead of heading west, it was turning in an easterly direction—straight at us! I'd heard

These two remarkable photographs show (top) a 'doodlebug' in its final dive after the engine cut out and (bottom) the cloud of smoke as it hits another London street.

vague rumours of these new weapons and 'old hare'* that I was, I reasoned it contained high explosive. I, my comrades and General Schill dived for cover. Just in time! There was a hell of a bang—and one wonder weapon never reached England![4]

Four of that first salvo, however, did reach England. Already hurtling across the south coast, they were heading straight for London.

At eight minutes after four that morning two members of the Royal Observer Corps, weary and bleary-eyed, spotted them as they streaked across the pre-dawn sky. The two—a grocer and builder in normal daily life—saw them from the top of a Martello tower at Dymchurch on Romney Marsh. Instantly reaching for the telephone they repeated the magic words that they had been practising for so long now: '*Mike two ... Diver! ... diver! ... diver! ...*'

Alarm bells started to jingle right across the country to Whitehall itself, as the four missiles cruised steadily towards the capital. Sentries at an American camp in the flight path blazed away at them merrily, but only succeeded in wounding one of their own comrades in their confused haste.

Flight-Lieutenant Perkins of 514 Squadron, stationed at Waterbeach near Cambridge, spotted one on his way for a dawn attack on Le Havre: 'It was a curious ball of fire, travelling below us and heading towards us, which I momentarily took for the moon and wondered whether we were flying upside down.'[5] Hastily he swung the plane out of the way of the 'thing, whatever it was'.

The first one landed miles from London, on agricultural land just north of the A2 Rochester–Dartford road. 'Some trees on the opposite side of the A2 (large oaks) had a great quantity of their leaves stripped off,' the Ministry of Home Security reported.[6]

The second landed a mile and a half from Duckfield, Sussex. It, too exploded without harm, cutting off the heads of standing wheat as if it had been mown down by a harvester. Still no human casualties.

The third landed—again without casualties—at Platt near Sevenoaks. This left only one heading directly for London, homing in on the aiming target set for all these 'cruise missiles' of 1944—Tower Bridge.

That dawn Edward Hunter was in charge of the Home Guard picket stationed at Customs House, Lower Thames Street, when he first heard what he thought was the sound of aircraft flying very low:

I dashed out onto the quay and there down the river to the east and flying out to West India Docks there was an aircraft on 'fire', as we thought, with flames belching from its tail. It crossed the river and disappeared behind the

silhouette of Wapping's warehouses. The engine cut out. We waited. Then came a loud explosion.[7]

What Mr Hunter had seen was the first of the 10,292 V-1s—'buzz bombs' or 'doodlebugs', as they became known—to be aimed at London in the next two weeks (though only 2,419 reached their target). They would succeed in killing 1,600 Londoners and injuring three times that number.

This first bomb introduced a totally new kind of warfare, the warfare of the future, struck a railway bridge over Grove Road. It carried the four tracks of the main line between Chelmsford and the LNER station at Liverpool Street. The bridge itself, a stout Victorian structure, stood up quite well to the impact of one ton of high explosive—but the houses nearby did not.

Mr J. Palmer, watching the strange new weapon, 'thought it was a plane'.[8] Next moment it crashed onto the bridge and his house was badly damaged. Cut severely by flying glass, he was taken for treatment to the Mile End Hospital, one of the fourteen first casualties, four dead and ten wounded.

Not really very many for a weapon on which so much time and money had been spent. Next morning Jimmy Langley shook Dr Jones's hand warmly and congratulated him on the accuracy of his prediction; it had enabled him, Langley, to win all his bets. Thereafter Jones went over to the Cabinet Office to see his former professor, Lord Cherwell, who chuckled maliciously at the insignificance of the German effort. 'The mountain hath groaned and given forth a mouse!' he said.

Jones was horrified by this reaction: 'For God's sake,' he urged, 'don't laugh this one off!'[9]

He was horrified too that Lord Cherwell would not warn Churchill that a major V-1 campaign was on the way. Once, at one of their meetings to discuss the flying bombs, Jones had heard Churchill say that 'the people of Britain would stand anything if you warned them in advance about what they were in for'.[10]

But nothing was said. The public was deliberately left in the dark—at first. The official communiqué that morning read: '*Two short alerts, the first since April 27th, were sounded in London today. Several people were killed during the second alert when bombs fell in a working-class area ... A raider was brought down in East London.*'[11] And that was all.

Thus for two whole days the authorities concealed this new type of warfare.

But Londoners were already growing suspicious. Richard Johnson, for instance, a Royal Navy man working at the Bush Radio Factory in Rover Road, Chiswick, making and testing airborne radar sets—'a real cushy number'—had started to wonder 'at the daring of the German pilots flying so low over London'.[12] How could they do it?

| * Soldiers' slang for a veteran.

Another Navy man, Mr H. Jones, was on a course at the British School of Telegraphy in Clapham and was passing the Common when he saw his first V-1 rocket late one night. He describes it today as a 'small plane with flames coming from the tail'. And he remembers: 'It crashed with a high explosion about half a mile away. At first I thought it had been shot down but as more came over, I realised it was something new. I remember a woman running down the road, shouting: "*God, what are they?*"'[13]

Gunner Pierce, stationed with the 4th AA Division at Cowes on the Isle of Wight, heard Lord Haw-Haw claiming that second week of June: 'Again our new weapons have been attacking the south coast of England. The Isle of Wight has been devastated.' Of course, it hadn't; but now Gunner Pierce understood why the higher command had been so 'tense and jumpy of late'.[14]

VAD nurse Dora Robertson had had four years of the blitzes and had long grown accustomed to the attitudes of many regular nurses and military doctors. While working for the Scots Guards at Pirbright, for example, the senior medical officer had told the new VADs that all he knew about them 'was how to handle their bodies if they were killed in action and that they were not allowed to wear silk stockings on duty'.[15] At the London Military Hospital the VADs had even been forced to hide dirty, blood-stained, post-operative patients in cupboards or bathrooms on 'colonel's inspection days' so that his tender Guardee's sensibilities would not be offended by the sight!

But Nurse Robertson was no fool. She had seen 'the early morning milk train loaded with bodies for the cemetery at Brookwood'. So when a strange object exploded only two fields away as she and a fellow nurse cycled to work in Croydon, she understood immediately what the postman had meant earlier on when he had hinted darkly, 'There's a new thing happening. Jerry's sending over planes without pilots ...'*[16]

It was not until June 16th that Morrison finally told the House of Commons the truth about the Germans' new bomb, and then he only gave them part of the truth: 'A small number of these missiles were used in the raids on Tuesday morning ... a large number were used last night and this morning.'[17] In fact, as he privately told the War Cabinet, some fifty people had been killed and 400 injured so far. And, he admitted, while it was true that the attacks were no worse than those of the previous February, their 'nuisance value was high'.

Just how high that 'nuisance value' was, he and his colleagues were soon going to see.

*In 1945, as some sort of recompense for the long hard years with the VADs, Nurse Robertson was informed that she was one of 25 VADs who had been lent a wedding dress donated by Mrs Roosevelt. That year she was married in it.

Another casualty is carried past blitzed buildings.

Throughout the night of Saturday, June 17th, the flying bombs had been striking home all over the capital's south-eastern boroughs—Croydon, Wandsworth, Streatham, Battersea. In Wandsworth alone, three of the missiles, while only killing two people and injuring thirty-eight, destroyed and damaged 3,000 properties.

So far, however, it had been the humbler boroughs that had suffered from this horrible new type of warfare. Westminster had not been hit yet. Now as Sunday morning turned out to be warm and sunny, those off duty or on leave, civilian and military, set off to visit friends in town, at least that part of it—Westminster—which had been preserved from the V-1s.

Writer Mrs Robert Henrey was one. Travelling up to town with her child by train, she shared her compartment with three young Guards officers, who 'talked about shows and restaurants, about fathers who paid their debts and practical jokes they played on their friends'.[18] Just before the train reached Victoria Station, two of them said they were going to attend morning service in the Guards Chapel in Wellington Barracks. It was regarded in the Brigade as a very fashionable thing to do.

Night-fighter pilot Jimmy Rawnsley was another who was taking time off this Sunday; he and his ATS wife were determined to have a few hours off in the country. Now the young couple stood in Victoria Station waiting for their train.

Mrs Churchill was on the move, too. Laden with flowers and strawberries she had brought up the day before from Chequers, she was on her way to visit her daughter stationed with her mixed battery in Hyde Park. Mary would appreciate the fresh fruit, she thought.

Dr Jones, who had done so much to alert the authorities to the new danger, was one of the few at work that Sunday. Together with his colleague, Charles Frank, he was busy in his office in SIS headquarters at 55 Broadway.

Gazing around at the soldiers and civilians who were packed into the Guards Chapel for the morning service, young ATS subaltern Elizabeth Sheppard-Jones let herself be distracted a little by the sight of a young Canadian lieutenant, who 'eagerly surveyed his surroundings as if to memorise the details that he might write them down in his next letter home'.[19] But there would be no more letters home for that young officer, or for many another present at that service.

Almost as if to herald what was to come, the weather suddenly changed. The sun vanished. It started to drizzle. Standing at Victoria Station, the young couple heading for the country wondered whether they should continue on their journey as the raindrops began to drip through the bomb-shattered roof.

Abruptly the trip was forgotten as they heard that familiar throbbing sound.

'I suppose it isn't done for ATS officers to lie down in public?' Jimmy Rawnsley joked.

'And I suppose it isn't done for Air Force officers to start running?' his wife retorted.[20]

Just then the guns at Hyde Park started to thunder and the two of them fled for the poor protection of the nearest train as the flying bomb went into its final dive.

Mrs Henrey in Piccadilly heard that bomb too, just after the church bells had ceased ringing at eleven o'clock. She took her child by the hand and ran out into the passage:

The noise was deafening and I knelt down, shielding his head ... The child, frightened for the first time, clutched my arms, crying, 'I love you! ... I love you!' Then a terrific crash and the building shook ... A heart-rending silence which lasted for thirty seconds, quickly followed by the sound of people running in the street.[21]

Jones and Frank had flung themselves under their desks as the flying bomb went into its final dive. While the room shivered and trembled under the tremendous impact, Frank kept asking: 'Are you all right? ... Are you all right?'[22]

Shakily Jones said he was and then they were up, running across the park towards the Wellington Barracks. The packed Guards Chapel had been hit!

Mrs Churchill and her daughter Mary watched numbly as the smoke rose in a black ominous mushroom above London into the dreary gray sky. There was nothing they could do. Soon she would return home, the day spoiled, to tell her husband, who was still in bed working: 'The battery has been in action and the Guards Chapel is destroyed.'[23]

It was. Writer and air raid warden William Samson described the shattered scene graphically:

To the first air party that soon arrived the scene in its subsiding dust looked vast and boxlike; impenetrable sloping masses of the grey walls and roof shut in the wounded; the doors were blocked; the roof crammed down; it was difficult to find an entrance; but there was one; behind the altar. From then onwards it became a matter for nurses and doctors to scramble up and down and in between the large intractable slopes and walls of chunked concrete ... These rocks of material had to be manhandled off casualties. While doctors were plugging morphia and nurses and first aid personnel were feeding bicarbonate solutions and wrapping on ... dressings, all rescue services, together with soldiers from the barracks ... began prising up the debris-blocks and carrying out the freed.[24]

There were many casualties. One of them, young Miss Sheppard-Jones, knew that she was seriously hurt. Yet she felt no pain. Nor was she aware of the heavy pieces of stone pinning her down and making her breathing difficult. Suddenly, however, she became aware that 'somewhere far above me, above the black emptiness there were people, living helpful people whose voices reached me, dim and disembodied as if in a dream'.

'Please, I'm here!' she shrieked, over and over again until her throat ached. At last her cries were heard:

Someone was frantically scraping the rubble from around my head ... Somewhere not far away from me, someone was screaming, screaming, screaming, like an animal caught in a trap ... My eyes rested with horror on a blood-stained body that, had my hands been free, I could have reached out and touched ... the body of a young soldier whose eyes stared unseeingly at the sky ... I tried to convince myself that this was truly a nightmare.

Finally her head was freed and she was given a shot of morphia. With painful slowness she turned her head to a young Guardsman who was clearing debris and asked hysterically: 'How do I look? Tell me how I look!'

'Madam,' he said enthusiastically, lying the best he could, 'you look wonderful to me.'[25]

Now they started to total up the casualties: 119 people, mainly servicemen, had been killed and 102 seriously injured (several of whom died later); thirty-nine others had received minor wounds.

'The news of this catastrophe in which so many gallant people lost their lives,' Mrs Henrey wrote later, 'spread rapidly. It cast a gloom over London for it was the first major tragedy occasioned by this new weapon in the heart of the town.'[26]

The government tried to disguise the extent of the casualties by requesting the quality dailies such as *The Times* and *Daily Telegraph* not to publish the obituaries

118

This damage to the famous Guards Chapel attached to Wellington Barracks in London was caused by a flying bomb.

of the dead all at once. They were filtered into the columns of those papers over the weeks. In the cheaper papers, too, the tragedy was glossed over as another 'serious incident'; and that was that.

But for Miss Sheppard-Jones that 'serious incident' would be with her for the rest of her life. Later, much later at St Mary's Hospital, she was told the truth about her injuries: 'My spine was fractured and spinal cord damaged ... I was paralysed from the waist down.'[27]

That walk she had taken across St James's Park, heading for the Guards Chapel with her friend (who was killed), was the last walk she would ever take.

THREE
"Eee, I've got now't on'

Never before had a people been subjected to this kind of warfare. Even today, forty years later, the British remain the only nation which has stood up to nearly a year-long missile bombardment.*

All London tensed daily now as they heard that first distant hum, growing to an ever-louder, harsh rattle, which either vanished as the 'buzz bomb' flew on, or stopped abruptly, followed a few seconds later by the roar of one ton of high explosive detonating. That twelve seconds' silence between the engine cutting out and the blast of the explosion seemed to be the hardest part to bear—that tense, electric, brooding silence when the same terrifying thought flashed through everyone's mind: *has this one got my number on it?*

Everywhere, people spotting one of the monsters would cry: 'Carry on, yer bugger!' or 'Not here mate, please!' On July 1st, Giles of the *Daily Express* drew a famous cartoon which summed up the tense waiting mood of London that summer. It depicts Londoners of all types in a busy city street, all of them adorned with a monstrous right ear, with below the caption stating: 'It's ridiculous to say these new flying bombs have affected people in any way!'

The missiles were causing enormous damage. Barely two weeks later, the Minister of Health could inform his colleagues that of London's 2,250,000 houses, some 554,000 had already been damaged, *about one-fifth of the total!* In this period 5,000 Londoners had been killed and 17,000 seriously injured, with thousands more wounded slightly and rendered homeless, with nowhere to go but the streets.

While Pile's guns had still not been moved and were firing away merrily at the flying bombs (something

which horrified Dr Jones, for the gunners might well stop the missile over London, if they were lucky enough to hit it) labour was mobilised all over Britain to help make emergency repairs to the ever mounting total of damaged houses. Mass evacuation was introduced; once again the north-bound trains, packed tight with women and children, set off every five minutes from Euston and King's Cross. It was 1940 all over again.

Lady Reading, head of the WVS, mobilised all her good ladies in green uniforms and strange hats and sent them to help out in the stricken capital. Between June and August, in addition to their canteen duties, these middle-aged volunteers set up 778 Incident Inquiry Points where they dealt with street-loads of people at a time who had nothing left but what they stood up in.

Mrs Churchill asked Lady Reading if she could see the work of her ladies. The Head of the WVS said she could. The two set off in Lady Reading's car, driven by her close friend and honorary chauffeuse Miss Pauline Fenno, heading for Paddington where a flying bomb had landed less than half an hour before. Tears came to Mrs Churchill's eyes as she saw the mangled bodies being dug out. They went on to Battersea, where another Incident Inquiry Point had been set up, and arrived just as a bomb came down 500 yards away. On to the East End, where three more bombs exploded in so many seconds.

By now Lady Reading was getting a little worried. She was exposing the Prime Minister's beloved Clementine to too much danger. They set off once more down the Old Kent Road.

Just then Miss Fenno heard that familiar putt-putt. 'Say,' she sang out, 'there's a doodlebug overtaking us!' In that same instant, a car in front of her braked to a sudden stop. Four men sprang out and flung themselves flat in the middle of the road. Miss Fenno swerved desperately to avoid them, but stopped obediently enough, as the flying bomb cut out somewhere overhead, at the next red light. 'Say, if I were in the United States,' she drawled, 'I wouldn't stop at things like this. What irks me is that if we get hit, I won't even have a decent obituary. It'll just be "Lady Reading, Mrs Churchill and *a friend!*"'

Of course, there was humour among the horror. A WVS observer noted, at a piano-dealer's in Greenwich, how two hearty WVS ladies lowered the owner by the legs into his shattered house while he tried to play 'God Save the King' on each piano to see if they still worked!

In Clapham, as doodlebugs dropped around and people raced for the shelters, one middle-aged man spotted his wife running back to the house. 'Wait a minute,' she cried, 'I've got to find my dentures!'

'Listen you,' the irate husband yelled back. '*They're*

---

* Later on, two Belgian towns were subjected to V-1 attacks (Antwerp and Liège) but never on such a massive scale as Britain.

'*It's ridiculous to say these flying bombs have affected people in ANY way.*
This cartoon appeared in the *Daily Express* on July 1st, 1944.

dropping doodlebugs, not sandwiches!' [2]

And in Ilford, the WVS helped to fight their way through the debris of a house which had been hit six hours before. Now as they battled towards what was left of the bathroom, where they knew the sole survivor was trapped, a woman's voice called in a broad Yorkshire accent: 'Ee, you'll get a surprise soon, lads. *I've nowt on!'* The unfortunate woman had been trapped in the bath.[3]

But there was more horror than humour this hot summer, as the chronicler of the WVS records:

At Mitcham a wedding party without the bridegroom was taking place. He was a sailor and had been held up on the way. Eighteen members of the wedding party were killed. When the would-be bridegroom arrived, he seemed completely calm. He is now in a mental home.[4]

Desperately the night-fighter pilots did their best to ward off these relentless attackers, just as their colleagues did during daytime. For now the Germans on the other side of the Channel were adopting a new technique: firing off salvoes of rockets just about the time when they estimated there would be a change-over of day and night-fighter squadrons.

Jimmy Rawnsley, who had seen the bomb drop on the Guards Chapel, was now flying as a navigator in a Mosquito piloted by an old friend, Peter Green, trying to stop the doodlebugs off the coast. Towards the end of July he took part in his first flying bomb 'kill', as the pilot levelled out behind one of them. To Rawnsley, it seemed 'there was something awesome and full of fiendish purpose in the unswerving flight of the bomb', but the pilot was undeterred. They hurtled down into the bomb's wake. They caught a quick glimpse of the fiery maws of the thing as their plane shook and rocked in that crimson tide. Still the pilot held on grimly, finger poised on his firing button.

'One thousand feet ... nine hundred feet ... eight hundred feet ...' the navigator called out the distances.

The pilot hesitated no longer. 'Right,' he cried, '*here goes!*' He pressed the button. The plane shivered. Tracer, glowing a bright red, zipped towards the bomb. It shuddered. It had been hit! Next moment it exploded with an awesome roar. The plane was suddenly filled with red-hot air. But they were still flying, and Rawnsley, who had ducked instinctively, sat up again and looked back: 'The air behind us was full of glowing red fragments still fanning out and floating downwards.'[5]

But it was not just the RAF that was making a determined attempt to stop the flying bombs reaching London; the Americans were too. The American AA Command (stationed on the south coast, with a good dozen anti-aircraft battalions), like the pilots of the US TAC Air Force who flew daily missions over the beaches, did their best.

That summer Colonel Richard Turner, an ace Mustang pilot, spotted two of them as he was returning home from a mission, flying over the Channel between Dover and Calais. For ten minutes he chased the first and succeeded in knocking it out of the sky with the last of his ammunition. Now what was he going to do with the second one? Let him tell the story in his own words:

This bomb must have been moving more slowly than the first one, for I almost overran it as I pulled out of my dive. As I flew alongside of the little monster I had a new idea. I knew they were controlled by a gyro guidance 'brain' and perhaps this mechanism could be upset without gunfire. I carefully edged close to it and placed my wingtip about a foot under its tiny fin. Rolling my plane suddenly I neatly flipped the V-1 upside down and it promptly spun into the shallows of the Channel near the English shore where it blew a useless hole in the water.[6]

Jubilant with the success of his daring manoeuvre, Colonel Turner flew back to his field at Maidstone where he 'hastened to tell the other pilots of the new pastime I had discovered'.[7]

But success was not achieved without casualties. Rawnsley lost several comrades from his own squadron, and although most of them managed to bale out and save themselves when the exploding bombs destroyed their planes, a few did not.

Nor were they safe from Pile's gunners, even when they were on the ground. Number 3 Squadron, flying Tempests and stationed under canvas at Newchurch near Dungeness because the place was close to the spot where most V-1s crossed the coast, between Cuckmere Haven and St Margaret's Bay, found themselves harassed by 'shrapnel falling all over the airfield and going through our tents'.[8] Indeed, the squadron's first casualty of this new battle occurred when one of a neighbouring squadron's fighters, shooting up a doodlebug, fired a burst into a tent and wounded a sleeping airman in the hand.

But the squadron was hampered in other ways, too. By the workers at the Langley factory, for instance, where the much needed Tempests were being produced.

The gunners did what they could to destroy the missiles—this battery has just shot one down.

Due to a change-over from Hurricanes to Tempests, the piece-rate wage had been reduced; and so the workers called a strike. This at a time when RAF ground crews were working around the clock to enable their pilots to fly four or five sorties a day; when the pilots themselves were flying 800 hours a month or more, instead of the usual 500–600 hours—living, sleeping, eating next to their aircraft!

But the workers struck for their rights in the very same month that a French Spitfire pilot, due to marry his English bride a week later, sacrificed his life while trying to 'tip' a doodlebug and prevent it falling on a hospital near Benenden. He was recommended for the Victoria Cross, but nothing came of it. In the end the workers got their pay and went back to work. The battle continued . . .

Pile still had his guns stationed in and around the capital where they were a danger to both the gunners and the general public. Harold Atkins, an *Evening News* reporter doing a story on the 'Battle of the Buzz Bombs', pointed out that AA Command would be more effective and cause fewer casualties from falling shrapnel if there were to be 'a change of belts with all the guns on the coast, providing a wide firing area out to sea and more space inland for the intercepting planes, right up to the balloons'.[9]

Atkins never learned whether his suggestions reached Air Marshal Roderic Hill, Commander of the Air Defence of Great Britain. But on July 3rd, without any reference to higher authority, Hill ordered the redeployment of 1,000 guns to the coast.

Lance-Corporal Pearce was one of those gunners, moving from Dulwich to Clacton. His crew of gunners had been without sleep for forty-eight hours and were not inclined to handle the heavy railway sleepers needed to form a solid base for their guns. But they were shamed into moving by their sergeant, recently returned from the fighting with the Eighth Army in the Desert. He knew the urgency of the moment. 'Come on, you lazy sods!' he cried and, placing one heavy sleeper on each shoulder, 'doubled two hundred yards and dropped them in the gunpit while the troops sat there laughing and applauding, marvelling at the feat'.[10]

The strikers' and the gunners' attitude was typical of many who did not realise the urgency of the time. Pile was horrified, for instance, to learn at the height of this new offensive that it was impossible to man the guns at one South Wales town 'because some of the personnel had gone away to shoot in a competition in which other anti-aircraft teams in the country are concerned'.[11] But even when his gunners were on duty, they were often asked to move because they endangered the local area or accused of not doing their best to defend it. After Eton was hit, the Provost for example, wrote an angry letter to Pile in which he said:

Why should we submit to have our buildings destroyed because the anti-aircraft authorities are unskilful and injudicious in their methods of defence? . . . It makes my blood boil that [Eton College] buildings should be imperilled, not by intended enemy action, but by the stupid and ill-conceived measures which the Military Authorities take for defence.[12]

Pile was not alone. Hill was censured too for his decision to move the artillery closer to the coast. The Air Council was very displeased, and as Pile wrote later, 'They left Hill in absolutely no doubt that he must take full consequences of the failure—for failure was forecast in their every word—attending upon his decision.'[13]

And still these new bombs continued to rain down on London, even though Pile's gunners made them run a gauntlet of 800 heavy and 1,800 light anti-aircraft guns, assisted by 1,750 balloon cables, while the fighters continued to risk their lives 'tipping' the missiles. Hundreds were downed, but hundreds more got through. Some of the capital's citizens had by now grown almost used to them. One told Mass Observation: 'I feel quite excited. Fancy this being the secret weapon! Here's us living right in the middle of H. G. Wells fantasy—pilotless planes and all that!'[14]

Another of Mass Observation's interviewees was less sanguine: 'Outwardly it doesn't seem to affect me—I carry on with what I'm doing in the day and I sleep at night. But my nerves seem edgy and I feel awfully sick before and after the thing explodes.'[15]

Mr Harry Penny was driving his No. 6 bus through London's streets at this time, and keeping a diary of what he felt and saw. 'What courage the daylight gives me,' he noted. 'With daylight very few people take notice of the warnings. Fate seems very queer for some people. Having spent their night in the shelters they lose their lives going about their business.'[16]

Someone else, a middle-aged woman, commented: 'It's wicked the way it goes on all night till morning and you keep listening all the time till you're tired out with it. And when those engines stop! I'd sooner be dead right out than stand the suspense. My girls have been sick all night.'[17]

That summer some anonymous person inserted a notice in the personal columns of *The Times*; it was the biblical quotation: 'Thou shalt not be afraid for the terror by night nor for the arrow that flieth by day.' But the long-suffering citizens of London who had stayed behind—over a million and a half had by now fled the capital—*were* afraid and exhausted. At West Hampstead, a housewife wrote in her diary, 'We do feel so tired; the strain is almost intolerable, but I keep as busy as I can in the flat to take my mind off. London is deserted . . . It gives me a queer lonely feeling.'[18]

And on August 24th, that same housewife, Dorothy

Cox, wrote: 'An alert made us look out of the window and to our horror, we saw a flying bomb making straight for us ... Suddenly it stopped and steadily dived, nose down. We were so spell-bound that we actually watched it for a few seconds, then realising our danger, dashed back into our hall for shelter. Immediately there was a violent explosion and a shattering of glass.'[19]

Every borough in London had by this time been badly hit. Stepney, Deptford, Battersea, East Ham, Bermondsey, Poplar, Hackney, Barking had all received 30 or more flying bombs. Camberwell, Greenwich and Lambeth had all been struck by between 40 and 80 of the terrible missiles, while Lewisham and Wandsworth had been hit by 117 and 126 respectively.

But the top of this league of death was undoubtedly the borough of Croydon, which had been the first London borough to suffer a serious attack back in the summer of 1940 when the airfield had been blitzed. Now, four years later, Croydon was going to have to endure a staggering 140 flying bombs. No other place in the whole of the United Kingdom, throughout the nine-month campaign, would ever see so many.

Betty Porlock's mother had had a recurrent dream ever since 1938 when she had moved from Portsmouth to Croydon: 'She would be sitting in a deckchair in the garden. She would hear a strange-sounding plane and look up to see it. She described it as being without a pilot when it landed near her in the garden.'[20] That dream had been related not only to the family but to friends, too.

Now as the campaign started against London that summer, Betty was talking one evening to a neighbour outside their house in Norbury Crescent when he said: 'That one is coming this way!'

Next moment there was a tremendous crash, as the bomb landed exactly where Betty's mother had always dreamt it would—*right at the bottom of the garden!*

The man talking to Betty was killed outright, but she and her family were untouched, save for a few scratches. But a little later Betty went into shock and was given an injection to calm her down by a 'doctor who shook more than I did'.[21]

Many strange things happened that summer in bomb-shattered Croydon. Mrs Dorothy Joslin-Smith was shopping one day with her children when the flying bombs started dropping all around. She caught a glimpse of Ernie Mills, the Olympic cyclist, marooned on the top of his staircase; the rest of his house had been blown away! Now the anxious mother sought any kind of protection she could find for herself and her children. As yet another flying bomb came hurtling down, the local fishmonger grabbed her and her children and thrust them inside his huge freezer!

Thus they survived. But Mrs Joslin-Smith's daughter was left with an eye defect due to shock and her other child 'had permanent heart damage'. And later that day they were evacuated to Doncaster because 'we were now homeless, as were hundreds of others'.[22]

PC William Holloway found himself tunnelling down into the smoking rubble of a gutted house to rescue a Mrs Wagstaff, her baby Nicola and an elderly nanny. Crouching there in the tunnel he told the shocked civilians that they'd better get out quickly; there was no time to lose.

Mrs Wagstaff, shocked as she was, refused. Her little girl Elizabeth was still buried somewhere in the rubble. PC Holloway said he would find her, but they *had* to get out while there was still time; the house might collapse at any moment. He himself admitted to being 'scared stiff, but twenty years of police service and discipline had taught me to face fear and overcome it'. Grimly he dug away at the debris, ignoring the ominous creaking and groaning of the ruin. At last he found the girl—but it was too late: 'I realised that Elizabeth would not survive. It was obvious her chest was crushed and I had seen death too many times not to realise that the end was very near.'

PC Holloway did not think himself a religious man, but he said the Lord's Prayer and as the dying girl opened her eyes, he whispered gently: 'It's all right, love. I'll keep the light of my torch on and we'll be all right.' Then, he says, 'She just smiled softly and closed her eyes.'

So the policeman and the little girl clung together there with the flying bombs landing all around and the ruin creaking and threatening to collapse at any moment until finally she passed away.

PC Holloway knew that if he called the heavy-rescue gang with their machines, the whole place would collapse on her poor sweet little face. So he built a little wall around her and placed his helmet over her dead face to protect it from any further falls. Now he set off through the blazing night to tell Mrs Wagstaff that her daughter was dead ...[23]

It was indeed the women, the old and the children who suffered most in Croydon's terrible attacks. Sylvia Fenton, then six, remembers her father throwing himself on top of her in a muddy trench as the doodlebugs rained down. Later her shocked and terrified mother told her, 'I spoke to a man. I didn't recognise him—it was your father!'[24]

WAAF Sergeant Barbara McMaster spent the night in the dark holding hands with a sick friend Joan, immobilised in bed with a severe back injury, as the bombs dropped everywhere and shook the walls of the sick bay frighteningly.

'Please God, let me live till morning,' Joan moaned.

'Yes,' Barbara echoed fervently, 'let her live till morning.' The room was 'stifling', she remembers, 'but Joan and I shivered the long hours away; both of us motion-less—pretending under the cover of darkness that the shivering was not happening'.[25]

Mrs F. Hobday was petrified as a doodlebug started to descend on her street in New Addington. Her husband was in the Army and she had four small children to look after. Should she hide them and herself under the stairs or chance it and run for the shelter? She took a chance. Together she and the children ran for the shelter. Just as she reached the shelter door, the doodle-bug's motor cut out. The explosion sent her flying through the air—right inside the shelter. 'The ARP men were there in no time and got us out. One man asked me where I'd like to go and I said indoors. He said, "You will not go in there again." When I looked there was a great empty space full of dust and glass ... That was the end of my house and home.'[26]

Like so many thousands of others in Croydon, Mrs Hobday was destined for the rest centre and evacuation, another family uprooted for the duration of the war.

That August, wartime mother Nina Searle counted ninety-one doodlebugs passing overhead as she tossed and turned with the agony of her labour pains as she gave birth to her daughter Gina; while a little way off a kind neighbour tried to help Mrs Wagstaff overcome the shock of having lost her daughter Elizabeth by making a painting of the dead girl from a picture.

Forty-odd years later, the dead Elizabeth smiles down from the wall of Mrs Wagstaff's rebuilt home—'We have never forgotten Elizabeth'—and less than a mile away, Gina, born in the month that Elizabeth died, is herself a mother.

And then it was September. Finally Colonel Wachtel's gunners had been driven out of France, firing their last salvo from French soil on the first day of that month. Now his regiment was on the run, part of the great retreat of the shattered Wehrmacht from France—a headlong flight across Belgium, with the Allied tanks at their heels, finally coming to rest in Holland and West-phalia in Northern Germany, safe at last, but sadly de-pleted. The terrible bombardment seemed over at last.

On the morning of September 6th, housewife Mrs Cox wrote in her diary: 'Blissful peace with no sort of bombing. It is strange to look up into the sky, innocent of enemy machines of destruction. Everyone looks so happy and cheerful, expectant of a real peacetime any time now ... However, a gorgeous, but stormy sun-set.'[27]

They were prophetic words. It was not over yet, not by a long chalk.

A flying bomb (V-1) has just fallen in the suburbs of London.

FOUR
The Battle of London is over

That summer of 1944, 'near panic' had reigned inside the Cabinet, as the threat of the V-2, against which there was no defence, grew ever closer. Morrison, who was in Dr Jones's opinion the most terrified of Churchill's ministers, wanted the immediate evacuation of a million people from London. Indeed, 'he had already tried on July 11th to have our Invasion forces diverted to land in the V-1 launching area.'[1]

Only Lord Cherwell refused to flap. He at first contended that the rockets photographed at Peenemunde were dummies, meant to fool the Allies. Now he conceded that there were real missiles in existence, but pooh-poohed the idea that they would ever be fired at London.

Desperately Jones worked on the politicians. Naturally he wanted to keep them aware of the danger; but on the other hand he did not want them to panic. On the basis of his own researches he concluded that the V-2s could not be launched before mid-September and by then, with a bit of luck, the German supply lines would be overrun by Allied troops. Besides, it had been estimated that the V-2 had a range of only 200 miles— and by now the victorious Allies were eating up German territory at a rate of twenty, even fifty miles a day! Already it was being confidently predicted in high circles that the war would be over by Christmas. Montgomery even made a five pound bet with General Eisenhower that the war would be over by the end of 1944.

Thus it was, as the V-1s started to peter out and none of the new weapons had arrived, that optimism replaced the earlier panic.

On September 7th, Duncan Sandys gave a press

Although these shelters stood up well, they could not always withstand the relentless bombing.

conference on the subject of the 'revenge weapons' campaign. That evening he announced to the assembled reporters: 'Except possibly for a few last shots, the "Battle of London" is over.'[2]

At 6.43 on the night of the 8th, with a clap like thunder, the first V-2 fell on Chiswick, killing three people and seriously injuring seventeen more.

Dr Jones was in his office, together with his colleague Charles Frank, when they heard that supersonic double-crack for the first time. Today we are all familiar with it, but this was the first one a startled London had heard. They looked at each other and said simultaneously: *'That's the first one!'*[3]

That first V-2 had been fired from the Hague's *Koekoekslaan** in Holland. But the egg that this particularly monstrous steel 'cuckoo' had hatched was anything but pleasant.

It had been aimed at the Fire Station in Southwark Bridge Road, but this first V-2 of the 1,190 missiles to be fired at the UK missed and struck Stavely Road, Chiswick, eight miles off target.

Now, after having survived being bombed out three times, Mrs Whiting and her daughter were killed. The last her son Bill, now an officer in the Royal Marines, saw of the place where she had lived was a huge crater. A veteran of the early blitz himself, he wondered at the size of the bomb which could cause such a huge crater, but 'could find out nothing'.[4]

The War Cabinet had ordered a security blackout. London was not to be told what had hit the city. Richard Johnson, the Royal Navy man who lived a mile away from Chiswick, 'heard the explosion and the supersonic boom which accompanied it, which was terrifying'; but later, when he tried to find out what had caused the explosion, he was 'met with a wall of silence'.[5]

So were the bewildered locals who tried to file a War Damage Claim at Chiswick Town Hall. They were turned away with the explanation that the damage to their homes had nothing to do with the war; it had been caused by an 'exploding gas main'. In fact, the gas main story became the standard official and unofficial explanation for many of the explosions to come.

Lord Cherwell, who had left England with Churchill for the Quebec Conference, received a personal description of the event from London and once again the exploding 'gas main' featured in it. There had been 'two explosions close together, one slightly fainter than the other', his correspondent said, and then went on: 'The Bishop of London told me yesterday that when he heard the explosion he thought the doodlebugs had started again; but he heard it was a gas main. One of the drivers heard the same story.'[6]

Cherwell's informant added maliciously: 'There is

going to be criticism of Morrison and Sandys for having crowed too soon. I thought the above might amuse you ...'

We do not know whether Lord Cherwell was amused or not, but there was no criticism of Morrison or Sandys because the public was simply not told what had happened.

London's population started to rise once more. The 'doodlebug' danger was over and evacuated people started to flood back into the capital at the rate of 10,000 a week. After all, who cared about a few exploding gas mains?

In the event, the Germans were slow to use this terrible new weapon. By September 18th they had only fired 18 V-2s at the capital, which killed—or so the authorities claimed later—56 people.

* 'Cuckoo's Lane'.

Mr William Harrison (head bandaged) lost his wife when one of the first V-2s fell on his house.

It was fortunate for Britain that this was so, for the only counter-measure which offered itself was to maintain constant armed reconnaissance over suspected launching sites in Holland. In the first few days of the new offensive, the Allied air forces flew 1,000 sorties over the area, shooting up any suspected launching site and supply vehicles, etc.

In the end, to escape this constant air attack, the Germans moved some of the V-2s to Stavern in Friesland. From here it was difficult to hit London, so Norwich was set as the new target; for this was where the Germans thought a major Allied army was being kept in reserve. Thus on September 25th, the first V-2 was fired at a provincial target. It missed Norwich, and fell instead on Suffolk.

Meanwhile, as Montgomery's armies failed to achieve his great thrust at Arnhem and the Allies advance began to bog down all along the German frontier, the Germans returned to their Dutch bases. The offensive against the targets in East Anglia swiftly came to an end, for Hitler now directed that rocket fire was to be concentrated solely on London and Antwerp, the Allies' major supply port in Belgium. The campaign against East Anglia had not been successful anyway. Forty-three rockets had been fired at Norwich and not one of them had hit the city (though one had struck Ipswich).

So London came under fire once more—yet still the authorities maintained their silence.

Those in the know were terrified by this new weapon. Charles Snow, the civil servant novelist, wrote later:

The rockets frightened me much more than the others. Quite unrealistically in fact. As you know, if one had been hit by a rocket one wouldn't have known anything about it. Most people took them more calmly than I did. This was purely subjective. They hadn't a big enough warhead to be

131

really dangerous, but somehow the idea that fate was above one without one knowing anything about it—that I found disturbing.[7]

By the first week of November 1944, some 200 rockets had been fired at London, of which 96 had reached their target. They had killed 456 people. Nothing, it seemed, could stop them. Their mobile launching sites in the Hague were difficult to hit from the air without inflicting damage on the Dutch,* and all efforts to interfere with the rocket's radio-controlled mechanism had proved fruitless. All the Allied planes could do was to concentrate on the German transports supplying the missile-launching crews; and here, too, they were hampered by the fact that these measures cost a serious loss of life among Dutch civilians.

Londoners soon began to suspect that these strange double-bang explosions could not all be caused by exploding gas mains. Some people actually saw a V-2 which failed to explode. Donald Ketley, for instance, then a thirteen-year-old schoolboy, passed a house one morning where a V-2 had just landed. But the warhead had not exploded and the monster had buried itself upright in someone's garden: 'The man of the house was standing, open-mouthed, in his doorway, staring in amazement at this enormous gleaming tower which had suddenly appeared in his yard.'[8]

Jimmy Rawnsley also saw one while he was flying over Hertfordshire, just north of London, at 10,000 feet:

... then like a sudden blotch in the blue sky, there appeared a small reddish cloud about half a mile ahead and high above us. It had not formed slowly as most clouds do. At one moment there was nothing and then in a flash, it was there, complete, ugly and menacing. As we flew on, gazing in astonishment at this phenomenon, smoky tendrils spread outwards and downwards from its billowing heart.[9]

What he and his pilot had seen was a V-2 exploding prematurely. They held on for dear life as bits and pieces fell off their plane, watching farm workers down on the ground racing to find souvenirs.

'I wonder how hot that thing is?' the pilot queried.

Next moment he had his answer, as the farm worker who had gripped a piece of the casing suddenly dropped it 'and started hopping around sucking his fingers'.[10]

On November 9th, 1944, Churchill told the nation at long last that for over two months now a V-2 offensive had been waged against the country.

Two weeks later, on November 25th, the worst incident of the year occurred when a V-2 landed between Woolworth's and the Co-Op in New Cross Road,

London, at lunch hour. One hundred and sixty were killed and many more seriously injured.

Surprisingly enough, now that the public knew what they were, they were little talked about. Unlike the V-1s, they attracted no nicknames and no jokes. They were openly hated and feared. As one Essex woman remembers (four hundred fell in her county): 'There was no anticipation with the rockets, so that when the explosion was heard that was the first one knew—and one was either alive or dead.'[11] Indeed if one heard the bang, one probably survived.

And when the Ketley family, out for a Sunday walk on the plateau above Chigwell, witnessed twenty V-2s plunging down on distant London, Mr Ketley senior remarked: 'You know, if the Germans had had those things in 1940, I think we might have cracked.'[12]

And still the war went on. Admittedly there were visible signs that it was ending on the Home Front. That winter it was announced that the Home Guard would no longer be needed. After a march-past in front of King George VI in December they would be stood down. That autumn too, the black-out was officially changed to a 'dim-out'. Now, it was joked, randy soldiers would no longer find themselves mistakenly chasing Scotsmen in kilts; now they would actually be able to see the painted faces of the 'Piccadilly Commandos' without having to shine a torch on them!

The politicians who had contributed by their pre-war folly to the present sad state of the nation—with already 50,500 men, women and children killed and 61,400 seriously injured in the conventional bombing alone—now began to prepare themselves for the coming post-war election. Labour and Conservative, all alike were looking to the future. The war was nearly over, they reasoned, so their chief concern now should be how to ensure their own political survival ...

But still the V-1s and V-2s came plunging down with dismal regularity, and still Air Marshal Hill and General Pile racked their brains trying to assess what the Germans might do next. Pile had already learned that the Germans were trying a new technique of launching their V-1s from Heinkel IIIs flying off the coast; it was perfectly possible, then, that any new offensive against Britain might be launched in the north, for the south was too well defended by now. He guessed that 'the enemy might conceivably be able to launch attacks simultaneously from North Foreland to Yorkshire'.[13]

On November 2nd, therefore, he sent a reconnaissance party up to the bleak east coast to check out the area between Skegness in Lincolnshire and Whitby in Yorkshire, looking for suitable sites for a redeployment of his forces to meet any attack on the northern cities. But manpower was short, as always, and in the end he had to be satisfied with a new line, divided into three central sections: one near Bridlington in Yorkshire; the second one on both sides of the River Humber; the third one based at Louth in Lincolnshire.

*In fact the Allies never located the main site—the area of the Duindigt racecourse.

The hurriedly organised sites were very primitive indeed. One VIP visitor to a site in Yorkshire said that it reminded him of Flanders in the Old War with mud right up to his knees. Indeed, one brigadier assembled 1,000 of his girls and told them he did not think it right for them to have to work under such terrible conditions. He offered to find new postings for anyone who wanted to leave; but in the event only nine of the girls asked to be transferred—and they were all clerks.

Naturally enough, the politicians quickly spotted this opportunity for self-promotion. Labour Independent MP Tom Driberg, on a visit to one of the mixed batteries, casually asked the RSM who the camp's tents were intended for. The RSM told him they were for the ATS girls.

One day later, on November 14th, Driberg rose in the House and asked the Secretary of State for War whether he was aware that ATS girls were still sleeping under canvas on marshy ground. Sir James Grigg, the Secretary, explained the reasons for the poor conditions. But Driberg (who had a strange secret life of his own, known only to the Intelligence authorities) was not to be fobbed off with that. He was working on the serviceman's vote in the 'khaki election' to come.

'Is the Right Honourable Gentleman aware,' he thundered, 'that *I* visited these gun-sites only yesterday afternoon? ... It is quite incorrect to say that double tenting has been provided; they are still sleeping under single canvas—and very leaky canvas at that!'[14]

Sir James was embarrassed and backed down; and Driberg had gained a few more future votes as the friend and defender of the 'rights of our lads and lasses in uniform'.

As for General Pile, who duly received a 'rocket' from the War Office, it only added one more headache to the problem of trying to defend the north before the Germans struck ...

At dawn on the morning of Saturday December 16th, the Allied front in the Belgian Ardennes was split apart by a great German surprise thrust: a quarter of a million men, comprised of two armoured armies and one infantry, striking some 80,000 surprised Americans. Almost immediately the greater part of one green US division surrendered and another inexperienced US division was badly mauled. By the 18th the Germans had broken through on a sixty-mile front, had sent the Americans reeling before them in confusion, and were advancing on the River Meuse. Their plan, it was stated, was to capture the key Allied supply port of Antwerp, split the Anglo-American armies in two and thus prolong the war so that they could finish off the Russians and obtain a better peace from the Western Allies.

The news shocked Britain. This miserable, cold, dreary December might not be the last Christmas of the war after all. But Britain was not only shocked by the

An official examines the rocket motor of a V-2 in Limehouse.

news; it was also profoundly alarmed. Wild rumours flew round the country. The Germans were developing even worse 'revenge weapons'. A mass breakout of German POWs was being planned, in which they would seize a key port. German parachutists were already being dropped by Colonel Skorzeny* similar to those already dropped behind the American lines in the Ardennes, to help the escaping POWs. Etcetera, etcetera. Alarm, fear, rumour and not a little war-weary despondency.

In London General Pile pleaded for permission to man the other sites he had picked for a redeployment on the north-east coast. The three already manned would not be enough if the Germans attacked in strength. But his pleas fell on deaf ears. For over a month the War Office refused to let him deploy his guns in the north. By the time they relented, it was all too late; 'the flying bombs never came that way again ...'[15]

Even after five years of war, the Home Front was going to be caught out again.

* Head of the SS Commandos.

FIVE
Somebody's gonna have a funny old Christmas present

HMS Caicos, which was used as a floating radar station.

Whoosh! The green signal flare shot into the dark sky and exploded in a burst of incandescence at the end of the runway. It was the signal they had been waiting for.

The first Heinkel III started to roll down the tarmac, gaining speed dangerously slowly. For the black-painted old fashioned bomber was heavily laden, its fuel tanks brim-full of high octane petrol, and with one ton of high explosive in the shape of a V-1 attached to its starboard wing. Ponderously it began to rise into the pre-dawn sky over Holland. Another followed and another. One by one, these fifty airborne launching pads lumbered into the air, while the sky to the south-east flickered a dull pink: the permanent barrage over the Belgian Ardennes. Now these young men of *Kampfgruppe 53* were going to make their contribution to the 'great struggle for life or death', as the Führer had called it. They were going to outflank General Pile's coastal defences and take the war to the north of England once more.

After all, on this day of all days, the Tommies would not be alert; their thoughts would be on plum puddings and all the other strange foods they ate at this time of the year. It was Christmas Eve 1944 and the Germans were coming back to Manchester after four years ...

For most of their flying time they flew at a couple of hundred feet above the sea to avoid British radar. For a mere seven minutes they would appear on the radar screens as they climbed to 1,500 feet in order to launch their missiles. At this particular time they were indeed highly vulnerable. But they were so slow that any Allied fighter that managed to reach the climbing Heinkel in time would either overshoot the German plane or simply fall out of the sky in a stall because its pilot had throttled back too much in order to keep in range.

Some weeks earlier, Jimmy Rawnsley remembers talking to one weary crew, who were not only exhausted after a long night patrol off the Dutch coast waiting for the Heinkels, but frustrated, too. 'We were close behind him for miles,' the navigator wailed, 'but he was so close to the water we just couldn't get at him without swimming. I had to watch the radar altimeter as well as the AI, while the skipper tried to spot him.'

'Didn't he pull up at all to launch the bomb?' Rawnsley asked.

'I'll say he did!' the pilot agreed bitterly. 'I closed in and spotted him ... I could even see the thing hanging under the wing. There was a dirty great flash as the bomb went whooshing off on its way and for the next five minutes I could see sweet Fanny. I had to pull up in case I hit the deck and that was that.'[1]

Up to quite recently the call had been for ever faster fighters. To meet this new danger, slower ones were needed. Obsolete Beaufighters were recalled for service. But most of these were not equipped with the latest air interception radar sets. So the frigate HMS *Caicos* was set up as a floating radar station and fighter control centre. In December ancient Wellington bombers which had flown the first raid on Germany back in 1939 (when their crews were warned severely not to drop bombs on 'private property') were brought back. They were equipped with ASV (air to surface vessel) radar in an attempt to pick up these low-flying Heinkels. Indeed, all the devices which would be employed in a far more sophisticated manner in the Falklands War nearly forty years later were already being used this December. But on this last Christmas Eve of World War Two, they met with little success. General Pile's flank would be successfully turned and over one hundred men, women and children would never live to celebrate the end of that long bitter struggle, after all ...

Then as the sirens spread the alarm further and further afield, the first V-1 was spotted on the outskirts of York. The Epworth ROC post there reported the sighting to the York HQ of the Royal Observation Corps just behind the General Post Office: 'The bugger's engine has stopped,' the observer telephoned excitedly, 'and ... if we go off the air, you'll know we've had it!'[3]

Fortunately for them, they didn't. The flying bomb came down some 500 yards away and shook their bunker like a sudden tornado.

Some of the bombs went wild, swerving away from their primary target. For instance, one was spotted at Dunham-on-Trent by the local ROC people and another was heard at a village near Worksop in Nottinghamshire. But the great majority of the surviving bombs were steadily winging their way across the snow-blown Pennines, as planned by Field Marshal Milch, heading for their primary target, the city of Manchester.

They landed at dawn that grey winter morning, dropping in a ring around their target. At Beighton in South Yorkshire and at Buxton in Derbyshire, some forty miles off the target; at Davenport and Hyde in Cheshire, eight miles to the east; and than at Worsley, Tottingham, Cheadle and Radcliffe in the area of Greater Manchester.

The casualties here were relatively slight, but the fear they caused was great. Mrs H. Reilly had been through the Christmas blitz on Manchester of 1940 and had become so immune that 'I generally slept through all air raid alerts so that my mother found it terribly difficult to rouse me.' But on Christmas Eve 1944 she was 'terrified because we'd all heard of the V-1s and V-2s and knew that these were the real thing ... I hid under the staircase and wept hysterically.'[4]

Skimming over the grey-green waters of the North Sea at 300 feet, the commander of *Kampfgruppe 53* gave his pilots the order to climb. Now came the worst part of the whole operation. Forty miles off the north-east coast, the Heinkels started to ascend to their launching height of 1,500 feet. All nerves were strained as the minutes ticked by with maddening slowness and the pilots, faces glazed with sweat in spite of the cold, urged their planes up to the necessary altitude.

At the underground radar station near Patrington, a few miles from Spurn Point, the first black dots appeared on the green-glowing screens. A quick confirmation. Yes, they were Heinkels all right, but as yet too far out for those AA gunners stationed on both sides of the broad Humber. Fighter Command was alerted and all night-fighters already out over the North Sea on standing patrol were ordered to intercept.

Five minutes ... Six minutes ... They were almost there now, the anxious German pilots told themselves as they stared at the altimeter needle, willing it to reach the desired height. Behind each pilot the rest of his crew peered out into the night, throats dry, eyes smarting, as they searched the darkness for the first tell-tale flame of an exhaust, which would indicate that the Tommy night-fighters had spotted them ... *Seven minutes!* They had done it! But there was no time to waste. Now came the most dangerous stage of the Heinkels' mission: the firing of the flying bomb's sparking plugs by means of a cable linking the plane to the V-1. In the past, some missiles had stubbornly refused to unlink; others, once fired, had threatened to down the planes themselves.

The sudden thunder of another engine. A burst of fiery-red flame. Grimly the pilot held onto the shaking controls. An abrupt lurching. Suddenly the first Heinkel fired its missile and went soaring up into the night sky, released of that one ton weight. One after another, the Heinkels hurried to get rid of their load before the Tommies caught them. Off the V-1s went, surging towards the north-east coast at a steady 400 mph, trailing that brilliant plume of fire behind them, while the Heinkels swooped low again over the cold North Sea, ready to make for home.

Five minutes later, the first of the night-fighters caught up with them. Too late. Forty missiles had been launched on a seventy-mile front between Bridlington in the north and Skegness in the south—at a cost of one Heinkel bomber shot down.

The north was still asleep as the first of the flying bombs crossed the coast and the sirens began to sound their shrill warning and the war returned to that sector of the Home Front for the first time for years.

On either side of the Humber, the gunners took up the challenge. Once again the battered citizens of Hull heard the heavy drum-roll of the ack-ack, saw the searchlights parting the night sky with their icy white fingers, and spotted the scarlet flames stabbing the darkness. 'There were seven of them,' remembers ex-gunner Holyrood, then stationed on the northern bank of the Humber. 'I remember counting them by the flames coming from their rear. Quite close together they seemed to me, but we did no good. We banged away at them for five to ten minutes, but then they vanished into the darkness and we were stood down. My mate said to me, as we had a quick spit-and-a-draw while we waited for the next batch which didn't come, "I bet somebody's gonna have a funny old Christmas present this day, Dave." '[2]

At first it seemed as if that unknown gunner would be proved wrong. Some of the V-1s had vanished, never to be found; perhaps they sank beneath the sea or buried themselves in the lonely moors of the area. Some came down without causing any great harm. One plunged into the black mud which lines both sides of the Humber estuary, its engine still running, near Reads Island. It is said that at low tide it can still be seen there. Another landed harmlessly near the village of Redbourne in Lincolnshire. All that survives of its passing today is a depression in a field which regularly fills up with rainwater in winter.

She was not the only one. Nora Ryder, who had also been through that horrific Christmas blitz four years ago, now had 'a Mrs Bryce and family from Wimbledon' billeted on her; the authorities had evacuated them to escape the V-weapons falling on the borough. They had arrived 'nervous wrecks', Mrs Ryder remembers; and when they heard 'the sirens and knew the V-1s were on their way they were terrified, completely frantic'.[5]

Yet again the attack had caught the authorities unprepared. In some areas the sirens never sounded, so the local Civil Defence personnel simply did not turn out. Instead they hugged the comfort of their warm beds in this coldest winter on record for twenty-five years.

Liverpool was particularly bad; like Bootle, Birkenhead and Wallasey, the city had apparently forgotten the lessons of four years before. After the raid, a stern warning was issued that 'all personnel must be definitely informed of their obligation to turn out on an alert, or on enemy action occurring ... and of the consequences

This damage was caused by one V-2.

which may follow a failure to report for duty.'[6] But by then it was too late.

Another city where the local authorities were later shown to be particularly lacking was Oldham. Although the attack was aimed at Manchester, as we have seen, only one flying bomb landed within the city limits; six struck home within ten miles of the centre and eleven more within fifteen miles. Oldham, however, which was not the main target, suffered the worst damage and the most casualties.

One V-1 came zooming in at ten to six that Christmas Eve morning, twenty minutes after the sirens had sounded. It slapped into an estate, demolishing twenty-three houses and severely damaging another twelve which had to be pulled down later, plus damaging a staggering 1,025 homes in a three-quarter mile radius! One bomb alone caused severe casualties: 28 killed

and 38 seriously injured, plus many more wounded. As the black mushroom of smoke started to ascend into the grey sky above the shattered Abbey Hills Road which the bomb had struck that dawn, it was clear that the Civil Defence organisation was not working.

The local control centre had been closed down for the night. The men and women who operated it were still in bed. The nearest first-aid post to the incident was not open. Many of the Civil Defence personnel had not turned out when the siren sounded, and even those who were on duty were not able to identify what had caused the tremendous explosion for a good ten minutes after it had happened.

Later Sir Hartley Shawcross, the Regional Controller, after the investigation into Oldham's Civil Defence, ordered the local authorities to forthwith prosecute any part-time warden who did not turn out for duty imme-

diately the sirens sounded, as required by law. But by then the damage had been done. As had been proved, year in, year out, in this long battle of the Home Front, the powers-that-be had been predictably slack and unprepared.

This raid, which had turned General Pile's flank so successfully and brought a new mood of gloom to the north, had an unusual aspect to it, too—propaganda.

Searching the still smoking V-1 crater at Epworth, near York, one ROC man found a wooden box. It contained an airmail version of the glossy Wehrmacht propaganda sheet, *Signal*, which showed on its front page a clock face with the hands standing at five minutes to midnight—a reference to the German phrase meaning that the hour of decision had come. But not only were

The V-1 campaign 1944–45.

Where the V-1s landed in London. The London Civil Defence Region as it was in June 1944. It included parts of several counties adjoining the County of London. The list shows the number of flying-bombs which landed in each borough or urban district within the Region during the main attack, from June 13th to September 1st, 1944.

Where the V-1s landed outside London: all those counties in which flying-bombs landed between June 13th, 1944 and March 29th, 1945. The names and boundaries are as they were at the time, not as they are today. The map shows the number of flying-bombs in each county, excluding the County of London and those parts of other counties included inside the London Civil Defence Region.

CUMBERLAND

DURHAM 1

WESTMOR-LAND

YORKSHIRE 7

LANCA-SHIRE 8

CHESHIRE 6

DERBY 3

NOTTS 1

LINCOLN-SHIRE 2

STAFFORD

SHROPSHIRE 1

RUTLAND 1

LEICESTER-SHIRE 1

NORTHANTS 4

HUNTS 2

NORFOLK 13

WORCS

CAMBS 8

SUFFOLK 93

HEREFORD

BEDS 10

BUCKS 27

HERTS 82

ESSEX 412

OXFORD-SHIRE 4

GLOUCESTER

BERKS 12

KENT 1444

WILTS

SURREY 295

SOMERSET

HAMPSHIRE 80

SUSSEX 880

DORSET

Isle of Wight

1 Bushey 1	49 Hackney 36
2 Elstree 2	50 Shoreditch 7
3 Potters Bar 1	51 Finsbury 5
4 East Barnet 6	52 Holborn 4
5 Enfield 20	53 The City of London 17
6 Cheshunt 6	54 Stepney 30
7 Waltham Holy Cross 11	55 Bethnal Green 9
8 Uxbridge 5	56 Poplar 39
9 Ruislip 4	57 Leyton 24
10 Harrow 11	58 West Ham 58
11 Henden 13	59 East Ham 36
12 Barnet Urban District 4	60 Barking 37
13 Southgate 6	61 Dagenham 28
14 Edmonton 7	62 Esher 35
15 Chingford 8	63 Kingston 8
16 Chigwell 20	64 Malden 21
17 Yiewsley 3	65 Richmand 8
18 Hayes 6	66 Barnes 9
19 Southall 7	67 Wimbledon 33
20 Ealing 11	68 Wandsworth 122
21 Wembley 14	69 Battersea 34
22 Willesdon 15	70 Lambeth 71
23 Finchley 6	71 Camberwell 80
24 Friern Barnet 1	72 Southwark 14
25 Hornsey 15	73 Bermondsey 30
26 Wood Green 5	74 Deptford 30
27 Tottenham 4	75 Greenwich 73
28 Walthamstow 17	76 Woolwich 77
29 Wanstead 23	77 Erith 12
30 Ilford 34	78 Surbiton 20
31 Staines 7	79 Merton 35
32 Sunbury 4	80 Mitcham 43
33 Feltham 5	81 Croydon 141
34 Heston 15	82 Penge 17
35 Twickenham 27	83 Beckenham 70
36 Brentford 13	84 Lewisham 114
37 Acton 7	85 Bromley 37
38 Hammersmith 14	86 Chislehurst 45
39 Kensington 20	87 Bexley 25
40 Fulham 15	88 Crayford 11
41 Chelsea 3	89 Epsom 29
42 Westminster 29	90 Banstead 35
43 Paddington 5	91 Sutton 34
44 St Marylebone 12	92 Carshalton 27
45 Hampstead 8	93 Beddington 36
46 St Pancras 19	94 Coulsdon 54
47 Islington 15	95 Orpington 63
48 Stoke Newington 7	

copies of *Signal* found at many other sites, there were further 'airmail deliveries' to be discovered that Christmas Eve morning.

In Oldham, police sifting through the wreckage of Abbey Hills Road found what was perhaps the strangest delivery of Christmas greetings in history, even more curious than the balloon-borne post flown out of a besieged Paris in 1870–71—missile-delivered letters from British POWs from Stalags in Germany!

This 'POW Post' was a cunning idea. Each packet contained several facsimile letters from the men behind barbed wire who had homes in the area, plus reassuring comments from a German officer. With each bundle there was a covering note stating that the original letters were being sent via the Red Cross through normal channels, but would any finder send the letters to the addresses supplied.

The police quickly seized the letters, for they realised they did not just have a propaganda effect, but a military aim, too. Any recipient, German Intelligence hoped, would write back to the loved one in the POW camp explaining where the letter had been originally found. This would enable Intelligence to pin-point the areas where their V-1s had landed.

So the recipients did not receive those Christmas greetings till long afterwards. Even those which slipped through the hands of the police were caught by Post Office sorters, who had been ordered to open all letters addressed to people named in the missile-borne post. Thus the wife of Captain Coulthard of Thorne near Doncaster did not receive, until much later, the letter from her wounded husband, hoping this would be 'our last Christmas apart' and wishing her 'a happy Christmas, darling, knowing that I am right, completely cured and thinking of you and that we shall be together soon. I love you. Always your own Jim.'[7]

For Captain and Mrs Coulthard it was indeed their last Christmas apart; but it would be another long dreary six months before they saw each other again—in a changed world.

'That Christmas, I was fourteen and a great reader of the comics that were given to us by the Yanks stationed near us,' remembers Mr R. Bielby of Manchester. 'I was specially keen on Buck Rogers and the 25th Century and all that science fiction stuff, but when they fired the V-1s at Manchester and I heard that in Oldham they'd killed a whole wedding party, together with the bride and bridegroom, I went off science fiction and the future for good. Blast the 25th century, I thought! I don't think I've ever been so miserable in all my life as that last Christmas of the war . . .'[8]

An ATS girl gives comfort to a little girl.

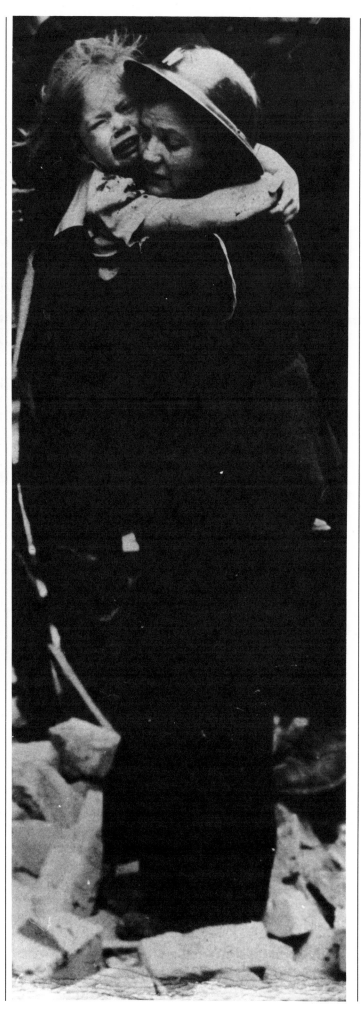

V: DEATHRIDE, 1945

'God bless you all. This is your victory ... Everyone, man or woman, has done his best. Everyone has tried. Neither the long years nor the dangers nor the fierce attacks of the enemy have in any way weakened the independent resolve of the British nation. God bless you all.'

Winston Churchill, Victory Day 1945

A postman asks about casualties after a V-1 bomb has hit a block of flats.

ONE
'This war is not over'

It was the custom of the staid 'Old Thunderer' to publish on the first day of the New Year a picture of the last sunset of the old year. On January 1st, 1945, *The Times* stuck to its custom. That day it depicted the sun setting over the village of Chartwell in Kent. The caption underneath the traditional picture did not mention the fact, but most of the paper's readers knew who was the village's most famous resident—*Winston S. Churchill!* For some that—perhaps unwitting—prophesy was exciting: this year he would go. For many, however, it was unsettling.

Inspector Walter Thompson, who had guarded the Great Man night and day for twenty years, already suspected that a fickle nation might be preparing to discard their war-time saviour. He believed that his beloved master thought so too, and was 'prepared to take what came'.

'Well, Thompson,' Churchill told him one day, 'there's a Cabinet meeting tomorrow. If they throw me out, I'll come right back here [Chartwell] and be happy as a sandboy.'[1]

In Thompson's opinion—and he had known the sorrow of losing his own son during the great conflict—*this* was the nadir of the war on the Home Front.

The people still held on, but the hours, the blackout, the queueing, the rationing, the loss of rest and holidays, loss of homes and children, the great dead areas without fun or change—all this finally begun to grind down our nerves.[2]

Many people would have shared that opinion. It was the coldest winter in twenty-five years. Coal, gas and electricity were in short supply. No one was actually starving—although even potatoes were scarce—but food was generally dull and uninspiring. Even the victories announced almost daily over the BBC did little to cheer up the Home Front this grey, grim winter. The knowledge that, as long as he was alive, Hitler would continue to deal out punishment on the Home Front soured those triumphs.

'Just as all these wonderful sounds [the victories] were coming over the air,' wrote social worker Vera Hodgson that January, 'behold, I heard a rocket bomb drop in the distance! It was a long way away, but it was there to remind us that there were still some very unpleasant things about and that THE WAR IS NOT OVER!'[3]

Indeed it wasn't. The V-1s and V-2s were still arriving, dropping on London and surrounding areas with dismaying regularity.

Essex was particularly hard hit. One house in Ilford was hit by a V-1 and a little girl was trapped in the Anderson shelter in the garden. A doctor appeared on the scene and had a few grave words with the driver of the WVS canteen already serving tea to the rescue workers, before he hurried off at a run.

'What's he doing?' asked one of the heavy rescue men waiting for orders.

'He's gone to get his instruments to amputate the girl's leg,' the WVS driver replied sadly, eyeing the shattered garden and the shelter in which the little girl was trapped.

'Listen,' the heavy rescue man said, 'if you girls will go on giving us tea, we'll *amputate* the shelter.'[4]

And they did.

All over southern England, similar tragedies and heroic rescues were enacted. On January 15th, the *Daily Telegraph* reported how rescuers had been working all night to drag people from a bomb-hit block of flats:

At one time a tunnel more than twelve feet in length was made beneath the smashed masonry. Dead and injured were brought out through this perilous escape way. In the middle of the work, it collapsed and three firemen were trapped. When they were brought out they were found to be badly injured. Volunteers took their place. The tunnel was cleared again and the work went on . . . to bring out alive, two brothers, one aged eight and the other five.

As if the V-1s and V-2s were not enough, on January 14th General Pile heard that Milch was now planning a large-scale conventional raid on southern England. Ultra had definite information, he was told, and it was confirmed by Luftwaffe prisoners who said they'd been told their raids would be comparatively safe because the Tommies' AA defences had been considerably reduced. This was true. So General Pile anxiously set about re-organising his defences yet again.

Meanwhile, as Colonel Wachtel's flying bomb regiment retired to remote prepared positions in the well-wooded Eifel, just over the German border with

A V-2 rocket in Trafalgar Square.

Belgium (where they would never be found by the Allied air forces), and V-1 firings consequently ceased for a while, the V-2s still came raining down. In January they killed 198 people and injured 1,629. In February the figures were 151 killed and 1,152 seriously injured.

Farringdon Market was struck one day at noon when the stalls were crowded with shoppers; 110 people were killed and 123 injured seriously. Two blocks of flats at Hughes Mansions in Stepney were hit; another 134 were killed and 49 seriously injured. At Folkestone Gardens in Deptford, a surface shelter was hit one day in March: 52 people were killed and 32 seriously injured. Another V-2 struck Packard's Factory on the Great West Road, Brentford, and the resultant fire caused great damage and loss of life . . .

Then, on March 3rd, Colonel Wachtel's men started firing their V-1s again. Now the misery intensified, with ever more casualties and damage to homes. By the time it was over, the two revenge weapons would have caused the deaths of 6,184 civilians and 2,917 servicemen (some of them killed in attacks on the various launching sites), while 17,981 civilians and servicemen would have been seriously wounded, and twice this number lightly injured. Indeed, more people would be killed and wounded by the V-1s and V-2s than had been in all the three Allied armies attacking Normandy in battle on D-Day!

That same day, March 3rd, Churchill was in Germany to celebrate the capture of the Siegfried Line; after five long years the Reich's last defensive position had been breached. Together with the top brass he journeyed to the headquarters of the US Ninth Army, where General Simpson asked him if he wanted to visit the 'men's room' before they set off for the Siegfried Line. How long would it take to get there, Churchill wanted to know. Simpson told him it would take about half an hour; whereupon Churchill beamed and said: 'I'll wait, then.'

On their way they were stopped by a speeding jeep bearing a red-faced courier who had brought a small package for Churchill. In a matter-of-fact manner Churchill undid it, shoved his forgotten dentures into his mouth and gave Simpson another beam.

A little later the cavalcade stopped at a bridge over a small ravine. Simpson explained that the ravine marked the boundary between Holland and Germany.

'Let's get out,' Churchill commanded and dressed as he was in the uniform of a colonel of the 4th Hussars, the regiment he had joined as an eighteen year old in the previous century, he stumped across the bridge, down the river bank to a long row of 'dragons' teeth' (concrete tank-traps) running across the countryside like the vertebrae of a stone monster. 'Gentlemen' he announced, big grin on his face, cigar tucked into the side of his mouth, as he fumbled clumsily with his flies,

Five people were killed when a rocket fell on Wemyss Road, Blackheath in March 1945.

144

'I'd like you to join me. Let us all urinate on the Great West Wall of Germany!'[5]

Field Marshal Alan Brooke, not normally one of Churchill's greatest admirers, was standing next to him at that moment, and later remarked: 'I shall never forget the childish grin of inner satisfaction that spread all over his face as he looked down at the critical moment.'[6]

In that instant of great triumph, with nothing but the Rhine to stop the Allied armies now from beating Germany totally and overwhelmingly, fifty miles away in the Eifel, just above the little township of Wittlich, Wachtel's men were still firing their V-1s at the south of England.

Another hundred miles further on, German conventional bombers made their final preparations for the raid General Pile had been dreading. But, contrary to his expectations, they were going to arrive over England in broad moonlight—and again the enemy had a trick up his sleeve to confuse and overwhelm the defenders.

On the night of that Saturday, March 3rd, 500 RAF heavy bombers were returning from raids on Cologne and the Ruhr, where they had been paving the way for the Allied capture of that city and the crossing of the Rhine. Waiting for them were 80 German fighter-bombers. But they had no intention of shooting down the 'furniture vans', as they called the great lumbering four-engine bombers. They meant to use them as a means of infiltrating AA defences over the eastern part of England.

And the new tactic succeeded. Slowly they were borne across the North Sea together with the unsuspecting RAF bombers, skirting the newly 'dimmed out' cities and towns where Pile's AA gun-defences were mainly concentrated. Even where his gunners recognised German aircraft overhead, there was little the frustrated ground defenders could do. As General Pile himself wrote later: 'Mixed up with the stream of friendly bombers, it was almost impossible to distinguish friend from foe in the confusion which followed.'[7]

That night the German fighter-bombers ranged far and wide. Attacks were made not only on bombers and RAF airfields, but on towns, villages, rail and road transport, even on London itself. The Luftwaffe was giving Britain a taste of the kind of medicine the Reich had been receiving these last few months.

A railway signalman, Thomas Inman, was killed when the empty train in which he was returning home was machine-gunned by a low-flying Messerschmitt. A Fire Service tender trying to dowse a fire in a lonely part of the countryside was shot up and its crew members severely wounded. A couple of fighter-bombers sprayed an East Anglian town with cannonfire, wounding the chief warden. A village in the north-east was attacked and similarly shot up. 'We heard the roar of a plane and the machine-gunning started,' one resident, a Mr Wolfe, told the press a day later. 'I was standing in the kitchen beside the pantry door when something hit me in the side and leg and I was knocked out. After a few minutes I recovered and found I was bleeding from cuts.'[8]

Not far away an ROC man, Mr J. Kelway, was killed instantly when one of six German planes was shot down and crashed into his car in flames and exploded. None of the crew survived.

In comparison with the massive 1,000 bomber raids carried out by the British and Americans in 1945, that last German conventional raid meant little. It caused several score casualties and damaged a few hundred houses. But it had a cruel psychological effect on a people already reaching the end of their tether. What did Churchill's victories mean when London could again be bombed by conventional aircraft, not to mention the V-weapons, and the blackout had had to be re-introduced?

In his diary for March 6th Goebbels noted maliciously: 'Sinclair, the British Air Minister, takes a very serious view of our renewed air raids on the British homeland ... By all accounts they are lowering British morale still further,' he gloated. And he went on:

Strikes in Britain are mushrooming again. The British workers are clearly under the impression that by and large the war is already won and that the time has now come for them to press their social demands. In London alone 10,000 dockers are on strike. Troops had to be used to load vital war material.[9]

There was indeed a dockers' strike at Avonmouth and signs of industrial unrest in several other industries. At Avonmouth it had been discovered that dockers had been earning a staggering £47 a week (about ten times the weekly pay of an infantry soldier currently fighting in Germany) and the dockers did not like the thought that the good times were almost over; for peace loomed ahead. As a result they struck. The national solidarity which Churchill had created was slowly crumbling ...

But General Pile had no time that month for strikes or crumbling national morale, which was not helped any by these last raids and the V-weapons. He had other, more urgent, problems. On the Continent, a Luftwaffe officer taken prisoner had told his interrogators that Goering, through Milch, had informed what was left of the Luftwaffe's decimated squadrons that soon they must expect orders to set out on a mission against England from which there would be no return.

As soon as Pile received a transcript of that interrogation, he had made his own guess as to what the Germans were about. They were going to make the kind

In Islington, seventy-two people were killed by this V-2 rocket.

of kamikaze raid on England that the Japanese were already employing in the Pacific against the Allied fleets. But what was their target to be?

Eventually the harassed General and his staff came to the conclusion that the suicide raid would be directed against the heart of London—Buckingham Palace, Westminster and Whitehall. Further they decided it would be a raid of about 300 aircraft which would crash on their objectives, perhaps even deliberately. Their route, Pile thought, would be 'at roof-top level along such well-defined highways as the Thames estuary or the main railways lines'.[10]

So in the middle of March he ordered a massive movement of light ack-ack guns to the threatened area and the route along which the Germans would come. In one day 100 HQs and 272 detachments were set up and equipped with 412 light flak cannon. Two dozen half-inch Browning machine guns were posted on the roofs of Westminster. Two hundred barrage balloons were readied for the same area. Finally, the code-word—which, if the Germans came on this last desperate suicidal mission, would flash out and alert all units: *Death-ride.*

TWO
'No bombs ... ain't it lovely?'

Now the ammunition of General Pile's coastal gunners was almost exhausted. The new wave of flying bombs, heading for London and crossing the coast between the Isle of Sheppey and Orfordness, was taking its toll. Every bomb that was shot down cost AA Command 150 rounds. Thus, in the first stage of the new contest, the gunners had expended 3,500 of their precious shells; and only a limited amount of ammunition was available that March. Pile ordered that his deadly new T-98 shell (with a highly lethal and secret proximity fuse) should be rationed, and prayed that the almost beaten Germans could not still mount a flying bomb campaign of the kind they had staged the previous summer.

His prayers were answered. On March 10th the US 76 Infantry Division marched into the little Eifel town of Wittlich. Four miles beyond it, Colonel Wachtel's gunners stationed there in the wooded hills, abandoned their launching sites and fled across the River Moselle, where they would attempt to go into action again from the Hunsruck Mountains. They never did.

It was not just General Pile who was relieved when the flying bombs stopped arriving from the Eifel; the locals were too. For months now, flying bombs aimed from the site at London and Antwerp had malfunctioned, circled around alarmingly, and come crashing down on the villages and hamlets of that remote area. Indeed, they were known locally as the '*Eifelschreck*' ('terror of the Eifel') and still loom large in the area's folk memory forty years later.*

Wachtel's other sections, however, continued firing from that part of Holland still in German hands, just as the V-2 launching pads did. But as the Third Reich

---

* Even today their firing mechanism is still occasionally found in the area and the local engineers have to go out and explode the rusting fuses.

writhed in its death throes, their efforts were becoming weaker and weaker.

On March 12th, the V-2s in Holland temporarily switched their attentions from Britain's Home Front to a more urgent target: 'the most famous bridge in the world', as it was being called that month, the one and only bridge to have been captured over the Rhine, the Remagen Bridge.

The Americans had been holding it for ten days now and pouring division after division across it to hold their narrow bridgehead on the Rhine's eastern bank. For those ten days, the bridge had been subjected to artillery attacks, dive-bombing, underwater sorties by German frogmen, and even a barrage by the 'Karl Howitzer'—a monster which weighed 132 tons and fired an enormous 4,400-pound shell. But after a few rounds that failed to hit the bridge, it was withdrawn for repairs.

Now it was up to the V-2s. Between March 12th and 17th, eleven of them were fired at this target, some 200 miles away. Several landed in the Rhine. One wrecked a building near the Apollinaris Church overlooking the bridge, and another landed in a nearby farmyard, killing three soldiers billeted in the farm, plus an assortment of animals (though the family dog survived and, after disappearing, duly limped home in a shaken condition after the war was over—clever dog).

On the morning of March 17th another V-2 landed near the bridge and finally helped to bring about its destruction. That afternoon the whole structure started to groan and shake alarmingly. The engineers trying to repair the morning's damage to the structure ran for their lives. In an instant they found themselves labouring upwards as the end section tilted at an alarming angle. And then, with a huge rasping throaty noise, the Remagen Bridge collapsed into the Rhine, taking with

it twenty-eight American engineers.

The destruction of the Remagen Bridge proved to be the V-2's only real tactical victory. It was essentially a terror-weapon. 'I aim for the stars,' its inventor Werner von Braun often said, when he later became the power behind America's post-war space effort. A cynic might have retorted: '*Yes—but sometimes hit London!*'

The terror resumed, but it was not for much longer now. Shortly before the Western Allies crossed the Rhine in Montgomery's set-piece operation between Rees and Wesel, seventeen V-2s were aimed at the capital in the short space of fourteen hours—the highest number of the whole attack on the Home Front. Apart from the many domestic and business properties already destroyed or damaged by the V-2s, over 45 London churches and 35 hospitals had now been hit, including the Erith Sanitorium which was destroyed; St Peter's Hospital, Stepney, which was seriously damaged; and the Central Eye Hospital, St Pancras, which suffered considerable damage.

But already the V-2 gunners were packing their bags and preparing to run for their lives back into the shrinking Reich.

On Palm Sunday, March 25th, Churchill himself crossed the Rhine, together with General Simpson—who was very worried that he might be responsible for having the British Prime Minister killed in this moment of victory; for the enemy was still fighting stubbornly only a few hundred yards away.

This did not worry the old warhorse. He scrambled nimbly onto the girders of a wrecked railway bridge, while the shells dropped ever closer, creating great brown spouts of water; it was as if the enemy gunners knew that he was there.

A junior aide ran up to Simpson. 'General,' he gasped, 'we're bracketed already! One or two more tries and they may hit you!'

Simpson went across to the Great Man. 'Prime Minister,' he said very formally, 'there are snipers in front of you, they are shelling both sides of the bridge and now they have started shelling the road behind you. I cannot accept responsibility for your being here and must ask you to come away.'[1]

The look on Churchill's face at that moment reminded Field Marshal Alan Brooke of a small boy being called away from a sand castle on the beach. He grasped a girder with both arms and peered over his shoulder as if defying them to pry him loose. But then, to everyone's relief, he let go and allowed himself to be taken back.

Repeatedly Churchill had told Brooke, the soldier: 'The way to die is to pass out fighting when your blood is up and you feel nothing.' Now it seemed to Brooke that Churchill was determined to take every possible risk, as if a sudden soldier's death at the front would have suited him better than the worries of an uncertain future.[2]

Two days later the last V-2 dropped at Orpington, Kent at six minutes to five that Tuesday afternoon. It killed one civilian and wounded twenty-three.

By now Colonel Wachtel had only one solitary site in operation near Delft, Holland. But still it kept firing what was left of its supply of V-1s. Now on Wednesday

The devastated East End of London in March 1945.

March 28th, Wachtel's gunners started their last full day's bombardment of London. Two came down that morning, one at Waltham Cross, twelve miles north of the aiming point, Tower Bridge, and the other at Chislehurst, roughly the same distance to the south-east.

Around nine thirty that evening the Germans began their final bombardment. The last gunners gamely fired their remaining twenty-one flying bombs at London. There Pile gave out the code-word, *Deathride*. This must be it, he thought; this must be the last bombardment.

On the coast the AA gunners fired furiously, reckless of their ever diminishing supply of ammunition, destroying the V-1s one by one, while over the Channel the fighters zoomed back and forth playing their part too.

In the end only one V-1 evaded the guns and the fighters. It exploded at nine o'clock on the morning of March 29th, 1945, at Datchworth in Hatfield in Hertfordshire—aptly enough in a sewage farm!

All that long day Pile and his gunners waited for the worst—that massed suicide attack on the City, that Wagnerian ride of the Valkeries that would herald the end of the doomed Third Reich. It did not come. London was saved. There would be no *Deathride*.

'No bombs ... ain't it lovely!' wrote Vera Hodgson on April 11th, 1945.[3]

It was indeed. The long ordeal was over. Field Marshal Milch's attempt to bring Britain down to her knees had failed. There would be no more sirens, no more enemy planes; no one need fear that lethal silence as the doodlebug's engine cut out and it prepared for its final descent, or the thunder from General Pile's ack-ack. Just as his gunners—and the fighter-pilots—had beaten the conventional bombers, they had beaten Milch's V-1s, too, knocking 4,262 of them out of the sky in the ten-month campaign.

The war as it affected General Pile's AA Command was finished. His gunners had been the first to go into action. Never since the outbreak of war, five and a half years ago, had they ceased to be on the alert. They had fought the Battle of Britain, the Battle of London, the Battle of the Ports and Provincial Towns, the Baedeker Raids, the Little Blitzes, the Battle of the Flying Bombs ...

But now Pile's gunners were fading into obscurity. When Pile asked that his gunners, who had done so much to defend the Home Front, be awarded the 1939–45 star like their comrades who had gone overseas to fight, he was turned down by Parliament. Instead he was told that the AA Command would be allowed to share—with any civilian who had endured three months of fire-watching*—the Defence Medal with its 'two black stripes representing the black-out'.[4]

That medal was all the thanks they got, those men and women who had moulded an out-of-date and ill-equipped defence machine—bequeathed to the country in 1939 by the same politicians who now refused them their campaign medal—into the epoch-making army that had finally defeated the first all-out missile attack in history.

One month later the war was won; and two months after that, Churchill was on his way out. The first post-war election was in progress. In Manchester he was greeted by cheering crowds, but the Labour candidate—*Captain* Harold Lever—noted that 'in working-class areas his reception was cool'.[5] Churchill himself thought this was because ordinary people felt the city had not been adequately prepared for the 1940 attacks, and 'people blamed the Conservatives for this'.

In Woodford, his own constituency, which his beloved Clementine had risked her life to visit while the V-1s had been dropping, he was again received by a tremendous welcome. Here the Liberals and Labour had agreed not to put forward a candidate to oppose him. But it didn't help. An obscure farmer, who stood as an Independent, beat him.

In the East End, where five years before he had waved his stick and cried 'Are we downhearted?' to a tremendous ovation, they booed him for minutes on end, so much so that he cried angrily at the 'socialist woolgatherers', mocking 'their idiotic idealism, philosophic dreaming of Utopian worlds which will never be seen except with improvements in the human heart and head!'[6] Then he sat down, flushed with rage, unable to speak any more—and the booing continued.

But there were no 'improvements in the human heart and head'. On July 5th, 1945, Labour won a resounding victory over Churchill's Tories. Winston Churchill, so the electorate thought, had no role to play in this brave new world of sweetness and light that the socialists promised. So a new era began. It would not be so pink and warm and promising as the victorious Labour supporters hoped.

Churchill retired to lick his wounds and hope for another and better day. His old crony and doctor, Lord Moran, suggested that he had been scurvily treated by the nation he had saved. Was he not a victim of base ingratitude?

The Great Man would have none of it. He shook his head. 'Oh no,' he replied in that familiar growl, which once had roused the nation to standing cheers, 'I wouldn't call it that ... They have had ... a very hard time ...'[7]

---

* The author received it, too, for a rather peaceful spell of fire-watching as a fourteen-year-old schoolboy.

(Right) The British spirit!

SOURCES

Introduction
1 Quoted in Richard Collier: *1940—The World in Flames* (Penguin Books, London 1975).
2 Miss Madge Faulkney (personal interview).
3 Ibid.
4 Mrs H. Ryder (letter to author).
5 Mrs B. Reilly (letter to author).
6 Miss U. Compton (letter to author).
7 Mrs B. Hardcastle (letter to author).
8 *Sunday Telegraph*, July 29th, 1984.

BOOK I
Chapter One
1 Leonard Mosley: *The Reich Marshal* (Doubleday, New York 1974).
2 Personal interview.
3 Quoted in A. McKee: *Strike from the Sky* (New English Library, 1972).
4 *Der Volkische Beobachter*, September 1940.
5 Personal interview.
6 Letter to author.
7 Heinz Becker (personal interview).
8 Letter to author.
9 Personal interview.
10 Ibid.
11 Hans Fruehauf (personal interview).
12 Quoted in Angus Calder: *The People's War* (Panther, London 1971).
13 Ibid.
14 Letter to author.
15 Personal interview.
16 Mrs Hunter (personal interview).

Chapter Two
1 Personal interview.
2 E. Reeves (letter to author).
3 F. Pile: *Ack-Ack* (Harrap, London 1950).
4 Ibid.
5 Ibid.
6 Quoted in Ian McClaine: *Ministry of Morale* (Allen & Unwin, London 1963).
7 Ibid.
8 John Watson (personal interview).
9 Quoted in Angus Calder: *The People's War*.
10 D. Flowers: *The Taste of Courage* (Harper, 1968).
11 Ibid.
12 Personal interview.
13 Ibid.

A congregation of city workers gives thanks for victory in Europe in the shattered church of Saint Mary Le Bow. St Paul's can be seen through the once-stained-glass window.

14 *Daily Express*, November 3rd 1940.
15 Personal interview.
16 Quoted in Calder, op. cit.
17 Letter to author.
18 Personal interview.

Chapter Three
1 Letter to author.
2 Ibid.
3 Ibid.
4 Ibid.
5 Ibid.
6 Ibid.
7 *Daily Telegraph*, April 24th, 1984.
8 Letter to author.
9 Ibid.
10 Ibid.
11 Ibid.
12 Ibid.
13 *Daily Telegraph*, December 22nd, 1983.
14 'Our Blitz', *Manchester Evening News*, 1941.
15 Letter to author.
16 Ibid.
17 Ibid.
18 Ibid.
19 Ibid.
20 Ibid.
21 Ibid.
22 Ibid.
23 Ibid.
24 Ibid.
25 Ibid.
26 Ibid.
27 Ibid.
28 Ibid.
29 'Our Blitz', *Manchester Evening News*.
30 *Daily Telegraph*.
31 *Yorkshire Evening Press*, December 22nd, 1983.

Chapter Four
1 Quoted in Ian McClaine: *Ministry of Morale*.
2 Personal interview.
3 Quoted in R. Minns: *Bomber and Mash* (Virago, London 1979).
4 Barbara Nixon: *Raiders Overhead* (Gulliver, 1943).
5 Ibid.
6 Bill Whiting (personal interview).
7 Ibid.
8 Ibid.
9 Mary Hemingway: *How It Was* (Weidenfeld & Nicolson, London, 1976).
10 Letter to author.
11 Quoted in Richard Collier: *1940—The World in Flames*.
12 Bill Whiting (personal interview).
13 Personal interview.
14 Collier, op. cit.

15 Collier, op. cit.
16 Ibid.
17 Quoted in A. McKee: *Strike from the Sky*.

BOOK II
Chapter One
1 Personal interview.
2 Quoted in *Front Line 1940–1941* (HMSO, London 1942).
3 Ian McClaine: *Ministry of Morale*.
4 Ibid.
5 Ibid.
6 Quoted in F. Wintle: *The Plymouth Blitz* (Bossiney Books, 1983).
7 Ibid.
8 *Western Morning News: The Plymouth Blitz*.
9 Ibid.
10 Quoted in H. P. Twyford: *It Came to Our Door* (Underhill, Plymouth 1946).
11 Quoted in Wintle, op. cit.
12 Ibid.
13 Ian McClaine, op. cit.
14 Ibid.
15 Quoted in Wintle, op. cit.
16 Ibid.
17 Christopher Sykes: *Nancy: The Life of Lady Astor* (Collins, London 1972).

Chapter Two
1 Ian McClaine: *Ministry of Morale*.
2 Ibid.
3 Quoted in Angus Calder: *Home Front* (Collins, London 1968).
4 'After the Blitz', *Picture Post*, May 3rd, 1941.
5 Personal interview.
6 Letter to author.
7 Ibid.
8 McClaine, op. cit.
9 Ibid.
10 Ibid.
11 Letter to author.
12 Ibid.
13 A. Firebrace: *Fire Service Memories* (Collins, London 1945).
14 Letter to author.
15 *Liverpool Echo*, 1980.
16 Letter to author.
17 Ibid.
18 Ibid.
19 Ibid.
20 Ibid.
21 Ibid.
22 Ibid.
23 Ibid.
24 Ibid.
25 Ibid.
26 Ibid.
27 Ibid.
28 Ibid.
29 Ibid.
30 Madge Faulkney (personal interview).
31 McClaine, op. cit.
32 Ibid.
33 Letter to author.
34 Ibid.

Chapter Three
1 Quoted in Richard Collier: *The City That Wouldn't Die* (Collins, London 1959).
2 Ibid.
3 Ibid.
4 Personal interview.
5 Quentin Reynolds: *Once There Was A War* (Harper & Row, New York 1943).
6 Mary Hemingway: *How It Was*.
7 Quoted in Angus Calder: *The People's War*.
8 *Churchill's Great War Speeches* (Corgi, London 1946).

Chapter Four
1 Personal interview.
2 F. Pile: *Ack-Ack*.
3 Personal interview.
4 Ibid.
5 Ibid.
6 Ibid.
7 Ibid.
8 Ibid.
9 Quoted in *Front Line 1940–1941*.
10 *Sunday Telegraph*, April 1973.
11 Letter to author.
12 Ibid.
13 Ibid.

BOOK III
Chapter One
1 Personal interview.
2 Ibid.
3 Quoted in Kessler and Taylor: *Yorkshire At War* (The Dalesman, 1976).
4 Letter to author.
5 Ibid.
6 Quoted in Kessler and Taylor, op. cit.
7 Personal interview.
8 Letter to author.
9 Ibid.
10 Ibid.
11 Ibid.
12 Ibid.
13 Quoted in A. Calder: *People At War*.
14 Quoted in Max Hastings: *Bomber Command* (Michael Joseph, London 1981).
15 Ibid.
16 Ibid.
17 D. Saward: *Bomber Harris* (Cassell, London 1984).
18 Pathé newsreel, March 1942.
19 Hastings, op. cit.
20 Saward, op. cit.
21 Hastings, op. cit.
22 *Goebbels Tagebucker* (Bertelsmann, 1976).
23 Ibid.

Chapter Two
1 F. Pile: *Ack-Ack*.
2 Ibid.
3 Letter to author.
4 *Der Volkische Beobachter*, April 1st, 1942.
5 Pile, op. cit.
6 Ibid.
7 Letter to the author.
8 Ibid.
9 Ibid.
10 Ibid.
11 Ibid.
12 Ibid.
13 Ibid.
14 Ibid.
15 Ibid.

Chapter Three
1 *Yorkshire Evening Press*, April 28th, 1942.
2 Personal interview.
3 *Yorkshire Evening Press*, April 28th, 1978.
4 Ibid.
5 Ibid.
6 Personal interview.
7 Letter to author.
8 Personal interview.
9 Ibid.
10 Ibid.
11 Ibid.
12 Ibid.
13 *Yorkshire Evening Press*, April 30th, 1942.

14 Ibid.
15 Quoted in Norman Longmate: *How We Lived Then* (Hutchinson, London 1971).
16 *Yorkshire Evening Press*, April 28th, 1978.
17 Ibid.
18 Personal interview.
19 *Churchill's Great War Speeches*.
20 Ibid.

Chapter Four
1 F. Pile: *Ack-Ack*.
2 Ibid.
3 Ibid.
4 Ibid.
5 L. Mohan: *Historical Sketch: 71st Monmouth Home Guard*. Locally printed.
6 Personal interview.
7 Leonard Mosley: *London Under Fire* (Pan, London 1971; originally published by Weidenfeld & Nicolson as *Backs To The Wall*).
8 Personal interview.

BOOK IV
Chapter One
1 F. Pile: *Ack-Ack*.
2 Quoted in Leonard Mosley: *London Under Fire*.
3 *Daily Telegraph*, March 4th, 1943.
4 Mary Hemingway: *How It Was*.
5 Quoted in Mosley, op. cit.
6 C. Baekker: *Luftwaffe Diaries* (Ballantine, New York 1972).
7 Letter to author.
8 C. Babington-Smith: *Evidence in Camera* (Penguin, London 1968).
9 Letter to author.
10 Quoted in Mosley, op. cit.

Chapter Two
1 M. Edelman: *Herbert Morrison* (Praeger, New York 1968).
2 Ibid.
3 Personal interview.
4 Ibid.
5 Letter to author.
6 Norman Longmate: *The Doodlebugs* (Hutchinson, London 1982).
7 Letter to author.
8 Ibid.
9 R. V. Jones: *Most Secret War* (Hamish Hamilton, London 1980).
10 Ibid.
11 *Daily Telegraph*, June 14th, 1944.
12 Letter to author.
13 Ibid.
14 Ibid.
15 Ibid.
16 Ibid.
17 *Daily Telegraph*, June 17th, 1944.
18 R. Henrey: *The Siege of London* (Right Book Club, 1948).
19 Longmate, op. cit.
20 Rawnsley and Wright: *Night-Fighter* (Corgi, London 1972).
21 Henrey, op. cit.
22 Jones, op. cit.
23 Mary Churchill: *Clementine Churchill* (Hutchinson, London 1984).
24 Quoted in Longmate, op. cit.
25 Ibid.
26 Henrey, op. cit.
27 Quoted in Longmate, op. cit.

Chapter Three
1 C. Green: *Women in Green* (Heinemann, London 1953).
2 Ibid.
3 Ibid.
4 Ibid.
5 Rawnsley & Wright: *Night-Fighter*.

6 Richard Turner: *Mustang Pilot* (Kimber, 1968).
7 Ibid.
8 Norman Longmate: *The Doodlebugs*.
9 Letter to author.
10 Ibid.
11 F. Pile: *Ack-Ack*.
12 Ibid.
13 Ibid.
14 Quoted in McClaine: *Ministry of Morale*.
15 Ibid.
16 *Evening Standard*, May 1984.
17 Ibid.
18 Ibid.
19 Ibid.
20 Letter to author.
21 Ibid.
22 Ibid.
23 Ibid.
24 Ibid.
25 Ibid.
26 Ibid.
27 *Evening Standard*, May 2nd, 1984.

Chapter Four
1 R. V. Jones: *Most Secret War*.
2 *Daily Telegraph*, September 8th, 1944.
3 Jones, op. cit.
4 Personal interview.
5 Letter to author.
6 Quoted in David Irving: *The Mare's Nest* (Kimber, 1968).
7 Quoted in Leonard Mosley: *London Under Fire*.
8 Ibid.
9 Rawnsley & Wright: *Night-Fighter*.
10 Ibid.
11 Quoted in Mosley, op. cit.
12 Letter to Author.
13 F. Pile: *Ack-Ack*.
14 Ibid.
15 Ibid.

Chapter Five
1 Rawnsley & Wright; *Night-Fighter*.
2 Letter to author.
3 Quoted in Norman Longmate: *The Doodlebugs*.
4 Letter to author.
5 Ibid.
6 Quoted in Longmate, op. cit.
7 Ibid.
8 Letter to author.

BOOK V
Chapter One
1 Walter Thompson: *Assignment Churchill* (Popular Library 1956).
2 Ibid.
3 Quoted in Mosley: *London Under Fire*.
4 Letter to author.
5 Ibid.
6 Ibid.
7 F. Pile: *Ack-Ack*.
8 *Daily Telegraph*, March 5th, 1945.
9 *The Goebbels Diaries*, edited by H. Trevor-Roper (Secker & Warburg, London).
10 Pile, op. cit.

Chapter Two
1 Letter to author.
2 Ibid.
3 Leonard Mosley: *London Under Fire*.
4 F. Pile: *Ack-Ack*.
5 T. Pocock: *1945* (Collins, London 1984).
6 Ibid.
7 Ibid.

INDEX

All numbers in *italics* refer to photographs.

Mrs Eals tells the King and Queen how she was saved by taking cover in an Anderson shelter when her house was bombed.

159

ACKNOWLEDGEMENTS

I would like to thank the editors of the following newspapers for their assistance in tracking down the survivors of the Battle of the Home Front: the *Church Times, Hull Daily Mail, Withernsea Gazette, Liverpool Echo, Manchester Evening News, Croydon Advertiser, Norwich Mercury* and the Scottish Gazette Group.

I should also like to thank most warmly the several hundred people who wrote to me—many of whom are pensioners on a low income—telling me of their experiences and enclosing treasured memories of that battle fought so long ago. In particular, I am grateful to those who gave of their time for a personal interview.

C.W.

The publishers are most grateful to the Imperial War Museum for permission to use the photographs which appear on pages 14/15, 20/21, 22, 25, 29, 31, 33, 40/41, 44/45, 48/49, 53, 54/55, 56/57, 63, 67, 69, 71,73, 77, 79, 85, 89, 105, 106/107, 109, 110/111, 112/113, 115, 117, 119, 122/123, 128/129, 131, 133, 134, 136/137, 144/145, 147; to the BBC Hulton Picture Library for those appearing on pages 9, 16/17, 19, 26/27, 37, 39, 43, 47, 50/51, 87, 148/149, 157; and to the Topham Picture Library for the photographs which appear on pages 2, 7, 10/11, 59, 65, 90, 93, 126/127, 139, 140/141, 143, 151, 152.

We also thank the author for the use of the photographs which appear on pages 13, 82/83, 94, 97, 101, 102/103, 138 and the *Daily Express* for the cartoon which appears on page 121.